In more specific relation to political science, there has also been a mood of disenchantment. The unity, cohesiveness, and commonalities of the field seem to be in eclipse; perhaps they have already been abandoned.[2] This is a common theme in many of the essays that follow. Frequently, the approaches or substantive concerns that have held a subfield together and contributed to its distinctiveness are now in doubt. There is change in the redefinition of boundary areas, in what is significant and should continue to be so in contrast to what has been considered important in the past. The subfields are in flux: some are assuming greater importance; the interest in others is declining. Political science is a discipline in transition.

The question of seeking a broader identity for the field is raised in varying contexts by a number of authors. What distinguishes political science as an integrative whole, a bounded and coherent intellectual pursuit? What makes the discipline distinctive? What constitutes its particular problems? What should be the central focus and common bonds among its practitioners? These concerns are addressed in differing contexts and, in particular, served as the basis for those contributing to Volume 1, *The Theory and Practice of Political Science*, arguably the most contentious of the four. These questions are the mega-issues, the ones that concern all of us as practicing academicians. Whether it is preferable to achieve the coherence, stability, and self-assurance that some found in the past, or whether a more eclectic, exploratory, and innovative practice is preferable is debatable. Whether conceptual approaches ("power," "politics," "markets," "representation," "democracy"), subject matter (the study of government, institutions, political behavior), or definitional guides ("the authoritative allocation of values," "who gets what, when, and how") are the best indicators of relevance is also arguable.

Both approaches have their costs: in one, smugness, perhaps, and a hint as to what can or "should" be done, contrasted in the other with a disparate, shotgunlike scattering of interests that raises questions about the interests or bonds that political scientists share. What distinguishes political scientists from sociologists, economists, historians, or anthropologists (or, for that matter, from those who work in professional schools of law, journalism, management, or policy)? Should distinctions among them be made? Can they communicate intellectually with each other? What do they have to share, borrow, or contribute that is distinctive to their respective disciplines? Or, conversely, are those valid concerns? Some believe that each subfield should follow its own road. Eventually, they argue, all—or at least knowledge writ large—should prosper. The role of graduate education—what skills and perspectives are transmitted to future generations of pra[...]tional[...] scheme is unclear—a further sign of a discipline [...]

lieve that this indecision typifies the mood that has been progressively enveloping the discipline over the last generation.

The questions raised in the essays that follow are basic. No effort has been made to supply answers—should they even exist at this point in time—on which the balance of contributors might agree. The purpose is to encourage critical thought at a convenient summing-up point in a discipline's development.

Finally, a note on what the essays that follow are not. They are not intended to be comprehensive reviews of the literature in any given area.[3] In fact, the authors were specifically asked not to do this. These instructions, however, did not exclude the compiling of bibliographies to many of the essays that might provide a reasonable starting point for serious inquiry into the subfield being discussed. Many of these are extensive.

The authors were also asked not to restrict themselves to the need to present a balanced or thorough examination of their respective fields. This type of directive is a little unusual in academia. One result may be the intentional omission of works of stature, the contributions of major scholars. The editor, not the authors, takes full responsibility for such deficiencies. Rather than comprehensiveness, fairness, or balance, we wanted ideas—a freshness of perspective, a personal signature on the observations made. The goal has been to raise issues of significance for discussion and debate. Where are we? Where are we going? What could prove useful to us as we move toward an uncertain future? These are the comments that unite the chapters.

The papers were commissioned for a special series of theme panels held at the 1989 annual meeting of the Midwest Political Science Association. At that time, William Crotty was serving as president of the association and assumed the principal responsibility for organizing these panels. Alan D. Monroe served as program chair for the meeting. In addition, significant support was provided by Richard P. Farkas, then executive director of the Midwest Political Science Association, and Catherine E. Rudder, executive director of the American Political Science Association.

The idea behind the theme panels was to have a distinguished practitioner in a field prepare a paper on his or her specialty written in the context described above. A panel was then built around each paper and included three to four discussants, also individuals of prominence in the subfield, who commented on the paper, challenging its assumptions and often advancing alternative explanations, relevant criteria, or scenarios for future exploration. Most of the individuals who contributed in these ways are acknowledged by the authors in their essays.

The papers were then read before a group presumed to be expert in most cases, or at least interested enough as teachers or researchers in the area under discussion to participate in such a specialized critique. In general, the sessions were well attended. Surprisingly, perhaps, many of the panels had standing-room-only audiences, and in a few cases the meeting rooms were unable to accommodate all those wishing to attend. In most cases, too, the exchanges were lively, perhaps indicating that the issues being addressed and the questions raised reflected generally felt concerns in the discipline.

The authors were asked to incorporate into their essays the points they considered most relevant from the resulting exchanges and, specifically, to address in some fashion any issues that might appear to have been deficiencies in their original presentations. In some cases, the editor also advanced suggestions, but always with the understanding that the author's judgment as to relevance and importance, and the issues and themes that he or she preferred to emphasize, took precedence. No two essayists address the same questions within the same format. Some of the papers are lengthy; others are relatively brief. Some are opinionated; others preferred to mute their approach while allowing their personal preferences to remain clear. Some are cautiously optimistic; others are not. Some attempted to document their arguments extensively; others opted for a simpler thematic presentation. All in all, though, we trust that the essays taken together serve to highlight many of the most significant issues facing the discipline today, and that they provide a starting point for a serious discussion about where we as political scientists now are, what we have to contribute, and where we, as a discipline, may be headed.

IN THIS VOLUME . . .

Donald M. Freeman ("The Making of a Discipline") reviews the history of political science as a discipline, giving particular attention to the dilemmas and issues that have helped shape its growth. Freeman traces the evolution from studies in law and government through the influence of the early founders and the major departments—Columbia University, Johns Hopkins University, and the University of Chicago. The University of Chicago is considered the cradle of the scientific movement within political science.

He examines the influence of the behavioral movement and the scientific method in researching political phenomena, orientations that have generated the most divisive continuing debates in the field. Also discussed is the influence exerted by émigré scholars escaping Nazism and the emphasis on reality and relevance resulting from the experience of social scientists working in the government during World War II.

Freeman critiques a number of the major schools of thought, publications, and research undertakings that have shaped the field. Included is an account of the evolution of the survey method as a research tool and the dominance in behavioral studies of the "Michigan School" and its approach to structuring political inquiry. He looks at the Caucus for a New Political Science's challenge to the prevailing orthodoxies in the profession and its contributions to the rethinking of goals and the opening of the association's deliberations to broader influences.

The interests of political scientists continue to expand at a time when the field itself has shown signs of contraction. The postbehavioral period has witnessed an explosion of specialized knowledge, a greater distancing between subfields, and a fragmentation of concerns. The continuity and cohesiveness that marked the discipline in an earlier age is not so apparent today. Less appreciated also is an understanding of what the many subfields have generated in terms of knowledge and how well it advances our understanding of the traditional concerns that have guided inquiry.

In a related essay, J. Donald Moon ("Pluralism and Progress in the Study of Politics") addresses head-on the question of fragmentation—the intellectual and substantive decentralization of the discipline—and the unease this has evoked. Some—possibly many—feel that the integrity of the enterprise is under attack; that the answer is to return to the cohesiveness that bonded broad concentrations of scholars together in their inquiries into problems of commonly accepted importance from related value, theoretical, and methodological perspectives.

Moon's position is quite different. He argues that a plurality of approaches and concerns is desirable; it generates knowledge and it encourages flexibility and innovation. Moreover, such a diffusion of goals and perspectives is inevitable; wanted or not, it is the sign of a maturing discipline. A shared intellectual heritage is important, but efforts to bound the field or require conformance to any type of reigning orthodoxies, however benign or promising, are unproductive. Moreover, the search for such coherence of intellectual approaches is fanciful; it cannot succeed. As much as any, this represents a fair statement of where we are, and more than likely, what the future should hold.

A diffusion of approaches is unavoidable because of the differing conceptions of what the subject matter of political inquiry is and what it includes. Prescriptions as to what constitutes acceptable political science change with time and respond to societal experiences. Knowledge is reflexive; it influences the way people behave and what they expect by transforming the political environment that is the focus of attention. Each contributes to change. The old will not suffice; new theories of explanation must be found.

Unfortunately, the institutionalization of knowledge within professions and universities can serve to discourage creativity and innovation;

in effect, it presents a look at what has been done as a guide to further research. A pluralism of purpose and approach challenges these barriers, pragmatically calling on whatever is useful wherever it may be unearthed.

The cumulative advance of a discipline, marked by a common set of problems to be explored and criteria to judge research, may be hindered by a fragmentation of concerns. A degree of standardization and an agreed upon history of development in a discipline is both desirable and needed to set standards of commonly accepted relevance. The stakes are high for contending schools of thought that seek to historically re-create the discipline and its past within its image of relevance. Nonetheless, whatever the orientation of disciplinary histories and the criteria they put forth as preferable, the pluralism of approach and purpose is unlikely to be deterred.

Fragmentation has its costs for a discipline, and they are substantial. But a diversity of perspectives and areas of concentration, and eclecticism and pragmatism of orientation has its rewards. The overall goal is a progression of knowledge; a deeper and broader understanding of political phenomena. A Kuhnian "normal science" approach may not be the best way to achieve such ends.

Moon ends with a checklist of objectives that analytic overviews of the discipline might achieve. The hope is that the chapters in the four volumes of this series will begin to realize some of these ends.

Terence W. Ball ("Whither Political Theory?") takes on the difficult and unenviable task of assessing where political theory has been over the last few decades, the contemporary situation it finds itself in, and where it may be heading.

Ball begins by referring to David Easton's famous 1953 work, *The Political System*, celebrating the end of normative or traditional theorizing in the discipline. The ensuing decades witnessed repeated declarations as to the "end of political theory" and the "end of ideology" as a force in American scholarship and culture. There were dissenters from these claims and eventually their views would come to prevail.

Societies, much less the study of politics, cannot exist without theories to explain—rationalize?—their values, their reward systems, the manner in which decisions are made, who is to make such choices, and how they are selected, what contributes to private as against public behavior. The questions are fundamental; coherent and encompassing political theories are needed to address them and to frame the bounds for political inquiry. What had fallen into disfavor was the study of classical theory, an activity that much of political science did not prize.

During the last few decades, political theory has enjoyed a significant rebirth of interest. The reasons for the revival are many: behavioralism and its philosophic base, logical positivism, came under attack;

ideology and ideological activism enjoyed a rebirth during the 1960s and 70s in the antiwar, civil rights, and women's movements; and a revived theoretical interest emerged in questions of immediate real-world interest, symbolized by John Rawls's influential *A Theory of Justice* (1971). These developments were accompanied by the introduction of new journals for theorists and political philosophers to exchange ideas.

The newfound popularity of political theorizing may contain the seeds of its own destruction. In particular, Bell finds the present state of theorizing in the discipline out of touch with the politics that should be its subject matter: overspecialized, concerned with questions of methods and techniques of interpretation, and unnecessarily arcane in its debates.

Bell advocates that theory return to a concern with society and its problems; that it explore questions raised by the relationship of humankind to nature, our obligations to ourselves and our descendants in preserving a livable environment; and that it seek a reintegration with empirical behavioral investigations. Political theory should "learn from" political life and reflect its complications, irrationalities, and richness of experience. Theory has much to offer; more than this, a society cannot function without it or a discipline prosper in its absence.

One of the most significant influences in the study of political phenomena over the last several decades have been theories of rational action. These are borrowed from economics and hold promise of formulating comprehensive, researchable, and explanatory models of behavior as powerful as any the discipline has known. At the same time, the theoretical emphasis has been controversial. It is well removed from the type of theory construction traditionally prominent in political science or from the socio-psychological assumptions implicit in much of the empirical and behavioral research. Critics have elaborated the weaknesses of rational modeling approaches, while proponents continue to emphasize their promise. Whatever the cost-benefit balance, its influence in reshaping thought within the discipline cannot be denied.

Kristen Renwick Monroe ("The Theory of Political Action: What is it? How Useful is it for Political Science?") explains what rational action theory is and what its assumptions are; provides an intellectual history of its evolution; and assesses concerns with its applicability for political science research and the weakness in its conceptual superstructure. She proposes three principal modifications of the approach that should make it more suitable in adapting to disciplinary concerns. It is a major undertaking executed in a crisp, balanced, and insightful manner.

Rational action theory as taken from classic economics assumes that individuals are the basic actors in society; they act in expectation of the highest utility return; they have access to information relevant to decisions to be made; and they can anticipate the consequences of different outcomes. A modification of the classic approach is offered in "bounded rationality"—that is, the limits imposed on action of the individual's process of decision-making. The emphasis in "satisficing" (choosing acceptable rather than maximizing alternatives) is one influential outcome of the bounded rationality school of thinking. In effect, these alterations represent not only a significant modification of the assumptions inherent in the original theorizing, but commentaries on its inflexibility.

Rational actor theory has also been criticized for its insensitivity to the restrictions of choice posed by cultural influences and social norms. In addition, research in cognitive psychology has shown that individuals do not process information or establish priorities in anything approximating the efficient manner that rational action theory postulates. This theory is also weak in accounting for unselfish behavior or collective action.

Monroe poses eleven fundamental questions that address assumptions in the approach and on which she believes future research might focus. She raises concerns as to the role of emotions in decision-making; the relevance of market concepts and the priority of economic concerns for explaining political behavior; and the implicit values hidden within economic theorizing. On each point she reviews the relevant thinking, indicating avenues that future research might explore.

Monroe concludes by arguing for three modifications in rational actor theory, relating to such considerations as self-interest, conscious choice, and the process of individual identity. Reconceptualizations of these dimensions would make the approach more applicable to analyzing political actions.

An evaluation of analytic theories and their derivative methodologies, the way the two interrelate, and the orientation provided methodological investigations by such models, is by its nature a most formidable enterprise. Such an assessment covers in one manner or another every subfield of political science. In addition, the methods and the theoretical models are borrowed from a variety of other disciplines, ranging from mathematics to engineering, necessitating a familiarity with their use in these contexts and the manner in which they have been adapted to political science ends. Yet this is exactly the type of intellectual journey that Paul E. Johnson and Philip A. Schrodt ("Analytic Theory and Methodology") embark on. It is a rich, complicated, and sophisticated venture.

The mathematical modeling of political behavior is relatively new for political science; it has enjoyed a life span of roughly three decades. The perspective has just begun to assume the position of a fully mature subfield within the discipline. The models employed in research have been broad-gauged, finding applications that cross the traditional boundary lines of disciplinary subfields and involving issues that range from legislative committee decision-making to the nuclear arms race. Thinking in the field has evolved from technique to substance, requiring an exacting methodological preparedness from practitioners. The clarity and precision of the research are attractive, as is the clarity of the scientific criteria used in judging investigations. The likelihood is that a reliance on such modeling and the statistical processes that are associated with it will increase in the future; their impact is just beginning to be broadly felt.

The models that Johnson and Schrodt explore are abstract, explicit, deductive, and empirically testable. They include those active in guiding political research, to which most attention is given; those once important but now fallen into disuse; and those employed in other disciplines to good effect but rare or unknown in political science. Most of these have been developed or applied within political science only since the 1950s. They fall into three major areas of inquiry: public choice and political economy approaches; systems modeling; and artificial intelligence or computational modeling.

The authors analyze the diversity of modeling approaches and their results in a variety of substantive areas: voting models of legislatures and elections, including references to the "new institutionalism" as it affects social choice; games and decision theory, and the variety of conceptual and definitional problems that concern modelers who employ different gaming strategies; dynamic modeling as evidenced in the arms race and computer simulations, among other applications; stochastic models of varying types (statistical, poisson distributions, and Markov chains); and the broad category of artificial intelligence simulations, employing among other problem-solving assumptions, rule-based, precedent-based, and natural-language-based propositions. It is an impressive overview, indicative of the technical virtuosity of the practitioners and the increasing relevance of modeling to a variety of political science applications and real-world problem-solving.

Johnson and Schrodt close by directing attention to a set of issues that they feel must be addressed for analytic modeling to continue its contributions to disciplinary explanation. These range from emphases in developing noncooperative gaming strategies in game theory to the relationship between modeling aggregations of preferences to explain macrobehavior patterns. Political behavior is less predictable and more episodic and its impacts on collective action more troublesome than the behavioral patterns experienced in other social sciences. The field would benefit from models and explanatory tools that take explicit account of the peculiar problems faced by the political scientist. As it is, these approaches are progressing nicely, in the process giving back to other disciplines distinctive contributions to the thinking concerning their own modeling and explanatory needs.

The women's movement of the 1960s brought gender to academic attention as a focus of intellectual concern. Within a short period of time, gender-based research appeared in quantity. Such research has developed in comparable stages throughout the social sciences. First, sex as a variable of importance was appended extending traditional research designs. Next gender perceptions and behavior were explored from a female point of view. And finally, the role that gender played in theory constructions and the assumptions underlying explanations of political behavior were analyzed.

Virginia Sapiro ("Gendered Politics: The State of the Field") reviews these developments and raises issues with which those who research gender-related questions should concern themselves. Gender studies are not a clearly defined subfield within the discipline, yet gender-relevant studies can be found in most of the conventional subdivisions of political science. The volume of work in print, the multiplicity of approaches employing the focus, the potential role of gender in forming research inquiries, and the areas and research investigations that omit or deemphasize its role combine to set a broad agenda for consideration.

Sapiro approaches the task by isolating six areas of concern in gender research. Each is notable for the inclusiveness of the problems addressed and the potential for further research of significance. In some cases, the areas have been developed more innovatively in other disciplines; political science is running to catch up. In others, the contributions of political science, while subject to continuing enrichment, have been distinctive.

The problem areas developed begin with identity politics and gender consciousness, the exploration of gender and sexuality as they relate to political ends. They include efforts to establish a division of the personal from the political, the private from the public. Such a rethinking of conventional perspectives—a task underway—holds the greatest promise for forcing a reevaluation of what constitutes politically relevant behavior. The role of power and the unpowerful, or the various ways in which influence is exercised in a world of political inequalities by those with a disproportionately limited sphere of authority, is a concern of researchers in the field and one with applications clearly not strictly related to women. The ambivalent attitude toward the intervention of the state in society constitutes a traditional concern of those who study government. It is significant for women, many of whom have historically favored an activist state role to redress grievances while opposing government dependency roles. An examination of gendered states, or the association and interpretation of certain activities, positions, concepts, and policy issues (war, defense, power, decision-making, competition) with maleness, others (education, family, welfare, child care, peace) with femaleness, is also of major concern. Neither politics nor government is gender neutral. There is an opening here for alternative constructions and perspectives. And finally in this context is the need for the grounding of an understanding of gender issues, and political science questions more generally, in an awareness of the relevance of historical studies for appreciating the complexity of change, and the role of conflict and collection action in seeking political expression.

The research agenda, while partial as would be expected, is rich in promise. The output for the study of gender problems is substantial and its relevance for reconceptualizing political inquiry and political science thinking extends well beyond an understanding of the immediate focus of the research.

In discussing the current state of the discipline in relation to the study of African-American politics, Michael C. Dawson and Ernest J. Wilson III ("Paradigms and Paradoxes: Political Science and African-American Politics") find ambivalences. Some reflect those found in society more generally; for others no readily apparent explanations exist. Dawson and Wilson make the following points: that the exploration of race as a part of American politics is separated from mainstream disciplinary concerns, receives relatively limited attention, and, while important in real-world politics, is treated by political scientists in such a manner that it adds little to an understanding of political life. They argue that there is a division by race in the study of black/white politics more pronounced than in related disciplines such as sociology or history. In addition, when political scientists engage in crossover research, and more specifically when white political scientists study African-American political questions, they produce distinctively different types of research. They ask different questions and employ different criteria to judge the significance of what they uncover. As Dawson and Wilson indicate, these findings were not anticipated. Yet the tendencies identified are pronounced. The authors also, of course, find them discouraging.

The study of Afro-American politics could be at a critical juncture. The significance of black movements and political efforts over the last generation, from the civil rights marches to the recent black mayoral successes in major cities and the Jesse Jackson presidential campaigns, has begun to reshape the political landscape. At the same time, inner-city crime, drug use, the social disorganization of families, and the weakening impact of a number of leading black organizations point to problems of magnitude for both blacks and American society more generally. The trends being observed are complicated; their significance and outcomes are unclear. The challenge is to capture these dimensions through first-quality research that engages the entire political science community and contributes directly to an understanding of American political life.

As for the current research on Afro-American politics, they observe a number of deficiencies. There is evidence of a general failure to employ theoretical models as a starting point or for explaining the behavior under investigation. They also find a lack of attention to rules of evidence and scientific (or other) criteria as standards against which to judge the value of outcomes or to test propositional inventories relevant to an understanding of black political behavior. The research undertaken can be rudimentary. The authors find little formal modeling or sophisticated quantitative analysis available in this field. These observations could be made in varying degrees concerning the work being done in many subfields of the discipline; the authors believe they are particularly applicable to research on questions relevant to black politics.

Dawson and Wilson indicate a number of problems open to investigation. These range from the implications of structural changes in Afro-American communities and its political ramifications to gender differences in political role playing among blacks. Increasingly also there has been a political isolation of blacks within American society. The political consequences of such changes have not been fully developed.

The authors assess the contributions of a variety of intellectual strains for understanding black political behavior. They review the major controversies in each area, as well as significant authors and their works, and they outline potential research agendas that could proceed from the shared intellectual perspectives. The canvas is broad, ranging from Weberian and Marxist analyses to pluralistic, modernization, social choice, and social stratification approaches. In all, they suggest a way of organizing the subfield and in the process capturing the most significant dimensions of the black political experience.

The conflicting pressures are great. Much can be done. The problem is to chart the way. This essay should engage the debate.

The volume concludes with brief biographical sketches of the authors.

NOTES

1. William G. Boyer and Julie Ann Sosa, *Prospects for Faculty in the Arts and Sciences: A Study of Factors Affecting Demand and Supply, 1987 to 2012* (Princeton, N.J.: Princeton University Press, 1989).

2. Gabriel A. Almond, *A Divided Discipline* (San Mateo, Calif.: Sage Publications, 1989), and idem, "Separate Tables: Schools and Sects in Political Science?" *PS* 21:828–42. See also Kristen Monroe, Gabriel A. Almond, John Gunnell, Ian Shapiro, George Graham, Benjamin Barber, Kenneth Shepsle, and

Joseph Cropsey, "The Nature of Contemporary Political Science: A Roundtable Discussion," *PS: Political Science and Politics* 23 (1):34–43.

3. These are needed and welcome. See, as examples, Ada W. Finifter, ed., *Political Science: The State of the Discipline* (Washington, D.C.: American Political Science Association, 1983), and Fred I. Greenstein and Nelson W. Polsby, eds., *Handbook of Political Science*, 4 vols. (Reading, Mass.: Addison-Wesley Publishing Company, 1975). See also Herbert S. Weisberg, *Political Science: The Science of Politics* (New York: Agathon Press, 1986). A guide to the relevant literature critiquing the discipline can be found in Donald M. Freeman's "The Making of a Discipline" in this volume.

REFERENCES

Almond, Gabriel A. 1989a. *A Divided Discipline*. San Mateo, Calif.: Sage Publications.

———. 1989b. "Separate Tables: Schools and Sects in Political Science?" *PS* 21:828–42.

Boyer, William G., and Julie Ann Sosa. 1989. *Prospects for Faculty in the Arts and Sciences: A Study of Factors Affecting Demand and Supply, 1987 to 2012*. Princeton, N.J.: Princeton University Press.

Finifter, Ada W., ed. 1983. *Political Science: The State of the Discipline*. Washington, D.C.: American Political Science Association.

Greenstein, Fred I., and Nelson W. Polsby, eds. 1975. *Handbook of Political Science*. 8 vols. Reading, Pa.: Addison-Wesley.

Monroe, Kristen, Gabriel A. Almond, John Gunnell, Benjamin Barber, Kenneth Shepsle, Joseph Cropsey, George Graham, and Ian Shapiro. 1990. "The Nature of Contemporary Political Science: A Roundtable Discussion." *PS: Political Science and Politics* 23(1):34–43.

Weisberg, Herbert F., ed. 1986. *Political Science: The Science of Politics*. New York: Agathon Press.

1

The Making of a Discipline

Donald M. Freeman

KNOWING A DISCIPLINE'S DILEMMAS

If there is one constant theme in the history of political science it is surely this: in each generation there has been at least one and sometimes several groups voicing discontent about things as they are in the discipline. Self-examination and criticism are healthy for the growth and maturity of a profession: as Bernard Crick (1959:xii) has written, "A discipline is known by the dilemmas it keeps." What is disturbing about American political science, however, is the tendency of the dilemmas it keeps to be converted into crusades notable for their sectarian divisiveness.

No doubt the most persistent dilemma for the discipline has been over political science as a science, a topic addressed later in this paper. Other, closely related debates have persisted over the last century, but interest in them waxes and wanes. I refer to the goals for undergraduate and graduate education in political science. What should be the content of the curriculum for the political science baccalaureate? Especially, what values should be taught in it, and how much socialization to democratic values should be included? Graduate education is linked to undergraduate education, especially in political science, because a large proportion, 80 percent or more of the discipline's doctorates, are employed in higher education. The primary question raised by critics of the typical doctoral graduate is: Should not graduate education include some training in teaching skills? Each generation of American political

I wish to thank panel members J. Donald Moon, Elinor Ostrom, and Anne Schneider for their comments and evaluations.

scientists has debated anew undergraduate and graduate curricular content, without resolution.

Since 1973, however, the American Political Science Association has published and distributed to members and departments information about undergraduate curricula and teaching innovations (beginning as *D.E.A. News* and most recently becoming *The Political Science Teacher*). In 1972, the association began publishing *A Guide to Graduate Study in Political Science* and more recently a *Directory of Undergraduate Political Science Faculty*. With these and other forms of communication within the profession, there is, minimally, a sharing that in earlier days was limited to special conferences or committees of the association and occasional panels at the Annual Meetings (see Somit and Tanenhaus 1967, 1982; Ricci 1984; Crick 1959; *PS* 5:51, 6:35, 446–49).

I have dealt briefly with the controversy over the goals of education for graduates and undergraduates in this introductory essay to illustrate a perennial subject over which critics of the state of the discipline can mount a protest. Please note that on the goals of undergraduate and graduate education, political science shares the dilemma with all the social sciences. However, political scientists act like their dilemmas are unique, unshared, and somehow indicative of an inherent weakness in our professional character.

Prediscipline Roots of Political Science

Perhaps the reason for the quarrelsome nature of political science, and the uncertainty that political scientists express about their true disciplinary identity, can be found in the complex history of the profession. Political philosophy can certainly be traced back to Plato and Aristotle, twenty-two to twenty-three centuries ago. In our more reflective moments, we political scientists claim our normative and empirical beginnings in these Greek philosophers. The works of these and other important political theorists, from their time to the present, have been taught in the political science curriculum. A great many of the early leaders in American political science were, in the main, political theory specialists, and the early importance of this field to our disciplinary heritage should not be overlooked.

While we have roots in political philosophy reaching back over centuries, political science is in reality a very young discipline. In William Anderson's introduction to Anna Haddow's remarkable history of political science education in the United States from 1636 to 1900, he says, "A perusal of Miss Haddow's work will also help to dispel the notion that political science is a 'new' or a 'young' subject in American colleges" (1939, 1969:x). There are roots that reach back well into the past, although the emphasis was different and the independence of inquiry suspect. The subjects being taught until the 1880s, almost exclusively at the undergraduate level, included moral philosophy, constitutional and legal history, and political economy. Before the Civil War, only one political scientist, worthy of the label, is identified—Francis Lieber, a German immigrant, who taught first at South Carolina College in 1835 and then at Columbia College from 1858 until 1872. In short, politics and government were not taught in an identifiable, independent curriculum.

When political science began to emerge as an identifiable discipline in the 1880s and 90s, German university education was the model Americans copied. All the social sciences, but especially history and political science, imitated the trend in the natural sciences to send their graduates to Europe for advanced study (Somit and Tanenhaus 1967, 1982:15, 16; Crick 1959:19–28). The inflexible and dry curriculum for what passed as graduate education in the United States in the nineteenth century did not inspire bright young scholars. On the other hand, in Germany there was freedom, excitement, and a commitment to original research. Students in history and political science were encouraged to use primary sources in their research, which meant newspapers, memoirs, documents, letters, and anything else that could be construed as a firsthand account. The German doctorate was a research-centered degree, featuring the seminar and the opportunity to pursue your research interests wherever they led you. The comparative, historico-analytical approach was invariably the style of research used in Germany, and it was carried back to the United States as the dominant pattern of inquiry for a couple of generations (Waldo 1975:23–30).

Burgess, Columbia, and Political Science

The "father" of American political science was a young Civil War veteran and graduate of Amherst, John W. Burgess. His postgraduate path led him first to law, next to teaching at Knox College, and finally to graduate study in Germany. Burgess returned to an appointment at Amherst, where he urged the administration and his colleagues to establish a German-style graduate program. When the Amherst project failed, he accepted an appointment (in 1876) to fill the chair vacated by the death of Francis Lieber. The graduate program Burgess had failed to sell at Amherst was approved at Columbia in June 1880 when the trustees established the nation's first school of political science.

Four years before Burgess got his graduate program approved, the Johns Hopkins University was established as an American version of a German-style (that is, devoted to graduate-level study as a principal duty) university, and Herbert Baxter Adams was selected to lead the department of history and political science. The program at Hopkins grew more slowly. Until well into the twentieth century, Columbia and Hopkins were the dominant sources of American doctorates trained in political science (Haddow 1939:171ff.; Somit and Tanenhaus 1967, 1982:11ff.; Waldo 1975:26ff.).

It is also significant that Columbia and Hopkins provided outlets for the publication of dissertations and research. By classic definition, the master's thesis was a modest contribution to knowledge and the doctoral dissertation a significant contribution. Dissertations were expected to be published, and when that did not become an automatic event, Adams established *The Johns Hopkins Studies in Historical and Political Science* (1883) and Columbia followed with its *Studies in History, Economics and Public Law* (1891). Shorter pieces, mainly historico-analytical articles and commentary, were published in Columbia's scholarly journal, the *Political Science Quarterly* (1886) (Haddow 1939:255).

At Columbia and Hopkins, under the leadership of Burgess and Adams, political science graduate education had a beginning in the United States, but little more than a beginning. In the Burgess school of political science, history, economics, geography, and sociology were commingled in an almost undifferentiated fashion.

A discipline or profession is much like a nation, and political science in the 1880s and 1890s was no better off than Lebanon is today. A discipline needs an identity, boundaries, control over those who practice within its ranks, a commonly accepted language, and a measure of respect from others who share the world within which the discipline is practiced. The first generation of political scientists faced an awesome task of nation-building, to carry the nation-state analogy one step forward. The first generation of American political scientists continued to use methods and approaches learned from German historians and political scientists. Often doctoral candidates traveled to Europe to further refine their education. It may be that the semipermanent identity crisis of political science is found in our disciplinary genes (Freeman 1977: ix, x).

Discipline-Building and Discontent

The American Historical Association, the American Economic Association, and the American Sociological Association were all organized and began publishing their journals in the 1880s and 1890s. Political scientists attended one or more of the annual meetings of their fellow social scientists until 1903. That year, in conjunction with a joint meeting of the American Historical and Economic Associations, in New Orleans, the American Political Science Association was organized, with Frank J. Goodnow as its first president. At first the association published only the proceedings of its annual meetings, but in 1906 it began to publish the *American Political Science Review,* which quickly became the preeminent journal of the profession and has remained so since (Haddow 1939:255–62).

Political science was still a small discipline. William Anderson reports that there were 287 individual subscribers to the *Review* in 1912 and 580 in 1932 (Haddow 1939:261). Moreover, political science was rarely represented in a freestanding and independent department in colleges and universities. Only gradually did political science escape the captivity of a joint department, usually with history. It was not until the post–World War II period that the discipline became broadly recognized as a distinct field of inquiry. Departmental status came first to the larger institutions and those offering graduate study—only thirty-eight institutions had separate departments in 1914 (Somit and Tanenhaus 1967, 1982:56).

Gradually, in the first decades of the twentieth century, there was an Americanization of political science. Somit and Tanenhaus (1967, 1982) note the fading of the requisite trip to Continental universities for graduate candidates, the increasing proportion of faculty posts filled by American-trained doctorates, and the proportionate decline of books published abroad to those published in this country in the book review section of the *Review*. There was also discontent with the comparative historico-analytical approach to studying politics and government. Among others expressing a displeasure over massaging dusty manuscripts and consulting legal records was Woodrow Wilson, a political scientist who went into university and party politics, eventually leading to the presidency.

Two books that were destined to have great impact on American political science appeared in 1908. One was written by a sociologist. It had little immediate impact and he soon abandoned academic life. The other was written by an Englishman. Both books were very critical of the style of research being carried out in the United States. Arthur Bentley's *The Process of Government* carries on the overleaf "This Book Is an Attempt to Fashion a Tool," the tool being a group theory of politics. In his short and devastating comment on political science, in chapter 4 Bentley says:

> We have a dead political science. It is a formal study of the most external characteristics of governing institutions. It loves to classify governments by incidental attributes, and when all is said and done it cannot classify them much better now than by lifting up bodily Aristotle's monarchies, aristocracies, and democracies. [Bentley 1908:162]

The real impact of Bentley's theory was to come years later in David Truman's rewrite of group theory in *The Governmental Process* (1951).

Graham Wallas, the English critic, had an immediate impact with his *Human Nature in Politics,* in which he offered this critique of the discipline:

> For the moment . . . nearly all students of politics analyse institutions and avoid the analysis of man. The study of human nature by the psychologists has . . . advanced enormously since the discovery of human evolution, but it has advanced without affecting or being affected by the study of politics. [Eulau, Eldersveld, and Janowitz 1956:9]

Not only did Wallas call for a study of human nature (informed by psychology) in politics, but he also waxed optimistic about future progress for a science of politics. Looking back at 1908, almost every student of the evolution of political science in the United States notes the importance of Bentley and Wallas for the emerging emphasis of a new science of politics (Crick 1959:109–11, 118–30; Somit and Tanenhaus 1967, 1982:66ff.; Storing 1962:152–224).

Charles E. Merriam, Advocate of Science

Before Merriam there were any number of scholars who discussed a "science" of politics, but the precise meaning of the idea is not to be found even in the writings of those who made lasting contributions to theory-building in the discipline. Rather than define or explain science, especially its methodology, Merriam was interested in "doing" science. Let the record show that, if his partisan political ambitions had not been destroyed in the Chicago election of 1919, and if his political fortunes had been quite good, Merriam might have become a second Woodrow Wilson in the profession. Instead Merriam channeled his considerable ambition and skill into advocating a science of politics. His efforts to redirect the discipline in the 1920s met resistance, and would have to be called a short-term failure. However, the battle he lost in the 1920s was won by his students after World War II.

Merriam was especially impressed with the methodology being employed by psychology, and he was quite willing to separate political science from the influence of history. In 1921 Merriam launched his crusade with an essay, "The Present State of the Study of Politics." He led three conferences on the science of politics (1923–1925) and he summarized his views and the work of the conferences in *New Aspects of Politics* (1925, 1970). Merriam was also a leader in the establishment of the very influential Social Science Research Council, which contributed to the progress of all the social sciences in the 1920s and 1930s. Later, during the heyday of behavioralism, the council was to fund retooling and training programs for social scientists and graduate students.

Merriam's greatest impact on political science came from research and graduate training that began under his leadership of the department at the University of Chicago. The faculty and graduate students at Chicago knew that something very special and exciting was happening there. A good faculty and good students attract more good students.

For Merriam there were no boundaries limiting cross-disciplinary training. The willingness to experiment, the cross-disciplinary fertilization, and the empirical quantitative style that was encouraged made it possible for Chicago to influence future generations of the discipline. Richard Jensen has said it well:

> Nowhere was the new science of politics more avidly studied than at Chicago, home of Merriam, Thurstone, and a host of brilliant scholars committed to the new behavioral paradigm. Under Merriam's tireless entrepreneurial leadership, Leonard White, Harold Gosnell, Quincy Wright, Harold Lasswell, Frederick Schuman, Roscoe Martin, V. O. Key, Gabriel Almond, Avery Leiserson, C. Herman Pritchett, Herbert Simon, and David Truman turned their talent to scientific behavioral research, often of a quantitative cast. . . . The first wave of enthusiasm for behavioralism did not change the tenor of publications and research in the discipline overnight, except perhaps at Chicago. A variety of institutional and technical factors slowed the transformation between old and new paradigms. [Jensen 1969:7]

Some historians of political science in the United States have found in Merriam a symbol of a sort of disciplinary schizophrenia. David M. Ricci, among others, finds an almost pathological condition for the discipline's value conflicts (*The Tragedy of Political Science* 1984:57ff.). Merriam advocated a science of politics, but he was directly involved in the subject he would "scientifically" study. Merriam, like many of his peers in the discipline, was involved in the middle-class reform movement called Progressivism. He like most of the profession was fundamentally committed to what Louis Hartz called "the liberal tradition," a set of internalized values unlikely to be set aside to conduct objective analysis. The American people, as a whole, and political scientists also, were the product of a culture that accepted the idea of progress, nationalism, and egalitarianism. Merriam was active in government, wished to manipulate it and its policies, and over time conducted research that would be applied to making a better society (according to his preferences). The conflicts many see in academics and in scholars like Merriam can be summarized in a famous sentence from the most important work by perhaps Merriam's most distinguished disciple: Harold Lasswell wrote in his *Politics* (1936), "The science of politics has no preferences."

Merriam was a prophet of science, but he wrote nothing about scientific method, and his kindest reviewers (for example, Barry D. Karl 1974) would not attribute to the leader of the "Chicago School" any sophistication in regard to the philosophy of science. It is likely that political science will go on debating and experiencing some tension about the subject: facts and values; analysis and advocacy; pure and applied research.

At the time that Merriam was trying to convert political science with his *New Aspects of Politics,* Thomas H. Reed and others were pressing the association to study government policy and commit resources to educate the young for proper civic duty. This is an old movement in the association. It commanded a good deal of attention in the 1930s and "education for democratic citizenship" has remained an important interest of the profession. Ultimately Reed was influential in establishing the Citizenship Clearing House (which became the National Center for Education in Politics), which fostered internships and experiential education of many sorts from 1946 until 1966, when its ability to raise funds ended. The values linked to CCH-NCEP live on today in political science through internship programs and schools of practical politics (for example, the Eagleton Institute at Rutgers). Most political scientists, I believe, find no professional value conflicts between a scientific orientation and sophisticated education for democratic citizenship (see Somit and Tanenhaus 1967, 1982:87–89, 195ff.; Waldo 1975:47–67; Dahl 1961:763, 764).

Crises and Growth

External events have shaped American political science from its beginnings. Indeed, the rise of the university in higher education and graduate education were the product of a post–Civil War period of nationalism, and the Columbia and Johns Hopkins programs were particular cases of a national trend. National crises, in the shape of two World Wars, the war in Vietnam, the Great Depression, and the black social revolution of the 1960s have influenced the discipline's growth in very special ways.

Dislocation in Europe between the two great wars caused what Dwight Waldo has called the "re-Europeanization" of American political science. Waldo gives a partial list of immigrants who contributed to a more vital and mature discipline in the 1930s: Hannah Arendt, Karl Deutsch, Alfred Diamant, William Ebenstein, Heinz Eulau, Carl Friedrich, Ernest Haas, Stanley Hoffman, Hans Kelsen, Henry Kissinger, Hans Morgenthau, Fritz Morstein Marx, Franz Neumann, Sigmund Neumann, and Leo Strauss (Waldo 1975:45). Robert Dahl has said that these immigrant social scientists brought with them their recent experience with theory-building. They were among the best political scientists and sociologists in Europe. Even though some of the immigrants would not be a part of the behavioral revolution, the knowledge they brought with them contributed to a new political science after World War II (Dahl 1961:764).

The rise of the social service state in the form of the New Deal and the total mobilization for World War II employed many social and behavioral scientists in advisory, planning, and management posts. From drawing up Franklin Roosevelt's court-packing plan to content-analyzing enemy communications, the work these scholars did ranged from constitutional-legal research to rather advanced empirical analysis.

Public administration had emerged in the 1920s as a field in the discipline. Its New Deal and wartime experience reinforced its conception of its value to practitioners and led to the creation of the American Society for Public Administration in the late 1930s. The publication of its *Public Administration Review* began in 1940. Two decades later public administration became the focal point of a major separatist movement.

The opportunity for government service challenged some social scientists and frustrated others who found their training inadequate. Many returned to academe ready to make changes in traditional political science. The next generation of social scientists would be nurtured on works like Samuel Stouffer and associates' four-volume *The American Soldier* (1949), a major breakthrough in the field of tests and measurements, and Alexander Leighton's *The Governing of Men* (1945), a study of the victims of the American relocation of the Japanese. Such innovative research provided a cafeteria line laden with propositions for testing in future research.

One site for service in the New Deal was a little-known Division of Program Surveys, located in the Department of Agriculture. In a fit of economy after the war, the Congress abolished the unit, leaving Rensis Likert and Angus Campbell looking about for an institution in which they could continue their trade of survey research. The University of Michigan gave these two future greats a place to work. Likert and Campbell became the first and second directors of the Survey Research Center of Michigan's Institute for Social Research.

The Bureau of Applied Social Research preceded the Survey Research Center. With a first life as the Office of Radio Research, beginning in 1937 at Princeton, it moved to Columbia under the leadership of Paul F. Lazarsfeld in 1940. The National Opinion Research Center was established at the University of Denver in 1941 under the leadership of Harry H. Field and relocated to the University of Chicago in 1947. These three opinion research centers refined and developed the survey as a tool in social research, but it was the Survey Research Center at Michigan that was to have an enormous impact on the postwar discipline.

Professionals using survey methods have always included those interested in both pure and applied research. The creation of the American Association of Public Opinion Research in 1946 brought together in one organization academics and "pollsters." The *Public Opinion Quarterly,* their official journal, preexisted AAPOR, first publishing in

1937. The appearance of the public opinion poll (beginning in 1935) and the development of the social survey made it possible for political scientists to study political behavior with a new set of powerful tools (Freeman 1977:221–23).

The successes of Angus Campbell and the creative young scholars who gathered around him at Michigan in the field of voting behavior reinforced the already considerable reputation of that university. Michigan became as important to the new, postwar political science as had been Chicago earlier, and Columbia and Johns Hopkins even earlier. However, the long-term importance of Michigan rests in the creation of the Inter-University Consortium for Political and Social Research (ICPSR) in 1962. Twenty-one of the nation's leading research universities in political science created a relationship between the Survey Research Center and the social scientific community to establish: 1) a data repository, 2) a summer training program for emerging scientists and to retread older professionals, and 3) a sharing of new technology and data management techniques. Those who created the ICPSR expected it to be a small holding company of the leading schools. It grew, however, under the leadership of Warren E. Miller until in the 1980s its members numbered over two hundred seventy colleges and universities in the United States and abroad. With the help of the National Science Foundation's continuing funding, the election studies have been institutionalized.

Data archives defy simple description. The data available from ICPSR alone come from all the social sciences. Its executive director for more than a decade has been a historian. The ICPSR is not alone: to mention only one other (of many data repositories), the Roper Center has a collection of public opinion polls dating back to 1935.

The several data repositories make their holdings available for secondary analysis, sparing graduate students and faculty the enormous costs of collecting their own data. For the first decade, and perhaps longer, of the consortium, Ann Arbor was a gathering place for some of the brightest and best young scholars and faculty. They came to attend 1) the annual meetings of delegates to the consortium, 2) the summer training programs, or 3) special conferences funded frequently by generous foundation support. The collegiality of these occasions was a source of vitality among empirical political scientists (Eulau 1989; ICPSR 1984; Freeman 1977:272–77; Rowdybush 1988).

The final pair of crises to shape American political science appeared together in the 1960s. These were the black social revolution and the war in Vietnam. Divisions over a proper professional response to these events created a form of two-party system within the discipline, with one faction led by those associated with the Caucus for a New Political Science. Again, political science was not alone in experiencing fraternal warfare within its professional ranks in the 1960s. All the behavioral and social sciences experienced the rise of a radical, leftist, or protest movement, but political science treated the caucus as if it were a unique and very special burden. The division within the profession followed an extraordinary expansion in political science, and all of higher education, following World War II.

Remember that the modal case for political science before World War II was for the discipline to exist in a combined department, most often with history. Rather rapidly after the war, independent departments appeared. With independence, and growing numbers of students enrolled in colleges and universities, departments expanded. That meant a demand for more faculty and an expansion of existing graduate programs, supplemented by many new graduate programs. Good, solid graduate programs expanded so rapidly that frequently the incoming students could not be assimilated. Time for the graduate faculty to interact with doctoral candidates was inadequate. A weak professional socialization was frequently the unintended consequence.

Association membership, as reported in the APSA *Biographical Directory 1968,* was doubling every ten years:

1938	2,090	members
1948	4,939	"
1958	7,065	"
1968	15,185	"

Of course, these figures included institutional, faculty, and graduate memberships, but the very rapid growth pattern was obvious. One year after the birth of the caucus, the executive director reported that 4,500 persons attended the annual meeting in Washington and 3,723 had registered. Only 872 persons had registered at the St. Louis annual meeting in 1958. The attendance at meetings was growing dramatically (Somit and Tanenhaus 1967, 1982:145; Kirkpatrick 1969:482). Unfortunately, the halcyon days of expanding membership and growth in enrollments in political science classes, both at the undergraduate and graduate levels, were ended in the 1970s by the declining birthrates and the popularity of applied programs.

SCIENCE AND POLITICAL SCIENCE, AGAIN

At the end of World War II, "traditional" political science was challenged by what Robert A. Dahl has called a successful protest movement, "behavioralism." Dahl's article in the *American Political Science Review* (1961) is surely the best short attempt to define and give the causes for the rise of behavioralism.

Dahl attributed the movement to: 1) Charles E. Merriam's "Chicago school," 2) the intellectual leadership of the European scholars who immigrated to this country (mostly in the 1930s), 3) the experience and frustration of political scientists who worked in government, especially during World War II, 4) the special leadership of the Social Science Research Council, 5) the rise of the survey and voting studies, and 6) the willingness of the large foundations to fund empirical research. Dahl could find little agreement among his peers as to the precise definition of "the political behavior approach," so he suggested it might be better called the "behavioral mood" or "scientific outlook" (Dahl 1961).

In a quiet and careful way, David Easton spoke for the behavioralist revolutionaries in his *The Political System* (1953). Given what others had a right to expect from the discipline in useful research output, the results had proven very disappointing. There was, he said, a need for more precise concepts; theory that had some relationship to the empirical or real world; a break with the discipline's hyperfactual past; and an end to the "immoderate neglect of general theory" (47). Easton mentioned the leading scholars in political theory and accused them of permitting their field to decline into historicism. What Easton borrowed from his fellow political theorists was the concept of "political system." The test of a sound and useful theory (be it from Marx, Locke, or anyone) for a traditional political theorist would be whether it included essential elements, such as the origin of the state, the locus of sovereignty, and such other venerable concepts. Easton offered a new approach to the political system, in which politics would be the "authoritative allocation of values." In a succession of books, Easton spelled out the details of his "model," or new approach, to a theory-guided empirical political science (Easton 1965a; 1965b).

There were many "converts" to the new "gospel" of behavioralism, and many spokesmen for the new science of politics. Still there was no orthodox set of tenets for what they believed. So many political scientists joined the protest movement, especially many leading scholars, that its importance became immediately apparent. A constant theme in the criticism of "traditional" (meaning anything in the past) research in the discipline was the embarrassment over the quality and importance of the research generated.

The meaning of behavioralism must be teased out of the often contradictory statements of the movement's chief protagonists. This means sorting through the views of Harold Lasswell, Gabriel Almond, David Truman, Herbert Simon, and David Easton. The extant literature argues that the discipline should adopt the methods, philosophy, and canons of evidence that had proven so fruitful to the natural sciences: therefore the discipline had to be methodologically self-aware. Faith in

the scientific method rested on the community nature of the enterprise—sharing, replication, and an acceptance of the self-correcting capacity of "science." Research was to be theory-guided, rigorous,
empirical, and, whenever possible, quantitative. As had been the case in
physics, the entire community's search would be for grand or general
theories from which many of the previously discovered "regularities"
could be deduced. The most neglected subject by traditional political
science had been individual political behavior; thus individual and individual interacting with other persons politically was to be a principal
focus. Research was to be value-free, detached, objective, and conducted
primarily to expand knowledge for its own sake. Interdisciplinary research was encouraged for its cross-fertilizing powers (Ricci 1984:
133ff.; Charlesworth 1967; Somit and Tanenhaus 1967, 1982:180ff.;
Isaak 1985; Eulau 1963; Seidelman 1985; Eulau 1969; Eulau and
March 1969).

The fresh spirit and unbridled optimism of behavioralism came at
the time graduate programs were expanding, curricula were being revised, and a larger political science profession was being fleshed out.
The first regional association, the southern, appeared in the 1930s and
began publishing its *Journal of Politics* in 1939 (Clark 1988). The other
major regional associations were established before World War II and
began publishing their official journals: *Western Political Quarterly*,
1948; *Midwest Journal of Political Science,* which became the *American
Journal of Political Science,* 1957; and *Polity,* 1968. Subregional associations also began to spring up around the country. The American Political Science Association, with a membership of over five thousand at the
time, modernized its organization and employed a small staff in a Washington office in 1950 (Somit and Tanenhaus 1967, 1982:150ff.). And
in the period from 1946 to 1967, at a time when the discipline was
growing in every aspect, Charles Merriam's disciples were spreading the
gospel of a new science of politics.

Old-style political scientists did not always accept the new movement: in some departments and at some professional meetings, the old
and new ways produced some unpleasant conflicts. The new, more quantitative articles and monographs were not, at first, welcomed at the editor's office. However, one by one, citadels of resistance retired from the
fray. Even the venerable *American Political Science Review* changed directions and did so rather dramatically, undergoing a change of editor, cover
design, and empirical-quantitative content in one year. There was a time
in the profession when articles certain to be printed in the *APSR* were
most likely to be Edward Corwin's case-by-case review of the decisions of
the term of the Supreme Court. By the 1960s, things had changed. The
most likely guaranteed publication, as the lead article no less, was the
Michigan group's most recent analysis of presidential voting.

Doing quantitative-empirical research, whether it was theory-guided or not, was a challenge in the years following World War II. Invariably, the early equipment to interpret data was rudimentary and usually belonged to departments of psychology or sociology. Humanists and traditionalists built coalitions at the large universities to resist efforts of the behavioral sciences to drop the traditional "reading knowledge of two modern foreign languages" requirement for the doctorate and replace it with requirements in statistics, computer application, and advanced research design modules. The "scope and methods" courses of the immediate postwar period assigned readings, not in political science sources, but in the publications of "cognate fields."

Of critical importance to the early years of behavioralism were the Free Press and one book in particular that it published, *Political Behavior*, edited by Heinz Eulau, Samuel J. Eldersveld, and Morris Janowitz. Published in 1956, the book had a subtitle, *A Reader in Theory and Research*, and introduced and reprinted examples of the research on which the new generation of political scientists trained. This volume was but one of many published by the Free Press, which for a time seemed to be the official house organ of the movement.

In these early years a number of books from the first generations were born again and had a greater importance in their second life than in their first. I have already discussed the importance of Arthur Bentley's *Process of Government* (1908). Stuart A. Rice's *Quantitative Methods in Politics* (1928), though written by a political sociologist, was used to suggest several lines of empirical research worth pursuing.

Credit should also be given to Northwestern University Press for publishing in the 1960s the first series of methodology books for political scientists (Anderson, Watts, and Wilcox 1966; Backstrom and Hursh 1963; Dexter 1970; Janda 1965; Madron 1969; North and others 1963). And the remarkable V. O. Key, Jr., published a small book on statistics for political scientists (1954). Other books appeared in the 1960s, but these stand out because of their signal contribution toward freeing political scientists from their methodological bondage to other social sciences. In the 1970s and 1980s many works in this vein prepared mainly for political science appeared; most of these appear in the bibliography at the end of this essay.

Other works were influential. Anthony Downs's *An Economic Theory of Democracy* must be mentioned prominently. Mancur Olson has suggested that political science is more of a social insight consuming, rather than producing, discipline. He has noted that the discipline is much in debt to such nonpolitical scientists as Kenneth Arrow, Anthony Downs, Gordon Tullock, James Buchanan, Charles Lindblom, and Thomas Schelling (Lipset 1969:xvii). Indeed the discipline is heavily in debt to this group for its development in formal theory and model-building. Within political science the appetite Downs created has been met best by William H. Riker and the young scholars he gathered around him at the University of Rochester. Today, the University of Rochester's political science department represents a peak of excellence in training young formal and positive theorists that places it in a class with Michigan, Chicago, Columbia, and Johns Hopkins in the evolution of American political science.

Finally in this section on behavioralism, the importance of the philosophy of science perspective must be mentioned. The first generation of behavioralists took seminars in the philosophy of science and devoured totally the works of Karl R. Popper, Hans Reichenbach, and Bertrand Russell. Logical positivist accounts of the history and methods of the natural sciences exposed mistakes along with noteworthy victories. The progress being made in political science research, exemplified by the voting studies, made imitation seem quite reasonable, especially if progress in science, as argued by Popper, rested on the cumulative, over-time effort.

The standards of the phenomenologists asked a good deal more from a science of politics—namely, that it explain not only the actions but also the meaning those actions had for citizens (Natanson 1977:517ff.).

Then came the impact of physicist and historian of science, Thomas S. Kuhn, and his landmark *The Structure of Scientific Revolutions* (1962). Kuhn's ideas had a delayed but important influence on political scientists. When Kuhn's book was read, behavioralists interpreted it their way: 1) scientific revolutions are about paradigm change, 2) a paradigm is an overarching or dominant view of the scope of a discipline and the way it will proceed to conduct inquiry, and 3) the behavioral revolution moved political science from a prescientific to a scientific stage in its development (Somit and Tanenhaus 1967, 1982:173ff.; Landau 1972:43ff.; Ball and Lauth 1971; Gutting 1980). Antibehavioralists, on the other hand, viewed a single, dominant view of the discipline and its work as closed, stifling, and dysfunctional (Ricci 1984:190ff.).

"My God: We Had a Motion from the Floor!"

For most of its professional life, the American Political Science Association has been run quietly, privately, and smoothly, if not in an open and purely democratic style. Before 1967, most association members delegated the operation of their professional affairs to leaders. These leaders conducted a smallish business meeting at the annual meeting held in the late afternoon while most members found other things to engage their attention. Such business sessions were tame, lifeless, and unlikely to provoke a fight. All that was about to change. To quote one surprised

APSA council member after attending one such business meeting at a 1960s convention: "My God! We had a motion from the floor! That has never happened before as far as I know." That year the antibehavioral-ists organized the Caucus for a New Political Science, an opposition movement determined to challenge "the establishment." The event had significance. Change was in the air. Discontent in the political science fraternity again organized to try to redirect the discipline's development. The caucus never came close to commanding the loyalty of a majority of political scientists. What it did accurately reflect was a well-organized and intense minority point of view.

Caucus members were opposed to things as they were. Unfortunately they were not always in agreement as to what they stood for. To some degree, their discontent conformed to a rising discontent in the nation: the peace movement had failed to end "Lyndon Johnson's war" in Vietnam, the black social revolution was being derailed by frustration over Vietnam, and public alienation was rising as unresolved social problems multiplied. Political science, the caucus argued, was either un-critically proestablishment (as a product of pseudoscientific objectivity) or irrelevant and without the capacity to help solve the nation's problems. In introducing their text, *Political Analysis: An Unorthodox Approach,* caucus leaders Alan Wolfe and Charles A. McCoy wrote:

> There is a deep-seated revulsion toward much of what passes as con-temporary political science. Many people consider it both amoral and irrelevant. This leads college students, and to an increasing extent their teachers, to regard political science courses as a colossal bore. [3]

J. Peter Euben argued (Green and Levinson 1969, 1970:3ff.) that political science was, in our time, "political *silence,* because it failed to speak out on the great issues and the crises of our time. To describe what is, uncritically, is to approve it." To quote McCoy again, this time writ-ing with John Playford in their *Apolitical Politics* (1967):

> As the title of this volume implies, it is the failure of the behavioralists to address themselves to genuinely significant political matters that con-cerns us most. By establishing methodology as the most relevant crite-rion for research they turn the students of politics into political science eunuchs. Yet important political questions will continue to be discussed by the poet, the Bohemian fringe, the propagandist and the opportun-ist. In fact, one is struck by the renewed interest in politics of students and the public at large; the only place where a discussion of politics is not likely to take place is in the political science classrooms. [9]

Thus, the litany of the caucus was that political science is apolitical, irrelevant, amoral, and boring.

Four of Leo Strauss's students joined him in writing *Essays on the*

Scientific Study of Politics (Storing, ed., 1962). It is a bitter critique of the writings of 1) the Columbia and Michigan voting studies, 2) Herbert Simon, 3) Arthur Bentley, and 4) Harold Lasswell. Written over five years before the caucus was formed, the book's closing words are:

> Only a great fool would call the new political science diabolic: it has no attributes peculiar to fallen angels. It is not even Machiavellian, for Machiavelli's teaching was graceful, subtle, and colorful. Nor is it Neronian. Nevertheless one may say of it that it fiddles while Rome burns. It is excused by two facts: it does not know that it fiddles, and it does not know that Rome burns. [327]

The caucus questioned the competence and relevance of what the behavioralists were doing. Most of the caucus supporters, but especially the Straussians, made these two points about a "science" of politics: 1) some things *can not* be studied scientifically, and 2) some things *should not* be studied scientifically (Landau 1972:6ff.). On the first point the argument is that the human being is more than an animal: the human being thinks, feels, and reacts in ways no laboratory animal would. The human being is too complex for simplified efforts at quantification. The enduring values that characterize humankind defy empirical assessment. The important things in life and politics cannot be measured in any conventional sense. And finally, the antibehavioralists contend that even if you could measure them, you should not; what can be measured can be manipulated and controlled. Such an effort would be unethical and it would be wrong (Surkin and Wolfe 1970; Somit and Tanenhaus 1967, 1982:180ff.).

The caucus "party" so frightened the APSA establishment "party" that the constitution was changed to settle elections and policy-related questions by mailed ballot. The business meetings initially were so volatile that the APSA employed the American Arbitration Association to assist in running them. The most lasting concession to the caucus was an accommodation in developing the program at the annual meeting: the year following the birth of the caucus, its panels and meetings were listed in the official convention program. The caucus lives on as a sort of moon to the APSA sun. Its business meetings and organized panels are a substantial part of the "courtesy listings" in the program at each convention and some of the nation's leading political scientists are active in its deliberations. For the last decade, the caucus has been little more than an interest group within the political science community.

Although a two-party system contesting for power had a short life within the profession, the caucus did have a salutary effect. Before 1950 there was no national office and staff for the APSA. The services offered individuals, programs, and departments were limited to periodic reports from conferences or committees officially sanctioned by the national organization. The association's affairs were managed rather privately.

The appearance of *PS* in winter of 1968 signified a change. First, the association simply publishing a communications vehicle such as *PS* was in itself noteworthy. The initial *PS* contained two ethics reports dealing with associational dalliances with the CIA and suggesting standards for conducting research abroad and for research contracted for by the United States government. And it announced the purchase of a national headquarters building in 1966. With the caucus monitoring the APSA professional life, it became more open, more inclusive of all of its members, more willing to affirmatively reach out to women, blacks, and other minorities, and more likely to provide services, including some planning for the future.

Since the early years, the APSA had periodically published a *Biographical Directory,* but in the next decade a departmental services program was established, manpower studies were begun, and a *Personnel Newsletter* was created. These were only the beginning of a long list of services the APSA would offer to its constituency. Clearly, the members of the APSA had been underserved by its national office. Many of these services were likely to be made available by a maturing association. Their earlier rather than later appearance may be attributed to the threat posed by the caucus to the traditional ways of conducting affairs.

The Post-Behavioral Era

The caucus leaders were quick to proclaim their victory over behavioralism and the arrival of a new age in the discipline. In *The Post-Behavioral Era* (Graham and Carey 1972), Ellis Sandoz, a caucus leader, wrote:

> It is rumored that positivist-behavioral political science is moribund if not dead. It is said that we now live in the post-behavioral period of political science; and credence need not be placed exclusively in the rumors among the disgruntled. For this is the talk not only of challengers outside the present "establishment" but, fascinatingly, the demise has been proclaimed by unimpeachable authority. That assertion constituted the thesis and central thread of David Easton's presidential address to the American Political Science Association in September 1969. [Graham and Carey 1972:285]

And that was the case. Easton, one of the leaders in attacking the old ways of studying politics, at least in traditional political theory terms, had thrown in the towel. In essence, Easton, a man of peace, had said it was time to end this fraternal warfare and to build a new and better political science. He challenged those present to get on with rethinking the nature of the discipline, including its posture toward relevance and action (Ricci 1984:188–90).

It is noteworthy that Theodore J. Lowi's *The End of Liberalism,* a book he himself called a polemic, appeared in 1969. As Lowi documented the shortcomings of pluralistic democracy, which political scientists had for many years described uncritically, he concluded: "interest group liberalism produces an apologetic political science" (312–13).

According to the victors, what was political science supposed to adopt as a new paradigm? There is simply no agreement in the literature. Clearly those who made this latter-day attack on behavioral orthodoxy wanted to restore political theory (as political philosophy) to an important place in the discipline. Some factions of the caucus were taken with the new critical theory and radical literature in the 1970s. Beyond this tendency, little direction comes from the caucus movement.

At best, the critique of behavioralism by the caucus never was more constructive than the warnings offered by Robert Dahl in 1961. At the end of his famous *APSR* article on the behavioral approach, Dahl said, if the main focus of the profession is empirical, to whom will we turn for a normative political appraisal and evaluation? In the political behavioralist's hurry to study "what is," Dahl continued, the scholar must find a way to make systematic use of "what has been"—namely, historical evidence. Those in the movement had to be bold in building general theory. This was needed to offset a noted tendency for the scientific outlook to stimulate caution, which would, in the long run, be likely to produce trivial findings. And, finally, he wrote that "empirical political science had better find a place for speculation" (Dahl 1961:771, 772).

The Caucus for a New Political Science was the last of the several great movements to redirect the profession. It opposed what was without offering a clear agenda of its own. It did not gain an ascendancy in the profession; instead it gradually declined in importance, itself becoming a part of the grand eclecticism that has characterized the discipline since 1968.

American Political Science: 1968–1988

There have been a number of broad trends in the discipline's history during the last twenty years. The post–World War II growth boom ended. Even with advanced warnings aplenty, the graduate departments continued to produce more Ph.Ds than there were new positions available to fill. The number of prospective students belatedly came into a rough balance with disciplinary needs. In recent years, political science has enjoyed about an 80 percent placement rate for newly minted Ph.Ds.

During this period, American political science dominated professional activity throughout the world. Writing in the 1970s, the long-time executive director of the association, Evron Kirkpatrick, reported:

> If there are 17,000 trained political scientists alive and working today, 14,000 of them are in the United States. Whatever the number of new books and articles produced each year, 95 percent are produced in the United States, even though significant increases are taking place elsewhere in the world. [Freeman 1977:5]

Since that date, political science has grown in other countries, and the International Political Science Association has expanded, but the ascendancy of the American version of the "master science" is clear.

New biographical directories were published by the American Political Science Association in 1968, 1973, and 1988. Roughly, 12,000 entries appeared in the 1968 *Directory* and 12,500 in the 1973 *Directory,* yet only 9,500 in the 1988 *Directory*. Membership in the association had peaked and had begun its decline.

Equally notable is that it had become increasingly difficult to find labels to classify members by field of interest. Only eight labels had been used in the 1961 *Directory* to categorize members by interests. In 1968 three broad fields (contemporary political systems; international law, organizations, and politics; political theory and philosophy) were supplemented by seventeen "specialized fields." By 1973 the editors were using an elaborate taxonomy borrowed from the *NSF Register of Scientific and Technical Personnel*. The 1973 typology was condensed to twenty-one fields in 1988. A maturing political science, while smaller, was more complex and heterogenous in its interests.

EXPANDING DISCIPLINARY BOUNDARIES

A doctoral candidate a generation ago would have come to preliminary writtens and/or orals expecting to be questioned generally in three fields in the discipline and one cognate field. The questions could cover virtually the whole literature in those fields and the journals. In the contemporary period, this is no longer possible: the literature in political science has exploded. No student can be expected to have command of the literature published in an entire field, so examinations are typically by subfields within fields. As illustration, in one small area, presidential elections, twenty to thirty books will be published on each electoral cycle. In addition, the number of articles and papers that appear concerning each election considerably outnumber the books. Whole new subfields have appeared. Some have grown into fields that bridge disciplinary boundaries: consider political psychology, policy studies, positive or formal theory, and critical theory.

Thirty years ago political scientists had to learn methods from writings in sociology and psychology. Although many scholars in the discipline still learn from other fields (for example, econometrics), since 1970 the discipline's poverty in methods literature has been turned to abundance. There are many good basic methods texts for students at the beginning level. Examples are William Buchanan's *Understanding Political Variables* (1974) and Lal Goel's *Political Science Research* (1988). The Dorsey Press and Sage Publications, especially, have made significant additions to the modern literature in methods.

Major contributions surveying the scope of the discipline have been made by Stephen L. Wasby (1970), Herbert F. Weisberg (1986), Herbert B. Asher and others (1984), Alan C. Isaak (1985), Donald M. Freeman (1977), and Ada W. Finifter (1983). The most important effort to survey the entire scope of the discipline is the eight-volume *Handbook of Political Science,* prepared under the editorship of Fred Greenstein and Nelson Polsby (1975). These works are joint efforts and if the names of the contributors were mentioned, rather than just those of the lead author or editor, the list would be impressively long.

The proliferation of journals is yet another litmus test of the expansive, almost boundless, interests of American political scientists since 1968. When Michael Giles and Gerald Wright decided to gather professional evaluations of journals relevant to the discipline in 1974, they selected a list of sixty-three. The number has increased since (Giles and Wright 1975). *Political and Social Science Journals* lists more than 440 journals in political science and related fields (ABC-Clio 1983). The *American Political Science Review* has remained the most important journal in the discipline. But neither the American Political Science Association nor its *Review* are now without rivals. A variety of associations and journals are available to political scientists, and many professionals have transferred their loyalties and journal interests elsewhere.

Departmental Reputations: Remarkable Stability

The most important development since 1970 has been the spread of solid, quality graduate education across the country. One of the grand indoor sports practiced periodically is ranking these programs. Whether done within the discipline or outside it, by reputational or objective criteria, the same cluster of top departments appears. There are twenty to twenty-five graduate programs that stand at the top. The exact order of the ranking may vary, and a few departments drift into and out of the fringes of the rankings, but it is impressive that for twenty years a stable pattern has persisted. Some have proposed a variety of different objective criteria for evaluating departmental performances, including citations of faculty in social science indices and activity in professional associations (papers, panel participation, office-holding). These confirm the pattern of leadership more than they disconfirm it.

Among the top ten, almost always are three clusters: 1) Yale, Harvard, MIT, 2) Michigan, Chicago, Wisconsin, Minnesota, and 3) Berkeley and Stanford. To these clusters in the east, midwest, and far west is added Rochester. Michigan and Rochester are of special importance to the discipline because of the way in which they have dominated trends in data collection/storage and formal theory building (Somit and Tannenhaus 1967, 1982; Bair and others 1988; Rudder 1983; Klingemann 1986).

New Item for the Professional Agenda: Ethics

The radicals who helped make the caucus a healthy challenge to the old APSA establishment would want political scientists to continue to ask themselves: "Is there a dominant public philosophy or view that we serve? Are we, collectively, neutral or proestablishment?"

The neoconservatives in our midst would remind the profession of its worldwide leadership responsibilities. Ideas have consequences, and there may be such a thing as academic or intellectual malpractice. One member of the profession, who also is a United States senator, wrote a case study of the Community Action Program to make the point (Moynihan 1969). The last decades have raised our awareness of ethics and social responsibility. The questions are easy to pose: For whom will I work? Why am I doing this research? What are my motives? What may I study, and at what potential social costs to human subjects? How might others use the research I am doing and reporting? Ethics units have appeared everywhere in graduate methods seminars and more frequently now in the undergraduate curriculum as well (Warwick 1980a, 1980b; Fleishman and Payne, 1980; Sjoberg 1967).

An Era of Good Feelings?

If a science of politics is not possible, as the caucus argues, the *idea* of science has been productive for the discipline. If the caucus had no particular agenda to substitute for the behavioral agenda, its protest was still productive of a more open professional association and perhaps one more sensitive to the environment in which we function. Robert Dahl warned in 1961 that there was a potential lack of balance on the part of the behavioralists and that some "traditional" training might produce a better, wiser "scientist." Indeed, antibehavioralists might do better research if they acquired empirical/quantitative training in methods. Perhaps the two groups need one another. An era of good feelings in which all are behavioralists and all are traditionalists would benefit both.

In the main, an era of good feelings prevails today, but it is produced by the eclectic quality of interests in the discipline. With so many different graduate departments of quality, and so many associations and journals committed to various specialties, political scientists can go in different directions and never challenge or learn from one another. Gabriel Almond has written recently of his concern that the discipline is dividing into at least four different groups, which he calls "separate tables," based on whether the groups are ideologically right or left (on one dimension) and methodologically hard or soft (on the other). He sees most political scientists as "methodologically eclectic" and wishing to avoid "ideological bias in the conduct of professional work." He is most concerned that groups that occupy these "separate tables" will end up writing our disciplinary history (Almond 1988:836). This may be happening, if we judge on the basis of recent works on the history of the discipline (Farr 1988).

Political science in the United States has had an exciting past. It should have a productive future. But as a learned discipline, it is becoming so large and grand in its proportions as to defy study and evaluation in any one study of its history. The discipline badly needs generalists! The eclectic path taken lately is productive, but the variety of literature being produced is fragmented. Anyone trying to study the evolution of the discipline becomes hyperaware of the many threads awaiting a masterweaver to blend together. We may have more weighty substantive and theoretically exciting findings in our literature than we (or other social scientists) have realized.

REFERENCES

ABC-Clio. 1983. *Political and Social Science Journals: A Handbook for Writers and Reviewers*. Santa Barbara: ABC-Clio.

Almond, Gabriel A. 1988. "Separate Tables: Schools and Sects in Political Science." *PS* 21:823–42.

Anckar, Dag, and Erkki Berndtson, eds. 1987. "The Evolution of Political Science: Selected Case Studies." *International Political Science Review* 8: 5–103.

Anderson, Lee F., Meredith W. Watts, Jr., and Allen R. Wilcox. 1966. *Legislative Roll-Call Analysis*. Evanston: Northwestern University Press.

Asher, Herbert B., Herbert F. Weisberg, John H. Kessel, and W. Phillips Shively, eds. 1984. *Theory-Building and Data Analysis*. Knoxville: University of Tennessee Press.

Backstrom, Charles, and Gerald D. Hursh. 1963, 1981. *Survey Research*. Evanston: Northwestern University Press. Second edition, New York: John Wiley.

Bailey, Stephen K., ed. 1955. *Research Frontiers in Politics and Government.* Washington, D.C.: Brookings.

Bair, Jeffrey H., William E. Thompson, Joseph V. Hickey, and Philip L. Kelly. 1988. "Elitism among Political Scientists: Subjectivity and the Ranking of Graduate Departments." *PS* 21:669–74.

Ball, Howard, and Thomas P. Lauth, Jr., eds. 1971. *Changing Perspectives in Contemporary Political Analysis: Readings on the Nature and Dimensions of Scientific and Political Inquiry.* Englewood Cliffs, N.J.: Prentice-Hall.

Ball, Terrence. 1976. "From Paradigms to Research Programs: Toward a Post-Kuhnian Political Science." *American Journal of Political Science* 20: 151–77.

Bentley, Arthur Fisher. 1908. *The Process of Government.* Chicago: University of Chicago Press.

Bernstein, Richard J. 1978. *The Restructuring of Social and Political Theory.* Philadelphia: University of Pennsylvania Press.

Bluhm, William T., ed. 1982. *The Paradigm Problem in Political Science.* Durham: Carolina Academic Press.

Buchanan, William. 1969, 1988. *Understanding Political Variables.* New York: Scribner's. Fourth edition. New York: Macmillan.

Charlesworth, James C., ed. 1962. *The Limits of Behavioralism in Political Science.* Philadelphia: American Academy of Political and Social Science.

———, ed. 1966. *A Design for Political Science: Scope, Objectives and Method.* Philadelphia: American Academy of Political and Social Science.

———, ed. 1967. *Contemporary Political Analysis.* New York: Free Press.

———, ed. 1972. *Integration of the Social Sciences Through Policy Analysis.* Philadelphia: American Academy of Political and Social Science.

Chomsky, Noam. 1969. *American Power and the New Mandarins.* New York: Pantheon Books.

Clark, Elizabeth Hughes. 1988. "The Genesis of the Journal of Politics." *PS* 21:674–78.

Collini, Stefan, Donald Winch, and John Burrow. 1983. *That Noble Science of Politics: A Study in Nineteenth Century Intellectual History.* Cambridge: Cambridge University Press.

Conway, M. Margaret, and Frank B. Feigert. 1976. *Political Analysis: An Introduction.* Boston: Allyn & Bacon.

Cowling, Maurice. 1963. *The Nature and Limits of Political Science.* Cambridge: Cambridge University Press.

Crick, Bernard. 1959. *The American Science of Politics: Its Origins and Conditions.* Berkeley: University of California Press.

Dahl, Robert A. 1961 . "The Behavioral Approach in Political Science: Epitaph for a Monument to a Successful Protest." *American Political Science Review* 55:763–72.

———. 1963. *Modern Political Analysis.* Englewood Cliffs, N.J.: Prentice-Hall.

Dallmayer, Fred Richard. 1981. *Beyond Dogma and Despair: Toward a Critical Phenomenology of Politics*. Notre Dame: University of Notre Dame Press.

Dexter, Lewis Anthony. 1970. *Elite and Specialized Interviewing*. Evanston: Northwestern University Press.

Downs, Anthony. 1957. *An Economic Theory of Democracy*. New York: Harper & Row.

Easton, David. 1953, 1964, 1971. *The Political System: An Inquiry into the State of Political Science*. New York: Knopf.

———. 1965a. *A Framework for Political Analysis*. Englewood Cliffs, N.J.: Prentice-Hall.

———. 1965b. *A Systems Analysis of Political Life*. Englewood Cliffs, N.J.: Prentice-Hall.

———. 1985. "Political Science in the United States: Past and Present." *International Political Science Review* 6:133–52.

Eulau, Heinz. 1963. *The Behavioral Persuasion in Politics*. New York: Random House.

———, comp. 1969. *Behavioralism in Political Science*. New York: Atherton Press.

———, ed. 1989. *Crossroads of Social Science: The ICPSR 25th Anniversary Volume*. New York: Agathon Press.

Eulau, Heinz, Samuel J. Eldersveld, and Morris Janowitz, eds. 1956. *Political Behavior: A Reader in Theory and Research*. Glencoe, Ill.: Free Press.

Eulau, Heinz, and James G. March, eds. 1969. *Political Science*. Englewood Cliffs, N.J.: Prentice-Hall.

Everson, David H., and Joann Poparad Paine. 1973. *An Introduction to Systematic Political Science*. Homewood, Ill.: Dorsey Press.

Farr, James. 1988. "The History of Political Science." *American Journal of Political Science* 32:1175–95.

Finifter, Ada W., ed. 1983. *Political Science: The State of the Discipline*. Washington, D.C.: American Political Science Association.

Fleishman, Joel L., and Bruce L. Payne. 1980. *Ethical Dilemmas and the Education of Policymakers*. Hastings-on-Hudson, N.Y.: Hastings Center, The Teaching of Ethics VIII.

Freeman, Donald M., ed. 1977. *Foundation of Political Science: Research, Methods, and Scope*. New York: Free Press.

Frohock, Fred M. 1967. *The Nature of Political Inquiry*. Homewood, Ill.: Dorsey Press.

Garson, G. David. 1971, 1976. *Political Science Methods*. Boston: Holbrook Press.

Germino, Dante L. 1967. *Beyond Ideology: The Revival of Political Theory*. New York: Harper & Row.

Giles, Michael W., and Gerald C. Wright, Jr. 1975. "Political Scientists' Evaluations of Sixty-three Journals." *PS* 8:254–56.

Goel, Madan Lal. 1989. *Political Science Research: A Methods Handbook*. Ames: Iowa State University Press.

Golembiewski, Robet T., William A. Welsh, and William J. Crotty. 1969. *A Methodological Primer for Political Scientists*. Chicago: Rand McNally.

Graham, George J. 1971. *Methodological Foundations for Political Analysis*. Waltham, Mass.: Xerox College Publishing.

Graham, George J., Jr., and George W. Carey, eds. 1972. *The Post-Behavioral Era: Perspectives on Political Science*. New York: David McKay.

Green, Philip, and Sanford Levinson, eds. 1970. *Power and Community: Dissenting Essays in Political Science*. New York: Vintage.

Greenstein, Fred, and Nelson Polsby, eds. 1975. *Handbook of Political Science*. 8 vols. Reading, Mass.: Addison-Wesley.

Gregor, A. James. 1971. *An Introduction to Meta Politics: A Brief Inquiry into the Conceptual Language of Political Science*. New York: Free Press.

Griffith, Ernest S., ed. 1948. *Research in Political Science*. Port Washington, N.Y.: Kennikat Press.

Gunnell, John G. 1979. *Political Theory: Tradition and Interpretation*. Cambridge, Mass.: Winthrop Press.

————. 1986. *Between Philosophy and Politics: The Alienation of Political Theory*. Amherst: University of Massachusetts Press.

Gurr, Ted Robert. 1972. *Politimetrics: An Introduction to Quantitative Macropolitics*. Englewood Cliffs, N.J.: Prentice-Hall.

Gutting, Gary, ed. 1980. *Paradigms and Revolutions: Applications and Appraisals of Thomas Kuhn's Philosophy of Science*. Notre Dame: Notre Dame University Press.

Haas, Michael, and Henry S. Kariel, eds. 1970. *Approaches to the Study of Political Science*. Scranton, Pa.: Chandler.

Haddow, Anna. 1939, 1969. *Political Science in American Colleges and Universities, 1636-1900*. New York: Appleton, Century.

Hyneman, Charles S. 1959. *The Study of Politics: The Present State of American Political Science*. Urbana: University of Illinois Press.

Inter-university Consortium for Political and Social Research. 1984. *Guide to Resources and Services, 1983-84*. Ann Arbor: ICPSR.

Irish, Marian D., ed. 1968. *Political Science: Advance of the Discipline*. Englewood Cliffs, N.J.: Prentice-Hall.

Isaak, Alan C. 1985. *Scope and Methods of Political Science: Introduction to the Methodology of Political Inquiry*. Homewood, Ill.: Dorsey Press.

Janda, Kenneth. 1972. *Data Processing*. Evanston: Northwestern University Press.

Janos, Andrew C. 1986. *Politics and Paradigms: Changing Theories of Change in the Social Sciences*. Stanford: Stanford University Press.

Jaros, Dean, and Lawrence V. Grant. 1974. *Political Behavior: Choices and Perspectives*. New York: St. Martin's Press.

Jensen, Richard. 1969. "History and the Political Scientist." In *Politics and the Social Sciences,* Seymour Martin Lipset, ed. New York: Oxford University Press.

Jung, Hwa Yol. 1979. *The Crisis of Political Understanding: A Phenomenological Perspective in the Conduct of Political Inquiry.* Pittsburgh: Duquesne University Press.

Kalvelage, Carl, and Morley Segal. 1976. *Research Guide in Political Science.* Morristown, Pa.: General Learning Press.

Kann, Mark E. 1980. *Thinking about Politics: Two Political Sciences.* St. Paul: West Publishing.

Karl, Barry. 1974. *Charles E. Merriam and the Study of Politics.* Chicago: University of Chicago Press.

Kessel, John H., George F. Cole, and Robert G. Seddig, eds. 1970. *Micropolitics: Individual and Group Level Concepts.* New York: Holt, Rinehart and Winston.

Key, V. O., Jr. 1954. *A Primer of Statistics for Political Scientists.* New York: Crowell.

Kirkpatrick, Erron M. 1969. "The Report of the Executive Director, 1968–69." *PS* 2:479–537.

Klingemann, Hans-Dieter. 1986. "Ranking the Graduate Departments in the 1980s: Toward Objective Qualitative Indicators." *PS* 19:651–61.

Kress, Paul F. 1973. *Social Science and the Idea of Process: The Ambiguous Legacy of Arthur F. Bentley.* Urbana: University of Illinois Press.

Kuhn, Thomas S. 1962, 1970. *The Structure of Scientific Revolutions.* Chicago: University of Chicago Press.

Ladd, Everett Carll, Jr., and Seymour Martin Lipset. 1975. *The Divided Academy: Professors and Politics.* New York: W. W. Norton.

Lakatos, Imre. 1978. *The Methodology of Scientific Research Programmes.* Cambridge: Cambridge University Press.

Landau, Martin. 1972. *Political Theory and Political Science.* New York: Macmillan.

Lasswell, Harold Dwight. 1936. *Politics: Who Gets, What, When, How?* New York: McGraw-Hill.

———. 1963. *The Future of Political Science.* New York: Atherton Press.

Laudan, Larry. 1977. *Progress and its Problems.* Berkeley: University of California Press.

Leege, David C., and Wayne L. Francis. 1974. *Political Research: Design, Measurement and Analysis.* New York: Basic Books.

Lerner, Daniel, and Harold D. Lasswell, eds. 1951. *The Policy Sciences.* Stanford: Stanford University Press.

Lipset, Seymour Martin, ed. 1969. *Politics and the Social Sciences.* New York: Oxford University Press.

Lowi, Theodore J. 1969. *The End of Liberalism: The Second Republic of the United States.* New York: W. W. Norton.

Madron, Thomas William. 1969. *Small Group Methods and the Study of Politics*. Evanston: Northwestern University Press.

McCoy, Charles, and John Playford, eds. 1967. *Apolitical Politics*. New York: Thomas Y. Crowell.

McCoy, Charles, and Alan Wolfe. 1972. *Political Analysis: An Unorthodox Approach*. New York: Thomas Y. Crowell.

Meehan, Eugene J. 1965. *The Theory and Method of Political Analysis*. Homewood, Ill.: Dorsey Press.

————. 1974. *The Foundations of Political Analysis: Empirical and Normative*. Homewood, Ill.: Dorsey Press.

Merriam, Charles E. 1925, 1970. *New Aspects of Politics*. Chicago: University of Chicago Press.

Merritt, Richard L. 1970. *Systematic Approaches to Comparative Politics*. Chicago: Rand McNally.

Merritt, Richard L., and Gloria J. Pyszka. 1969. *The Student Political Scientist's Handbook*. Cambridge, Mass.: Schenkman.

Moynihan, Daniel Patrick. 1969. *Maximum Feasible Misunderstanding: Community Action and the War on Poverty*. New York: Free Press.

Murphy, Robert E. 1970. *The Style and Study of Political Science*. Glenview, Ill.: Scott, Foresman.

Natanson, Maurice. 1977. "Philosophy and Social Science: A Phenomenological Approach." In *Foundation of Political Science,* Donald M. Freeman, ed.

North, Robert S., Ole R. Holsti, M. George Zaninovich, and Dina A. Zinnes. 1963. *Content Analysis*. Evanston: Northwestern University Press.

Ostrom, Elinor, ed. 1982. *Strategies of Political Inquiry*. Beverly Hills: Sage.

Palmer, Monte, Larry Stern, and Charles Gaile. 1974. *The Interdisciplinary Study of Politics*. New York: Harper & Row.

Patterson, Samuel C., Brian D. Ripley, and Barbara Trish. 1988. "The American Political Science Review: A Retrospective of the Last Year and the Last Eight Decades." *PS* 21:908–25.

Pool, Ithiel de Sola, ed. 1967. *Contemporary Political Science: Toward Empirical Theory*. New York: McGraw-Hill.

Rai, Kul B., and John C. Blydenburgh. 1973. *Political Science Statistics*. Boston: Holbrook Press.

Ranney, Austin, ed. 1962. *Essays on the Behavioral Study of Politics*. Urbana: University of Illinois Press.

————. 1968. *Political Science and Public Policy*. Chicago: Markham.

Ricci, David. 1984. *The Tragedy of Political Science*. New Haven: Yale University Press.

Rice, Stuart A. 1928. *Quantitative Methods in Politics*. New York: Knopf.

Riker, William H. 1962. *The Theory of Political Coalitions*. New Haven: Yale University Press.

————. 1977. "The Future of the Science of Politics." *The American Behavioral Scientist* 21:11–38.

Rogow, Arnold. 1969. "Psychiatry and Political Science: Some Reflections and Prospects." In *Politics and the Social Sciences,* Seymour Martin Lipset, ed. New York: Oxford University Press.

Rowdybush, Brinton. 1988. "The Roper Center: A National Archive of Public Opinion Research." *PS* 21:929–31.

Rudder, Catherine E. 1983. "The Quality of Graduate Education in Political Science: A Report of the New Rankings." *PS* 16:48–53.

Sabia, Daniel R., and Jerald T. Wallulis, eds. 1983. *Changing Social Science.* Albany: SUNY Press.

Schaar, John H., and Sheldon S. Wolin. 1963. "Essays on the Scientific Study of Politics: A Critique." Also "Response." *American Political Science Review* 57:125–50; 151–60.

Seeley, John R. 1896. *Introduction to Political Science.* London: Macmillan.

Seidelman, Raymond, with the assistance of Edward J. Harpham. 1985. *Disenchanted Realists: Political Science and the American Crisis, 1884–1984.* Albany: SUNY Press.

Sjoberg, Gideon, ed. 1967. *Ethics, Politics, and Social Research.* Cambridge, Mass.: Schenkman.

Somit, Albert, and Joseph Tanenhaus. 1964. *American Political Science: A Profile of the Discipline.* New York: Atherton Press.

————. 1967, 1982. *The Development of American Political Science: From Burgess to Behavioralism.* Boston: Allyn & Bacon; New York: Irvington Publishers.

Sorauf, Frank J. 1965. *Perspectives on Political Science.* Columbus: Charles E. Merrill.

Spitz, David, ed. 1967. *Political Theory and Social Change.* New York: Atherton Press.

Storing, Herbert J., ed. 1962. *Essays on the Scientific Study of Politics.* New York: Holt, Rinehart and Winston.

Surkin, Marvin, and Alan Wolfe, eds. 1970. *An End to Political Science: The Caucus Papers.* New York: Basic Books.

Van Dyke, Vernon. 1960. *Political Science: A Philosophical Analysis.* Stanford: Stanford University Press.

Voegelin, Eric. 1952. *The New Science of Politics.* Chicago: University of Chicago Press.

Waldo, Dwight, 1956. *Political Science in the United States: A Trend Report.* Paris: UNESCO.

————. 1975. "Political Science: Tradition, Discipline, Profession, Science, Enterprise." In *Political Science: Scope and Theory,* volume 1 of *Handbook of Political Science,* Fred I. Greenstein and Nelson W. Polsby, eds. Reading, Mass.: Addison-Wesley.

Wallas, Graham. 1908. *Human Nature in Politics*. London: Constable.

Walter, Oliver, ed. 1971. *Political Scientists at Work*. Belmont, Calif.: Duxbury Press.

Warwick, Donald P. 1980a. "The Politics and Ethics of Cross-Cultural Research." In *Handbook of Cross-Cultural Psychology*, H. C. Triandis and W. W. Lambert, eds. Boston: Allyn & Bacon.

―――. 1980b. *The Teaching of Ethics in the Social Sciences*. Hastings-on-the-Hudson, N.Y.: Hastings Center, The Teaching of Ethics VI.

Wasby, Stephen L., and others. 1970. *Political Science: The Discipline and its Dimensions*. New York: Scribner's.

Watson, James D. 1968. *The Double Helix: A Personal Account of the Discovery of the Structure of DNA*. New York: Atheneum.

Weinstein, Michael A., ed. 1972. *The Political Experience: Readings in Political Science*. New York: St. Martin's Press.

Weisberg, Herbert F., ed. 1986. *Political, Science: The Science of Politics*. New York: Agathon Press.

White, Louise G., and Robert P. Clark, 1983. *Political Analysis: Technique and Practice*. Monterey, Calif.: Brooks/Cole.

Willoughby, W. W. 1904. "The Political Science Association." *Political Science Quarterly* 19:107–11.

Wiseman, H. Victor. 1967, 1969. *Politics: The Master Science*. New York: Pegasus.

Young, Roland, ed. 1958. *Approaches to the Study of Politics*. Evanston: Northwestern University Press.

2

Pluralism and Progress in the Study of Politics

J. Donald Moon

In recent decades political science has come through a period of great disciplinary upheaval, first the "behavioral revolution" under the banner of science, followed by the rise of the Caucus for a New Political Science, with its calls for political engagement. Both of these movements left important stamps on the discipline of political science, but neither displaced what preceded it. Traditional institutional analysis and political theory are still practiced, in spite of the efforts of David Easton (1953), and the ideal of a disinterested science of politics based on the study of individual political behavior continues to guide a significant body of political research.

Today our field is characterized by no similar impulse. Our discipline is marked instead by a luxuriant growth of different fields, approaches, concerns, methodologies, and forms of political commitment. Another way of putting this, a way that leads to an often expressed concern, is that our discipline has come to be radically decentered or fragmented. This has led to calls for unifying the discipline in some way—perhaps through a common political concern, a common method or "paradigm," or through the emergence of political scientists who are generalists, who understand and build on a variety of approaches, and so bring them together in a unified whole.

This paper is an extension of remarks made at the "Evolution of the Discipline" panel. I appreciate the comments and insights of fellow panel members Donald M. Freeman, Elinor Ostrom, and Anne Schneider.

Perhaps responding to this sense of fragmentation, we have recently
seen the publication and wide discussion of a number of books, methodologies, and articles reflecting on the history and current state of the
discipline.[1] Although, as Farr observes, political science has always been
preoccupied by such questions, "during the past decade, political science has seemed to be even more state-taking than usual" (1988b:727).
The "state of the discipline" was the explicit theme of the 1982 annual
meeting of the American Political Science Association, and variations
on this theme have defined the focus of many other meetings, as well as
those of the regional associations—including the 1989 meeting of the
Midwest Association, and it is the occasion of this volume. This attention suggests a widespread concern for the coherence and integrity of
the field, and an effort to understand and to relate different communities of scholars, methods, and approaches to each other.

I would not wish to suggest that this interest in disciplinary coherence is misplaced. There are genuine costs associated with fragmentation, but I will argue that the existence of a plurality of approaches and
methods in political science is, in many respects, a good thing. Moreover, and perhaps more important, it is inevitable. Because it is inevitable, visions of a unified discipline that can practice what Kuhn (1970)
called "normal science" are chimerical. Critical analyses of the field and
its history can serve important functions in maintaining its intellectual
integrity and vitality, but there are very real limits to what such analyses
can be expected to accomplish.

THE INEVITABILITY OF PROLIFERATION

Political science (using "science" in the sense of a more or less organized body of knowledge) is subject to decentering—it will tend to be
characterized by the existence of specialized fields and approaches for at
least three reasons:

1) There are conflicting conceptions of politics—of the phenomena
we study. Consider Easton's (1953) view of politics as the authoritative
allocation of values, where the focus is on distributive conflict;
Schmitt's (1976) view of politics as the constitution of an "us" vs. a
"them," where the focus is on intergroup conflict and the self-definition
of a collectivity through such conflict; or the "classic" view of politics as
the deliberate and self-conscious creation of the structures and norms
governing our collective lives, where the focus is on the political as at
least potentially a sphere of human freedom (see, e.g., Arendt 1958).

These are all, it goes without saying, very general conceptualizations, and they give rise to different research agendas, different theoretical conceptualizations, and different ways of subdividing the field.

Consider, for example, the differences between Crozier's *The Crisis of Democracy* and Habermas's *Legitimation Crisis*. The former study falls broadly within the conception of politics as the authoritative allocation of values, while the latter conceives of political life in more "classic" terms. The subject matter of both works is similar. Both investigate the consequences for stable authority of various forms of social conflict and the incompatible demands they generate on the political system. Crozier and his coauthors see the principal problem to be one of intense conflict and the escalation of political demands leading to the paralysis and undermining of the institutions of governance. But Habermas envisions the transformation of politico-economic systems in accordance with self-consciously accepted norms that—in contrast with those of capitalist democracies—express generalizable interests.

2) Our understanding of political life, and what we take to be an understanding of political life, changes with crises of political life itself. It is hard not to see the behavioral movement as an aspect of the so-called postwar consensus; consider, for example, Dahl and Lindblom's *Politics, Economics, and Welfare* as an exemplar of both the "behavioral persuasion" and the understanding of political life as the piecemeal solving of problems, not the clash of grand ideologies. The rise of a politically engaged political science, on the other hand, can be directly traced to the Vietnam war, the Civil Rights movement, and the urban violence of the 1960s.

3) Social and political knowledge has a reflexive character: our understanding of politics can itself come to be part of the self-understandings of political actors, affecting their behavior, and so altering the phenomena that political scientists study and the theories and approaches appropriate to them. For a fairly specific example, consider the self-conscious application of such modes of analysis as "cost-benefit analysis" in public administration. These have altered the way in which public programs are administered and the ways public agencies function, creating a whole new set of issues for political scientists to study. (For a good example, see Hird 1987.)

Conflicting conceptions of politics, crises in political life, and the reflexivity of political knowledge: all lead to a political science that will include conflicting approaches, theories, and even definitions of the field of study. But this theoretical and conceptual pluralism raises the question of whether political science can really be considered a discipline. What prevents these fissiparous tendencies from destroying the discipline altogether?

There is an obvious answer: our material interests are rooted in the departmental organization of university life. Unfortunately, the departmental structure of university life is itself problematic, for it tends to stabilize and ultimately to ossify the structure of knowledge as it exists

at a particular point in time. It can constrain research and support every-
thing that is wrong with professionalism.

In the social sciences especially, these boundaries are quite artificial,
and can be serious impediments to creative work. And this brings me to
a reason why these fissiparous tendencies can be seen as desirable. The
pluralism that characterizes political science today is, to a significant
extent, a result of the formation of subfields or disciplinary clusters
where area and methods frequently overlap with those of other disciplines, thus helping to breach the walls between them imposed by the
departmental structure of the university. Consider such examples as:

> voting studies—bordering on psychology and sociology

> political economy—in its Marxist variant linking political
> science to Marxist schools in various disciplines and to
> institutional economics

> rational choice theories of politics—linking political science
> to microeconomics and to welfare economics

> gender and politics—linking political science to a whole new
> field of study in the social sciences and humanities

As a result of the fragmentation of the field, there are often colleagues in other departments who are closer to one's own field of work
than some colleagues in one's own department. In this way, communication between scholars in different departments, which tends to be im-
peded by the social structure of contemporary universities, is facilitated.

THE COSTS OF PLURALISM AND THE
PROGRESS OF THE DISCIPLINE

There are, then, important benefits of the pluralism of political research
today. But these benefits involve certain costs as well. A unified discipline has the advantage that its practitioners (by definition) accept a
common set of exemplars and standards with which to evaluate political
research. Further, as Kuhn (1970) argued, they accept a common set of
problems or questions to which researchers seek answers. Given common standards and questions, a field can make systematic and more or
less cumulative progress. Researchers will be able to exchange their results readily, healthy competition among different teams and institutions will spur their work, and little energy will be wasted in disputes
over the significance of different pieces of work. In a disunified (or in
what Kuhn perhaps mistakenly called a preparidigmatic) field of study,
different researchers will go off in different directions, the application of
different standards to the same piece of work will lead to contradictory

evaluations and sometimes acrimonious dispute, and there will be no rational or commonly accepted way to make crucial institutional decisions regarding the allocation of research funds, the training of new entrants to the field, the publication of results in "authoritative" or leading journals, or the award of professorial posts.

These considerations suggest an important reason why we might be concerned with developing some degree of unity or integration of the field of political science: the need to articulate criteria and standards with which to evaluate research and to make important institutional decisions. This may be one of the reasons why there has recently been so much renewed interest in the history of the discipline, and points to what is at stake in the competing interpretations of its history. As Almond argues, "Whoever controls the interpretation of the past in our professional history writing has gone a long way toward controlling the future" (1988a:835). By providing an account of political science that shows that certain approaches or research programs have been successful, and that others are dead ends, one can stack the cards in favor of one's preferred school. By vindicating certain criteria, one can influence crucial institutional decisions.

This use of disciplinary history has been advocated in a paper by Dryzek and Leonard (1988), who argue that disciplinary history is essential because there are no neutral or invariant criteria or standpoint from which we can evaluate political research. The "rational superiority" of a particular research program, they argue, "must be established through the writing of a disciplinary history in which it can be shown that one program provides an account that is able to explain both the successes and failures of its extant competitors" (Dryzek and Leonard 1988:1249). We need to attend to disciplinary history because there is no way to demonstrate the validity of a particular tradition or program of research by comparing it directly to the world. Rather, as postempiricist philosophers of science have insisted, such judgments must be historical in the sense that they involve comparing the progress or adequacy of different programs with each other, in terms of their ability to account for the phenomena in question.

It is not clear, however, that we can use disciplinary histories to vindicate programs or specific cases of political research in the way Dryzek and Leonard suggest. To see this, we must first draw a distinction between the problem of evaluating a particular research project and that of assessing a research tradition or research program. By a particular research project, I refer to specific theories, interpretive accounts of particular episodes or socio-cultural wholes, so-called case studies of one sort or another, and the like. By a research program or tradition I mean, following Lakatos (1970) and Laudan (1977), the broad conceptualizations of a set of phenomena that are implicitly or explicitly used to construct theories and other accounts. Parsonian structural-functionalism is a research program (see Parsons 1954); Parsons's (1969) account of voting behavior in America is a theory (charitably speaking) embedded in his larger research program. The rational choice approach is a research program; Downs's (1957) theory of party competition and convergence is a particular theory within it.

What is critical about this distinction is that the research tradition or program provides the criteria in terms of which specific research designs, theories, and findings are to be framed and evaluated. Someone working out of a rational choice approach, for example, is constrained to construct explanations and theories that are broadly consistent with the fundamental conceptualization of social and political phenomena embodied by this approach. Specifically, these phenomena are to be represented as the outcomes of the choices of individual actors, seeking to realize the objectives they hold, faced with a given set of alternatives, in which they act in such a way as to achieve as many of their ends as possible, given the options they confront. Similarly, scholars working within a Marxist framework may seek to explain political phenomena in terms of their functional relationships within a social formation in which the structure of class conflict, determined by the relationships different groups stand to the means of production, is vital.

The purpose of introducing this distinction is to signal the important differences involved in vindicating different kinds of scholarly work. Particular studies or theories are evaluated in terms of the research tradition of which they are a part, for these traditions specify the problems that the research is intended to address, and the criteria for a satisfactory resolution of these problems. The standard view—roughly speaking—is that new theories should enable us to explain all the data we could explain before we had the new theory and, in addition, it should enable us to discover new facts or to provide explanations that involve less "conceptual" strain—less tension with our other beliefs—than previous theories. Such justifications, then, are broadly historical in the sense that they are relative to the state of a discipline at a particular point in time, and are carried out with reference to theories that had been proposed prior to the work in questions.

These justifications, however, do not involve a very rich or interesting sense of history. They do not require anything like a historical account of the way in which the discipline has developed over time, reconstructing and interpreting the changing ways in which its practitioners have understood their work. In the first place, they are limited to accounts of a particular research program, and need not look beyond that to the discipline as a whole. And even within these parameters, these justifications will invoke earlier theories or accounts, not as it were historically, but as contemporary voices in an ongoing conversation.

Indeed, a paradigmatic example of this kind of justification is the practice of locating a particular study in the literature at the beginning of a scientific article.

We come closer to finding a function for disciplinary history when we consider the problem of justifying one's choice of a particular research tradition or program. Why adopt a rational choice model (see, e.g., Quattrone and Tversky 1988)? Why take the "state" as a principal focus of research (see, e.g., Almond et al. 1988b)? Why accept the "new institutionalism" as a framework for political analysis (see, e.g., March and Olsen 1984; Smith 1988)? Answers to questions such as these are historical in a richer sense than justifications of particular studies, since they require a comparison of a whole program of research with its competitors, and their relative progress over a period of time. Thus, they involve a much wider scope—perhaps going beyond even a "disciplinary" history—and something like a genuinely historical account, one in which the historically specific and changing understandings of researchers are recovered and identified.

Nonetheless, even in this context we must modify Dryzek and Leonard's account of the purposes of disciplinary history. The justification of one's choice of a particular research tradition cannot be based, contrary to their assertion, on its ability "to explain both the successes and failures of its extant competitors" (1988:1249). As Lakatos and Laudan have shown, it may be perfectly rational to accept a research program that has been less successful than its competitors if one has reason to believe that it has superior heuristic power—if it promises to grow more quickly.

As an example, Laudan offers the choice of the Galilean program over the Aristotelian program, which involved choosing a program that not only had fewer demonstrated successes, but also considerably narrowed the scope of research by completely abandoning inquiry into such matters as the final causes or purposes of phenomena. But such a choice was fully justified by the heuristic power of the new science— that is, by the rapid progress that was being made by its practitioners, progress that held out the promise that further work in this tradition would be fruitful (Laudan 1977:112ff.).

I suspect that in political science today the rational choice research program has a similar appeal. This is a body of work in which significant progress is being made through the extension of its methods to new areas, and through the continual development and refinement of its conceptual and theoretical apparatus. An excellent case in point is the extension of simple, game theoretical models to explain the development and persistence of norms—of forms of behavior that are ostensibly incompatible with the fundamental assumptions underlying rational choice theory itself (see, e.g., Axelrod 1985).[2]

There is a further reason, specific to the social sciences, why comparison between research traditions cannot be based simply upon their relative capacity to explain phenomena. As any number of commentators have pointed out, the social sciences differ from the natural sciences because social phenomena are in part constituted by the self-understandings, the concepts and beliefs, of social actors. The identity of an action, for example, depends upon the norms of the society and the intentions with which it is performed. The same set of physical movements, then, might constitute different actions depending upon the context in which they are performed.

An important task of political science, like the other social sciences (with the possible exception of economics), has been to provide interpretive or hermeneutical accounts of the concepts and beliefs, of the self-understandings, of social actors, in order to enable us to grasp the sense of meaning of what they do.[3] Interpretive studies of this sort, however, are difficult to evaluate in terms of the criteria of theoretical progress, since it may not be possible to order them in terms of their relative explanatory power. Not only is the notion of "explanatory power" problematic in this context, but different studies often deal with different cultures or historical periods, making them incommensurate in these terms.

Generally, of course, political scientists are not interested only in interpreting the self-understandings of social actors, but also in providing causal or functional explanations of events, institutions, or patterns of behavior that may or may not reflect the intentions of those who bring them about. These explanatory accounts can often be assessed in terms of the heuristic power of the research traditions in which they are embedded. However, because political science takes as its subject matter phenomena that are, as it were, preinterpreted, we face the possibility that different societies, or different periods of time, may contain qualitatively different and, in a certain sense, incommensurate phenomena. Forms of behavior may be specific to particular, historically specific ways of life, and the research programs and theories that we use often incorporate concepts that are part of, and specific to, a particular form of life. Any number of concepts in regular use in political science are of this sort, including such commonplace notions as the state, voting, political party, or terrorism. Such research programs may not apply to other contexts—other times and other cultures—and so may not compete with the theories and research programs developed to account for these other cases.

I hasten to add that it is possible that qualitatively distinct phenomena may be subsumed under more general categories, as for example different forms of authority may be subsumed under the notion of "hierarchy." Contrary to some claims, social science is not necessarily particularistic. But even if it is possible to develop general categories, it may be the case that the theories that can be framed in terms of them are so broad that they do not enable us to explain significant variations within the categories.

The incommensurability of political phenomena in different cultures cannot be established a priori—it depends upon the actual success of research programs based upon generalized categories in explaining political life in different contexts. Nonetheless, to the extent that, at any point in time, we lack cross-culturally valid categories useful in framing wide-ranging explanatory theories, we may not be able to compare the success of different research traditions in any straightforward way. It is possible that some programs enable us to explain political phenomena in certain societies, and other programs are effective in other contexts. If the "data" explained by different theories are qualitatively distinct, the research programs in which they are embedded cannot be compared in terms of their relative explanatory power.

Thus, the uses of disciplinary histories to guide political research are quite limited. Following Lakatos and Laudan, we may sometimes assess competing research programs in terms of their heuristic power, but even when we can do so, such assessments always have a "post hoc" character, and seldom yield definitive results. Further, to the extent that research is interpretive or hermeneutic in character, concerned with recovering and understanding the concepts and beliefs of social actors, it does not lend itself to assessment in terms of the idea of heuristic power. And to the extent that our research programs incorporate actors' concepts, there may be problems of incommensurability among programs that make the test of heuristic power difficult to apply. For these reasons, we cannot expect that even the most careful, the most disinterested, disciplinary histories could do much to overcome the pluralism of research styles and approaches we find in the discipline today.

CONCLUSION

Methodological pluralism is endemic to political science. In many ways, it is something to celebrate. It makes an invaluable contribution to breaking down the disciplinary barriers that separate political science from the other social sciences, and so contributes to the advancement of our knowledge and understanding of political life. There are, as I have argued, significant costs associated with the pluralistic or fragmented character of the discipline. In particular, it is much more difficult to make reasonable choices regarding the allocation of resources—of research support, faculty positions, and time—in a pluralistic discipline than in one in which "normal science" is possible. These costs can be reduced by thoughtful and critical efforts to think through the history and current state of the discipline, and so we should be grateful for the many studies that have been produced along these lines in recent years. But these costs cannot be eliminated.

In the body of this paper I have focused my attention on the problem of evaluating or assessing political research. This is an important problem, but this focus on evaluation also carries certain dangers with it. Indeed, I would argue that in the past our methodological concerns have been too narrowly focused on problems of evaluation, on determining whether certain theories or propositions are "true" or "acceptable." This concern reflected the preoccupation in the philosophy of science and epistemology with the justification of knowledge claims, with demarcating areas and styles of inquiry that were cognitively acceptable from those that were not. That program, it is widely agreed, has failed. Instead of being centrally concerned with determining when a proposition or theory is true or false, acceptable or unacceptable, contemporary philosophy of science focuses on the question of scientific progress, on deciding when we should abandon one proposition, theory, or perspective in favor of another. What is involved here is a shift from a "static" concern with truth, understood as correspondence with reality, to a dynamic concern with the growth or progress of knowledge, with the replacement of less adequate theories with more adequate ones.

My discussion of disciplinary history in this paper has been informed by this dynamic perspective, but its principal focus has been "static," with making judgments about which programs ought to be abandoned, or denied institutional support, because they are no longer viable. But there are other tasks that overviews and histories of the discipline can perform, and some of these can contribute significantly to its progress. Among these tasks are the following:

1) To identify the various programs or communities of research within the field.

2) To identify the problems they are facing; determine what implications the work being done within one area might have for work in another—that is, to see what they might be able to learn from one another.

3) To identify potentially useful changes in the way the discipline is structured—including organizational changes (e.g., in definitions of subfields) or conceptual changes.

Disciplinary histories oriented to these concerns need not be partisan efforts to capture the discipline for a particular school or approach, but can contribute to the learning and sharing of ideas that makes a pluralistic discipline such as ours so exciting.

NOTES

1. There has been a real outpouring of such literature, including full-length studies, articles, and reviews. For example, see Almond 1988a, Collini et al. 1983, Dryzek 1988, Dryzek and Leonard 1988, Farr 1988a, 1988b, 1988c, Finifter 1983, Janos 1986, Ricci 1984, Seidelman and Harpham 1985, and Weisberg 1986.

2. Although not intended as such, one might consider Laclau and Mouffe (1985) to be a critique of the Marxist research program, showing that it has persistently failed to deal with what they call "hegemony" in an adequate way, ultimately justifying a radical shift in the research program itself. While the recent history of the rational choice program is one of significant theoretical progress (even in the face of massive anomalies), Laclau and Mouffe's account of Marxism offers a picture of a research program in decline.

3. When I say interpretation is an important task of political science, I do not mean to suggest that political science or the social sciences generally must adopt an interpretive framework or method. There is no (satisfactory) a priori argument against radical behaviorism. But there are deep reasons for rejecting it, and virtually all political and social science is in fact committed to understanding social phenomena in terms of the self-understandings of social actors. For further discussion, see Fay and Moon 1977.

REFERENCES

Almond, Gabriel A. 1988a. "Separate Tables: Schools and Sects in Political Science." *PS* 21:828–42.

———. 1988b. "The Return to the State." *American Political Science Review* 82: 853–74.

Arendt, Hannah. 1958. *The Human Condition*. Chicago: University of Chicago Press.

Axelrod, Robert. 1985. *The Evolution of Cooperation*. New York: Basic Books.

Collini, Stefan, Donald Winch, and John Burrow. 1983. *That Noble Science of Politics*. Cambridge: Cambridge University Press.

Crozier, Michel J., Samuel Huntington, and Joji Watanuki. 1975. *The Crisis of Democracy*. New York: New York University Press.

Dahl, Robert, and Charles Lindblom. 1953. *Politics, Economics, and Welfare*. New York: Harper & Brothers.

Dryzek, John S. 1988. "The Once and Future Discipline." *Polity* 21:439–46.

Dryzek, John, and Stephen Leonard. 1988. "History and Discipline in Political Science." *American Political Science Review* 82:1245–60.

Easton, David. 1953. *The Political System.* New York: Knopf.

Farr, James. 1988a. "Political Science and the Enlightenment of Enthusiasm." *American Political Science Review* 82:51–70.

———. 1988b. "The States of the Discipline." *Polity* 20:727–33.

———. 1988c. "The History of Political Science." *American Journal of Political Science* 32:1175–95.

Fay, Brian, and J. Donald Moon. 1977. "What Would an Adequate Philosophy of Social Science Look Like?" *Philosophy of Social Science* 7:209–28.

Finifter, Ada W., ed. 1983. *Political Science: The State of the Discipline.* Washington, D.C.: American Political Science Association.

Habermas, Jürgen. 1975. *Legitimation Crisis.* Boston: Beacon Press.

Hird, John A. 1987. "What We Don't (and Should) Know about Cost-Benefit Analysis." Paper presented at the ninth annual research conference of the Association for Public Policy Analysis and Management, Bethesda.

Janos, Andrew C. 1986. *Politics and Paradigms.* Stanford: Stanford University Press.

Kuhn, Thomas. 1970. *The Structure of Scientific Revolutions.* Second ed. Chicago: University of Chicago Press.

Laclau, Ernesto, and Chantal Mouffe. 1985. *Hegemony and Socialist Strategy.* London: Verso.

Laudan, Larry. 1977. *Progress and its Problems.* Berkeley: University of California Press.

March, James G., and Johan P. Olsen. 1984. "The New Institutionalism." *American Political Science Review* 78:732–49.

Parsons, Talcott. 1951. *The Social System.* New York: Free Press.

———. 1969. " 'Voting' and the Equilibrium of the American Political System." In his *Politics and Social Structure.* New York: Free Press.

Quattrone, George A., and Amos Tvesky. 1988. "Contrasting Rational and Psychological Analyses of Political Choice." *American Political Science Review* 82:719–36.

Ricci, David. 1984. *The Tragedy of Political Science.* New Haven: Yale University Press.

Schmitt, Carl. 1976. *The Concept of the Political.* New Brunswick: Rutgers University Press.

Seidelman, Raymond, and E. Harpham. 1985. *Disenchanted Realists: Political Science and the American Crisis.* Albany: SUNY Press.

Smith, Rogers M. 1988. "Political Jurisprudence, the 'New Institutionalism,' and the Future of Public Law." *American Political Science Review* 82:89–108.

Weisberg, Herbert F., ed. 1986. *Political Science: The Science of Politics.* New York: Agathon Press.

3

Whither Political Theory?

Terence Ball

My assignment, as I understand it, is to supply some sort of forecast for the future direction and condition of political theory. This I am reluctant to do, if only because predictions about changing human tastes, actions, and practices are notoriously unreliable and almost always wide of the mark. One need not be a Hegelian to appreciate the point of Hegel's warning about the dangers inherent in attempting to go beyond the world one knows and inhabits:

> Whatever happens, every individual is a child of his time; so philosophy too is its own time apprehended in thoughts. It is just as absurd to fancy that a philosophy can transcend its contemporary world as it is to fancy that an individual can overleap his own age, jump over Rhodes. If his theory really goes beyond the world as it is and he builds an ideal one as it ought to be, that world exists indeed, but only in his opinions, an unsubstantial element where anything you please may, in fancy, be built. [Hegel 1967:11]

A warning well taken by the wise and prudent.

Hegel's warning notwithstanding, there is another adage that might apply to the present case: fools rush in where angels (and even Hegel) fear to tread. So, having accepted my assignment to go on a

An earlier version of this essay was presented as an invited "theme" paper at the 1989 Midwest Political Science Association in Chicago. I thank William Crotty for the invitation, and my discussants—Jeffry Isaac, John Nelson, and Arlene Saxonhouse—for helpful criticism. My thinking about these matters also owes a great deal to conversations with many persons, including Isaiah Berlin, William Connolly, Richard Dagger, Mary Dietz, John Dryzek, David Easton, Peter Euben, James Farr, John Gunnell, Russell Hanson, Norman Jacobson, Peter Laslett, Stephen Leonard, Steven Lukes, Donald Moon, and Quentin Skinner—none of whom will agree with everything I say here.

fool's errand, I propose to proceed in the following way. Believing that the past and present may be the best guides to (though not necessarily predictors of) the future, I shall begin by retracing some of the steps taken by political theory and its critics over the last three decades. Second, having said something about where we have come from, I want to say where I think we stand now. And third, I want to hazard a few half-educated guesses about where we might be headed.

Before beginning, I should say that I do not claim or pretend to speak for anyone but myself. Many, perhaps most, of my fellow political theorists would tell the story differently and some—Straussians, say, or Marxists or postmodernists—will doubtless take exception to what I have to say. And their objections can, and should, carry considerable weight. But my assignment is to call the shots as I see them, and to speak autobiographically where it seems appropriate to do so.

THE WAY WE WERE

From the mid-1950s until the early 1970s or thereabouts, it was de rigueur to celebrate (if you were a "behavioralist") or to lament (if you were a "theorist") the "decline of political theory" (Cobban 1953). In 1953 David Easton announced the end of political theory as it had been and, in a way that might bring the blush of embarrassment even to the cheek of H. G. Wells, predicted the shape of things to come. A "normative" political theory concerned with the structure and proper ordering of "the state" was at last being superseded. The "systems" approach discarded the concept of the state and bracketed, if not eschewed altogether, any merely normative concerns. Henceforth "the political system" was to be pared down and seen in proper perspective, as one of several "subsystems," each having its own characteristic "inputs" and "outputs" (Easton 1953). This, needless to say, was a language far removed from the idioms in which political theorists had been accustomed to speak.

Easton was not, of course, the only critic of "normative" or (as it was sometimes called) "traditional" political theory. A chorus of critics soon appeared.[1] To their voices were added those celebrating the "end of ideology," at least in the West (Shils 1955; Bell 1960). The major social problems had, it seemed, been resolved, or were at any rate well on the way to being resolved. A widespread normative consensus was said to pervade the Western democracies, and the United States in particular. The American "consensus historians" showed that it had always been thus, and that the dreams, schemes, and "theories" of "utopian" thinkers and "ideologues" were bound to come a cropper in an essentially pragmatic culture (see Noble 1989). Unable (or unwilling) to forego at least a scholarly interest in the unorthodox and the utopian, political theory was tarred with this very brush.

It was in this climate that Peter Laslett intoned, "for the moment, anyway, political philosophy is dead" (Laslett 1956:vii). (A curious kind of death, this; but then political theory is a curious kind of vocation.) And even those unwilling to write its obituary were wont to lament political theory's precarious position. Sheldon Wolin prefaced *Politics and Vision* with a lamentation for the near dead:

> In many intellectual circles today there exists a marked hostility towards, and even contempt for, political philosophy in its traditional form. My hope is that this volume, if it does not give pause to those who are eager to jettison what remains of the tradition of political philosophy, may at least succeed in making clear what it is we shall have discarded. [1960:v]

And what was about to be discarded, on Wolin's subsequent telling, is a pearl beyond price whose value only real swine could fail to appreciate.

Not all commentators were so pessimistic. Some, such as Isaiah Berlin and John Plamenatz, held that political theory could not die, at least while its parent—politics—lived. Both, however, prefaced their accounts with apologies, albeit assertive ones. In 1960, some four years after Laslett's obituary appeared, John Plamenatz wrote:

> Even in Oxford, which more perhaps than any other place in the English-speaking world is the home of political theory or philosophy, it is often said that the subject is dead or sadly diminished in importance. I happen to have a professional interest in assuming that it is still alive, and as likely to remain so as any other subject as long as man continues to be a speculative and enterprising animal. I do not think that I am biased; I do not think that I need to be. The importance of the subject seems to me so obvious, and the reasons for questioning the importance so muddled, that I do not look upon myself as defending a lost or difficult cause. [Plamenatz 1960:37]

At about the same time, Isaiah Berlin, in a similar spirit, began an influential essay on the fate of political theory with a question. "Is there," he asked bluntly, "still such a subject as political theory?" Before going on to answer affirmatively, Berlin voiced an oft-heard suspicion that his opening question had posed so directly. "This query, put with suspicious frequency in English-speaking countries, questions the very credentials of the subject; it suggests that political philosophy, whatever it may have been in the past, is today dead or dying" (Berlin 1961:1). Both Berlin and Plamenatz went on to deny that political theory was dead, or even moribund.

Who then is, or was, right—those who warned of the death or at any rate the imminent demise of political theory, or those who held that political theory was not dead and could not die? I want to suggest that each, in their own way, was entirely right. To put my point in paradoxical terms: political theory was in some quarters dead or dying; and yet it could not die.

We can resolve the paradox if we begin by drawing (and later withdrawing) a provisional distinction between first- and second-order theorizing. First-order theorizing arises in connection with the activity of attending to the arrangements of one's society.[2] So long as people live together in communities, fundamental questions—"theoretical" ones, if you like—will inevitably arise. No community can long exist without addressing and answering, at least provisionally, questions of the following sort. To begin with, there are questions about justice and fairness in the distribution of duties and resources. What is due to whom, and in what order? Questions about offices and authority are also likely to arise: Who is to resolve issues of common concern—all the members of the community, or only a few? If the latter, which ones and how, or by whom, are they to be chosen? There are, moreover, questions about conceptual-cum-political demarcation: By what criteria shall we distinguish between matters that are political or public and those that are nonpolitical or private? These, in their turn, give rise to questions about grounds and justification: Where do the aforementioned criteria come from and on what basis might they be justified (or criticized, for that matter)? Or consider questions about punishment: What shall we do with dissident or deviant members of our community—tolerate, exile, or execute them? And then there are of course questions about the extent and limits of obligation: Does every able-bodied citizen have an obligation to die for the state, if the survival of the state should seem to require it?

The list could continue to grow, but the point should be clear enough: the questions in which political theorists are interested are precisely those that any civilized community, or at any rate its more reflective members, must address and attempt to answer. The greatest political thinkers—an Aristotle or a Hobbes, say—have tried to elaborate theories on the basis of which such questions can be (re)framed, addressed, and perchance answered in a coherent, comprehensive, and systematic way.[3] But however magnificent or mediocre the minds of those who wrestle with questions about the proper ordering of society, the fact remains that political thinking or theorizing is in this sense an important, indeed a necessary, activity. Therefore Plamenatz and Berlin were right to suggest that political theory—understood as first-order theorizing—could not die, and a more recent commentator is quite correct in deeming it indispensable (MacIntyre 1983).

By contrast, much of what passes for political theory in the academy might, at a first and very imprecise cut, be termed second-order theorizing. It consists largely, though by no means exclusively, of the activity of studying, teaching and commenting on the "classics" of political thought. If first-order theorizing is well-nigh immortal, second-order theorizing is eminently mortal. It can die or disappear—or at least be discredited, discounted, or ignored, as happened in many departments of political science during the heyday of behavioralism. Political theory, as practiced in political science departments, was relegated to a kind of limbo, or living death: the worst kind. Many who practiced second-order theorizing were made to feel unwelcome, and some were even encouraged to ply their trade in the more congenial setting supplied by departments of philosophy or history.[4]

So, returning to the paradox posed earlier—How could political theory be both dead and alive at the same time?—we can now see that the paradox was only apparent and its resolution really quite simple. Those who, like Laslett, announced the death or imminent demise of political theory were speaking of it as a specialized academic discipline within departments of political science—as second-order theorizing, in other words. And they were at least arguably right in suggesting that political theory *in this sense* was in mortal peril, if not dead already. But Berlin and Plamenatz were no less correct in suggesting that political theory—understood as first-order theorizing—was neither dead nor dying, nor could it be. That activity is indeed indispensable.

As it turned out, however, all reports of the death of (academic or second-order) theory proved to be premature, if not perhaps wholly unwarranted in the first place. By the mid-1970s academic political theorists were wont to quote Mark Twain's remark upon reading his own obituary. "The reports of my death," Twain cabled to his distraught editor, "have been greatly exaggerated." What had happened? How and why was this academic Lazarus brought back from the dead?

THE REVIVAL OF POLITICAL THEORY

Several explanations, all partial and none entirely satisfactory, help to account for the revival, indeed the astonishing resurgence, of academic political theory in the last decade or so. The explanation most commonly given is that political theory has prospered as, and because, its nemesis, "behavioralism," fell on hard times. Although an adequate history of the "behavioral revolution"—and the larger history of political science of which it is an important part—still remains to be written, it would, at a minimum, have to include an account of the rise and demise of its philosophical foundation.[5] Although behavioralists were wont to draw a sharp distinction between philosophy and science, discarding the former in favor of the latter, behavioralism was in fact deeply dependent on a particular philosophy—positivism. For it was from positivism—or, as it was more commonly called, logical positivism or logical empiricism—that behavioralism drew many of its key categories and distinctions.[6] For the behavioralists, this borrowing took three important forms.

First, as an account of meaning, logical positivism distinguished three sorts of statements: "synthetic" statements of empirical fact ("the cat is on the mat" was a favorite); "analytic" statements of logical necessity ("all bachelors are unmarried males"); and a residual catch-all category of "normative" utterances that neither describe some state of the world nor state logically necessary truths, but serve only to express attitudes, feelings, preferences, or "values." Second, this theory of meaning in its turn supplied the basis for an "emotivist" theory of ethics, which holds that ethical utterances are cognitively empty and meaningless, but are merely (in A. J. Ayer's colorful if slightly salacious term) "ejaculations" expressive of nothing, save, perhaps, the speaker's subjective preference or state of mind. Thus the utterance "stealing is wrong" says nothing at all about the world, nor anything about relationships of logical entailment, but merely expresses the speaker's disapproval of stealing. And third, as a philosophy of science, positivism provided criteria for demarcating between science and nonscience. Science is not about any particular subject matter but about meaning and method. There can be a science of politics just as surely as there can be a science of chemistry or physics, provided that its statements are cognitively meaningful (i.e., synthetic) statements of ascertainable empirical fact and that its explanations conform to the requirements of the deductive-nomological (D-N) model. According to the latter, we can be said to have explained some phenomenon X if and only if a statement describing X (the *explanandum*) is deducible as a conclusion from premises containing one or more general laws, along with statements of initial conditions (the *explanans*).

Philosophical positivism served, so to speak, a normative or regulative function for behavioralism in that positivism defined for behavioralists what "science" is—and what political science ought to be, if it is to be a science. First, political science ought to distinguish between "facts" and "values." Second, it should be "empirical" instead of "normative." And third, it ought to be explanatory in the aforementioned sense. All genuinely scientific explanation, according to positivist criteria of explanatory adequacy, depends on the discovery and deployment of timeless universal "laws." Because most of "traditional" political theory did not conform to positivist criteria of cognitive meaningfulness and explanatory adequacy, it was dismissed as unscientific or, at best, prescientific and therefore destined to be superseded in due course.

But in the hands of behavioralist critics, the positivist's scalpel cut both ways, wounding those who wielded it. It soon became clear that virtually all of what passed for "empirical" or "scientific" political science did not conform to those positivist criteria on the basis of which political theory had been criticized and dismissed as meaningless because "normative." It required no great semantic skill to show that "values" lurked in the shadows of even the most sanitized "scientific" statements: there were in fact no normatively neutral or nontheoretical descriptive statements (or "protocol sentences," as earlier positivists had termed them). Worse still, there turned out to be no "laws" of political behavior. None—not even the oft-touted "laws" propounded by Michels and Duverger—could pass muster under positivist criteria.[7]

In the philosophy of science, meanwhile, the critics of positivism had carried the day, and by the mid-1970s all but the most die-hard positivists had conceded defeat. Asked by an interviewer in 1977 what the main defects of positivism had been, A. J. Ayer replied: "Well, I suppose the most important of the defects was that nearly all of it was false" (Magee 1978:131). Among the many false claims that positivism had made—and that behavioralists had borrowed—was the oft-heard chestnut that one cannot derive "ought from is." As it turns out, however, it is not only possible but actually quite easy to perform this purportedly impossible feat (Searle 1969; Anscombe 1968).

Beholden as it had been to one particular philosophy of science, behavioral political science's fortunes could not but be affected adversely by the demise of positivism. It would, however, be wrong, or at any rate one-sided and simplistic, to suggest that the resurrection of academic political theory can be traced exclusively to the declining fortunes of philosophical positivism and the allied decline of behavioralism.

Another factor that must figure in our explanation is what Alasdair MacIntyre termed "the end of the end of ideology" (MacIntyre 1971, ch. 1). From the mid-1960s on, it became abundantly clear that ideology had not ended, nor was it likely to; on the contrary, new political movements—among students, blacks, women, antiwar activists, and others—were raising new questions and setting new agendas. However haltingly and raggedly, first-order theorizing was being done in the streets and in classrooms (Miller 1987). From the Free Speech movement in Berkeley in 1964 to *les evénements* of May 1968 in Paris (which very nearly toppled the Gaullist government), old orthodoxies—including the end of ideology thesis—were being questioned and "unmasked" as "ideologies" in their own right. By the early 1970s the news had traveled even as far as Cambridgeshire. In 1972 the editors of the distinguished series *Philosophy, Politics and Society*—in whose first number Laslett's obituary had appeared—acknowledged:

We were never right to think in terms of such pathological metaphors, and it is clear in any case that they are no longer applicable. It has now become a commonplace that both the intellectual movements prevailing at the time of our first introduction [in 1956], in terms of which it looked plausible for sociologists to speak of "the end of ideology" and even for philosophers to speak of "the death of political theory," were themselves the masks of disputable ideological positions. [Laslett, Runciman, and Skinner 1972:1]

Our explanation of the revival of political theory would also have to include an account of the political consequences of a particular conception of the relation between social science and political practice—not in the abstract, but (to use a phrase once frequently hurled against academic political theorists) in the real world. The war in Vietnam, although undeclared, was real enough. It was a war not only fought by GIs but, more importantly, "managed" by experts. Called "the new mandarins" by their critics and "defense intellectuals" by their defenders, their claim to expertise was grounded in an instrumentalist and positivist view of social science and its relation to political practice.[8] The hope of establishing a positivistic policy science—an aspiration that can be traced back to Saint-Simon and Comte in the nineteenth century—was dealt a decisive if perhaps not mortal blow by the United States' experience in Vietnam.

But what has this to do with the rising fortunes of academic political theory? Just this: Vietnam raised anew and brought to the forefront the kinds of "normative" questions that political theory was supposed to address—questions about the rights and duties of citizens, about one's obligation to fight for the state, about just (and unjust) wars, about active and passive resistance, and related matters.[9]

History having some connection with biography, and vice versa, I should like to pause briefly for an autobiographical aside about how I came to be an academic political theorist. To put it bluntly, I got into this line of work not so much because I was enamored of philosophy or the history of ideas, but because of the war in Vietnam. From the age of twelve until my junior year in 1965, I was certain that I wanted to be a physicist, and most of my education had been directed to that end. My interest in history and philosophy was largely restricted to the history and philosophy of science. I called myself a positivist, regarded Russell and Ayer as my heroes, and felt somewhat superior to those lesser minds laboring in lesser vineyards.

But what a difference a war makes! The prospect of having to choose between going to Vietnam, going to Canada, or going to jail concentrated the mind wonderfully. The more I found out about the war, the more I believed it to be both misguided and unwinnable. Besides, it was being fought by the poor, the black, and the uneducated, none of whom had student deferments. That I, then a student at the University of California, did have such a deferment seemed unfair on its face. Conceding the point, the Selective Service agreed to end student deferments and inaugurate a lottery system. In the meantime, I thought, I might help to redress the unfairness by enlisting; but this would also make me complicit in a war that seemed patently unjust. Having never before faced a deep moral dilemma, I had few, if any, resources upon which to draw. What should I do? Where do my duties lie? Should I support my government even when I think its policies mistaken and misguided or, worse yet, patently evil? Is there something like a duty to resist? I did not know what to do, or even how to begin to think, about such troubling questions.

So I did what any overeducated white boy would do: I enrolled in a seminar in political theory—a subject I had heard about before but had dismissed as irrelevant to my interests—in which these questions were to be discussed and debated. We read Sophocles' *Antigone*, Plato's *Apology* and *Crito*, Calvin and Luther and Locke, Thoreau, Tolstoy, Gandhi, Camus, and Martin Luther King (who was then still very much alive and active, and not yet the safely dead martyr he has since become). Our discussions inside that seminar—and outside, through the wee hours of the night—had a special urgency for many of us. That seminar and those discussions did not make me decide on a course of action, although they did help to clarify the thinking that went into that decision.[10] As it turned out, my interest in political theory did not end there; it grew, it got deeper, and it became my vocation and life's work.

But enough of autobiography. I mention my own experience only because it was not, I suspect, unique—nor were such experiences unrelated to the revival of political theory through the 1970s. There were, in addition and closely related to the antiwar movement, the earlier and concurrent civil rights and women's movements (Evans 1979). Political theory thrived to the extent that it dealt with real political problems and the movements that raised and addressed them. In emphasizing the role of such extracurricular activities, however, I do not mean to deny or denigrate the very important contributions being made within the academy.

Political theory received a notable boost in the early 1970s with the publication of John Rawls's *A Theory of Justice* (1971). Unlike some who credit Rawls with having single-handedly revived political theory, I do not want to exaggerate his importance, considerable though it was, and is. But I do believe that his thinking about justice had a special importance and appeal for those who had lived through, thought about, and participated in the civil rights and antiwar movements. Despite its awesomely abstract formalisms—the "original position," the "veil of ignorance," and the rest—Rawls's theory was nevertheless closely connected with real-world politics. It dealt incisively with pressing questions of rights, duties, and obligations; with the justification of civil disobedience; and, with his wholly original inquiry into intergenerational justice, he spoke to the concerns of the fledgling environmental movement (Sikora and Barry 1978; Partridge 1981).

Although—or rather perhaps because—Rawls's theory was subjected to a good deal of critical scrutiny (Barry 1973), commentary (Daniels 1975), and attempted refutation (Nozick 1974), its publication and reception proved to be an important factor in the revival of political theory within the academy. Another, albeit rather different sort of importance must also be ascribed to the historical inquiries of John Pocock, Quentin Skinner, John Dunn, and others among the "new historians" of political thought; to the critical theory of Jürgen Habermas and the revived Frankfurt School; to the role of Ronald Dworkin and others in renewing interest in philosophy of law; and to Michel Foucault's important studies of the institutions (prisons, clinics, asylums) and other means by which modern men and women are constituted and disciplined.

Also important, albeit in a different way, was the launching in 1971—the same year that saw the publication of Rawls's *A Theory of Justice*—of *Philosophy and Public Affairs*, a journal dedicated to the proposition that issues of public concern often have an important philosophical dimension. The new journal's editors wrote:

> *Philosophy & Public Affairs* is founded in the belief that a philosophical examination of these issues can contribute to their clarification and to their resolution. It welcomes philosophical discussions of substantive legal, social, and political problems, as well as the more abstract questions to which they give rise. In addition, it expects to publish studies of the moral and intellectual history of such problems.

The aim of this new journal, its editors concluded, was to bring the "distinctive methods" of philosophy "to bear on problems that concern everyone" (Cohen 1971).

This launching was followed two years later by *Political Theory*, a journal generally devoted to the sort of political theory done not by philosophers but by those who plied their trade within departments of political science. To review the contents of back issues of that journal is to see how political theory began to be revived and reshaped from the early 1970s on. The first issues were devoted largely, though not exclusively, to the analysis of political concepts such as "power," "liberty," "equality," "interests," even "politics" itself. By the mid-1970s interest had shifted toward Rawls and justice, Habermas and critical theory, Marx and neo-Marxism, and other topics. One way of reading these old tea leaves is that by the mid-1970s or thereabouts theorists had ceased to play the part of handmaid, conceptual clarifier, or "underlaborer" to the larger discipline of political science and that political theory was well on the way to developing an identity of its own.

But this breaking away went unrecognized and unappreciated within many departments of political science. In a 1982 editorial, Benjamin Barber, then editor of *Political Theory*, observed rather peevishly that:

> Political philosophy continues to flourish within the discipline of political science—for which the discipline remains curiously ungrateful. For a number of years now, political theory panels have outdrawn all others at the American Political Science Association meetings by two to one, and various theory subgroups . . . continue to multiply. . . . At the same time, political science seems to have lost its bearings with declining membership in the professional associations and the lost sense of purpose following the demise of the positivist project as conceived in the early 1960s. . . . The discipline of political science would serve itself well if it . . . paid heed to the message found in the numbers to which it purports to pay homage. [Barber 1982:491]

Exactly what "message" was to be found in those growing numbers, Barber did not say. But one was led to infer that political theory was back, and bolder and more popular than ever.

TOWARD THE FUTURE

As measured by Barber's criteria, academic political theory continued to flourish through the 1980s and shows no sign of abating during the closing decade of this century. As one who teaches and writes about political theory, I am both amazed and pleased by this turn of fortune. It is, no doubt, well deserved and long overdue. But it is also troubling in ways and for reasons that I find difficult to articulate in any satisfactory way. Lacking any better way of saying it, let me be blunt in stating a strong and growing suspicion: political theory's newfound pride may presage a fall. Indeed, I see political theory following much the same trajectory that behavioral political science followed from the mid-1950s to the early or mid-1970s. It is by no means impossible that political theory might meet with a similar fate. Several signs, it seems to me, are too obvious to miss.

The first troubling sign is to be found in political theory's increasing isolation from its own subject matter, which it supposedly shares with political science—namely, politics. A second and closely related sign has to do with the growing specialization and professionalization of political theory. A third danger signal is to be found in political theorists' increasing preoccupation with questions of method and technique. And a fourth sign is discernable in our penchant for engaging in methodological or metatheoretical disputes. We are, in short, becoming the sorts of creatures we once criticized. Let me say just a bit more about each of these worries.

The best and most profound political theories, I tell my students, have been closely connected with politics and have generally been born of crisis. And in today's world there are crises aplenty. But if one takes the table of contents of successive issues of *Political Theory* as any indication of where political theory is or might be going, one is bound to wonder what is even remotely "political" about political theory. One finds a good deal of discussion about alternative approaches to textual interpretation, to questions of "subjectivity," and the like; but one would never know that there is a Third World debt crisis that raises profound political and moral questions for the citizens of creditor nations. Nor would one ever guess that there is an environmental crisis of global proportions that raises troubling questions about the rights of, and our duties toward, future generations.[11] One might instead infer that there is something called the textual-interpretation crisis, or the crisis of "the constitution of the subject." Strange crises for strange times. Amid real destruction—economic, environmental, ethical—we engage in deconstruction. One does not have to be a Straussian to say of much of political theory what Leo Strauss once said of behavioral political science: "One may say of it that it fiddles while Rome burns. It is excused by two facts: it does not know that it fiddles, and it does not know that Rome burns" (1962:327).

The aforementioned isolation of political theory from politics doubtless has a good deal to do with the dynamics of professionalization in the American academy. Political theory shows every sign of ceasing to be a vocation and of fast becoming a "profession," with all that this entails about the division of labor, the specialization of functions, and the like. Already we "theorists" have "our" specialized organizations—the Foundations of Political Thought group and the Conference for the Study of Political Thought—and "our" journals, including *Political Theory, History of Political Thought* (inaugurated in 1979), and, for the Straussians, *Interpretation*. And we have "our" panels and round tables at the APSA and other professional meetings. Such specialization is not altogether a bad thing; it has its advantages but also, and no less importantly, its disadvantages. Professionalization is a little like moving to the suburbs: one is less likely to be mugged; but one is also less likely to meet new people and more likely to talk only to people like oneself. Pretty soon, the suburb becomes its own little self-contained world—safe, secure, familiar, friendly, and utterly predictable.

In 1969 Sheldon Wolin criticized behavioralists for their "methodism," their preoccupation with refining their methods of measurement, statistical techniques, and the like, while giving short shrift to pressing political problems (Wolin 1969). Now, some twenty years later, the same criticism might well be leveled against many political theorists. We do not, to be sure, do very much measuring (although some of us do apparently keep a careful count of attendance at APSA political theory panels); but we do, of necessity, interpret texts. And so our method-ological disputes tend to rage around methods and techniques of "read-ing" or textual interpretation.[12] Historical "contextualists" dispute with "textualists" of various stripes, while postmodernists turn every-thing—wars, revolutions, gender relations—into "texts" to be decon-structed. The latter "approach" or "orientation"—we theorists are reluctant to talk openly of "method"—seems to have gained some ground of late. Some have welcomed this development while others, myself included, have doubts and reservations aplenty. The former view is well represented by William E. Connolly, the very able former editor of *Political Theory*. He points with pride to "young scholars [who] pres-ent exotic imports such as . . . deconstruction, dialogical analysis, ge-nealogy, or intertextuality, as if these orientations were part of an ongoing conversation somewhere or other" (Connolly 1989:4). Unfor-tunately that "somewhere," as it turns out, is not any politically perti-nent site, but is to be found wherever academic postmodernists gather to talk postmodernese to each other.

Postmodernism is not without its critics, of course. John Searle, for one, has averred that "this is the kind of philosophy that could give bullshit a bad name." One need not be as nasty as Professor Searle to have one's reservations about this particular "exotic import." One can even appreciate its initial appeal, at least in France, where the *lycée* sys-tem has long dictated not only what the canon is to consist of, but what each of its constituent texts "mean," sentence by sentence and word by word. If as a student I had been told that there is one and only one way to read or interpret Rousseau or Balzac or Victor Hugo, then I, too, would rebel and be tempted to deconstruct and to talk about "the free play of signifiers" and suchlike. But I am not a Frenchman, nor did I receive a French education. Nor, for that matter, did most self-styled postmodernists among American political theorists. Which is why their way of approaching political theory has an ethereal, free-floating quality that makes it ideal for an esoteric academic hothouse but ill suits it for engagement with a world full of real political problems.

For my part, I confess that postmodernism, or at least the version transplanted into the American academy, strikes me as militantly and arrogantly unworldly, not to say profoundly apolitical or antipolitical. Indeed, it seems to be a kind of intellectual autism, which leads those thus afflicted to fantasize that they can dispense with discipline (which they are wont to dismiss by deconstructing the word and its cognates) and remake the world in their own image. Their logic, such as it is, would appear to lend itself to succinct syllogistic reformulation, as follows: I have the power to interpret texts as I like; all the world's a text; ergo, the world is within my power. Right; and if wishes were horses, beggars would ride.

But this is not the place to criticize postmodernism or any other particular perspective. My assignment here is not to say where political theory should not go, but where it might and perhaps should go as we enter the last decade of the twentieth century. I therefore want to conclude on a more positive note by briefly tracing three possible and complementary routes that we might follow into the next century.

First, I believe that political theory can, and should, return to its rightful role. That role is not to ape the latest fad from Frankfurt or Paris, but to draw upon all available resources in reviewing, appraising, criticizing, and perchance occasionally appreciating, the arrangements of one's own society. As it happens, we students of political theory are especially fortunate in having at our disposal an extraordinarily wide and rich range of resources upon which to draw. The greatest of these is, I believe—and I am well aware of the arguments against this contentious claim—the tradition of Western political thought itself. Warts and all, it is the most valuable resource upon which we have to draw.

If you ask me, Why draw upon such a flawed resource?, I can only answer: Because there is no other—and certainly no perfect—alternative. There exists no Archimedian point outside our world, no Cartesian cogito, no ideal observer's vantage point from which to perceive and pass judgment on our world and its inhabitants. We can only work with, and on, materials already at hand. It is ironic, to say the least, that as Westerners increasingly ignore, deny, or denigrate their heritage, the people of Eastern Europe and the far East—I write this as hundreds of thousands of Chinese students and workers are in the streets criticizing one-party rule and calling for democracy—are eager to appropriate what they can from our tradition of individual rights, of freedoms of speech, press, assembly, and the like. No doubt they have something to learn from us; but so, I think, do we have a good deal to learn from them and their aspirations—and from their attitude toward political theory, which they take to be of immediate and immense importance.

This brings me to my second hopeful route into the future. An otherwise sympathetic reader might concede that the Chinese are faced with crises worthy of theoretical reflection, but that we are not so situated. Setting aside the comfortable but questionable assumption that we are as "democratic" as can be, there remain a number of crises that academic political theorists have, as yet, failed to recognize as worthy of theoretical attention and treatment. One that I mentioned earlier—that interconnected series of actual and potential disasters that often goes under the name of the environmental crisis—raises a whole host of questions to which we have so far paid scant attention. It raises questions about who we are and where we belong in the order of nature; about our obligations to other people, including the members of other cultures and unborn future generations; about our conceptions of private property and profit; and about the strengths, shortcomings, and limitations of our institutions and of the moral, political, economic, and religious traditions that we have inherited from thinkers long dead. And this we need to do not merely because these matters are interesting to a few oddball theorists, but because they are of pressing importance to all of us, as moral agents, as citizens, and as political inquirers. This is "first-order" theorizing with a vengeance.

My third route to the future is concerned with the last of these roles. To put it simply, the questions of political theory are too important to be left to those who call themselves, or are conventionally classified as, political theorists. We theorists have no corner on wisdom or insight. If we are to speak knowledgably about and intervene in the crises of our time, we will need at least some of the sensibilities of those among our fellow political inquirers who are conventionally classified as (empirical) political scientists. We—and I do not use the pronoun lightly—are in desperate need of each others' talents, techniques, and sensibilities. But if we are to get together, then we must overcome a number of old obstacles, many of which are legacies of the older behavioralism and of the antibehavioralist reaction. Old rifts are not bridged easily or without effort. But let me suggest one possible way of shouting across, and perchance bridging, a long-standing divide between two camps that have more in common than they might otherwise suspect.

The conventional curricular division of labor assigns to theorists the task of tracing and accounting for ideas, ideals, and beliefs, and leaves to empirical inquirers the task of describing and explaining the actual behavior of political agents. This division of labor suggests that there are two domains, one of thought or "theory" and the other of action or "behavior," each of which can be characterized without reference to the other. In fact, however, this picture is patently false. For the agent who holds certain beliefs is not separable from the agent who acts. Indeed, his or her actions are not even describable without reference to his or her beliefs, and vice versa. Thus the hope of devising a science of political "behavior" was every bit as misbegotten as was a detached "history of political thought." And this, as we so often see, is a truth more readily recognizable if we look to the past. As Alasdair MacIntyre reminds us:

> There ought not to be two histories, one of political and moral action
> and one of political and moral theorising, because there were not two

pasts, one populated only by actions and the other by theories. Every action is the bearer and expression of more or less theory-laden beliefs and concepts; every piece of theorising and every expression of belief is a political and moral action.

It is only because of the peculiar "habits of mind engendered by our modern academic curriculum," he adds, that we have arrived at the mistaken belief "that ideas are endowed with a falsely independent life of their own on the one hand and political and social action is presented as peculiarly mindless on the other" (MacIntyre 1981:58). Thus the "beliefs" studied by the theorist and the "behavior" studied by the political scientist are not two things, but one. This, then, might provide the basis for a rapprochement between political "theory" and political "science."

A CONCLUDING RETRACTION

In this spirit, then, let me conclude by reiterating and then withdrawing my earlier distinction between first- and second-order theorizing. The distinction is standardly made between those who *do* political theory and those who simply *study* or *talk about* it. In its most vulgar form, this amounts to a variation on the old chestnut, "those who can, do; those who can't, teach." In its more sophisticated form, the first- and second-order distinction demarcates between actors and observers, or, to put it another way, between a particular subject matter and its scholarly study. Even so, this more sophisticated statement of the distinction fails to do justice to what we do—or try to do—as students of political theory.

And why? Because, I believe, the distinction cuts in the wrong direction. The relevant distinction is not between first- and second-order but between first- and second-rate theorizing. We are not only scholars and students of political theory, but citizens interested in and concerned about the polity and the wider world in which we live. We therefore have reason to think critically and systematically—to theorize—about that world's problems, possibilities, and prospects. This is a job, or a vocation, in which we not only want but badly need to excel, or at least to do as well as we possibly can. We therefore have reason to consult, to draw upon, and to appropriate—though not simply to imitate or slavishly duplicate—the thinking of first-rate theorists. And this we do not because we are "second-order" but because we are second-rate and trying to do better. This does not, I hasten to add, mean that one must agree with those from whom one appropriates. Far from it. One can learn more from a first-rate thinker with whom one disagrees than from a thinker who simply ratifies or reinforces what one already believes. That is why conservatives should read Marx, and Marxists should read Burke.

And that, no less importantly, is why "empirical" political scientists should heed what "normative" theorists have to say, and vice versa. What this amounts to can, I suppose, be restated by drawing another distinction—we theorists are perhaps overfond of distinctions—between two types of learning: learning about and learning from. Too much of modern education is concerned with learning about, with acquiring information. But education is not merely a matter of acquiring information, of "learning about" some subject or other; it is, more importantly, a kind of *learning from*—of wrestling with, and critically appropriating, alternative perspectives that complicate and enrich one's view of the world and one's place in it.

As we look toward the twenty-first century, I can think of no better description of political theory or of the central task facing those who undertake this difficult, demanding, and unfailingly interesting vocation.

NOTES

1. See, e.g., Dahl 1958. Euben 1970 offers a synoptic overview of earlier disputes and Gunnell 1986 a more recent survey of the relevant literature.

2. The phrase, if not the sentiment, comes from Oakeshott 1962.

3. Note that I say "such questions," not *these particular* ones. This is an important point, because political theorists disagree over whether there are "perennial questions" (Tinder 1979) or whether these questions change over time. My own view—which owes much to Collingwood (1939:61f.) and MacIntyre (1966)—is that the questions themselves change, in part because the concepts constituting the moral languages or idioms in which the questions are framed have historically mutable meanings. For a defense and illustrations, see Ball (1988), Ball and Pocock (1988), and Ball, Farr, and Hanson (1989).

4. I should perhaps add that I am speaking more about others' experiences than about my own.

5. It is interesting, though perhaps not inexplicable, that the history of political science is nowadays being written by political theorists, among whom the work of Collini, Winch, and Burrow (1983), Gunnell (1988), Farr (1988a, 1988b), Leonard and Dryzek (1988), and Seidelman (1985) is particularly noteworthy.

6. These points were readily, indeed disarmingly, conceded by David Easton in our 1983 APSA round-table discussion on "Political Science: Is it 'Science'?" As I recall, our co-discussant, William Riker, did not agree, though for reasons that were then (and for me still are) unclear.

7. This, at any rate, was the conclusion I reached in a rather tortuous and turgid dissertation entitled "Laws and Explanation in Political Science" (Berkeley, 1973).

8. See Ball 1989 and the works cited therein.

9. Then, as now, the work of Michael Walzer seems to me to be exemplary, in that it shows, rather than simply says or asserts, how political theory can cast light on political actions and practices. See Walzer 1970, 1977.

10. Other friends made different decisions. Two of their names are now engraved on the Vietnam memorial in Washington, D.C.

11. The sole exception would seem to be a short note by Bertram Bandman 1982.

12. For a recent and engaging example, see Tully and Skinner 1989.

REFERENCES

Anscombe, G.E.M. 1968. "On Brute Facts," in *Ethics*, Judith Jarvis Thomson and Gerald Dworkin, eds. New York: Harper & Row.

Ball, Terence. 1988. *Transforming Political Discourse*. Oxford: Blackwell.

———— 1989. "The Politics of Social Science in Post-war America." In Lary May, ed., *Recasting America: Culture and Politics in the Age of Cold War*. Chicago: University of Chicago Press: 76–92.

———— and J.G.A. Pocock, eds. 1988. *Conceptual Change and the Constitution*. Lawrence: University Press of Kansas.

————, James Farr, and Russell L. Hanson, eds. 1989. *Political Innovation and Conceptual Change*. Cambridge: Cambridge University Press.

Bandman, Bertram. 1982. "Do Future Generations Have the Right to Breathe Clean Air?" *Political Theory* 10:95–102.

Barber, Benjamin R. 1982. Editorial, *Political Theory* 10:491.

Barry, Brian. 1973. *The Liberal Theory of Justice*. Oxford: Clarendon Press.

Bell, Daniel, 1960. *The End of Ideology*. New York: Free Press.

Berlin, Isaiah. 1961. "Does Political Theory Still Exist?" In *Philosophy, Politics, and Society*, second series. Oxford: Blackwell.

Cobban, Alfred. 1953. "The Decline of Political Theory." *Political Science Quarterly* 68:321–37.

Cohen, Marshall. 1971. Statement of Purpose. *Philosophy and Public Affairs* 1:1.

Collingwood, R. G. 1939. *An Autobiography*. Oxford: Oxford University Press.

Collini, Stefan, Donald Winch, and John Burrow. 1983. *That Noble Science of Politics*. Cambridge: Cambridge University Press.

Connolly, William E. 1989. Editorial, *Political Theory* 17:3–7.

Dahl, Robert, 1958. "Political Theory: Truth and Consequences." *World Politics* 11:89–102.

Daniels, Norman, ed. 1975. *Reading Rawls*. New York: Basic Books.

Easton, David. 1953. *The Political System*. New York: Knopf.

Euben, J. Peter. 1970. "Political Science and Political Silence." In Philip Green and Sanford Levinson, eds., *Power and Community: Dissenting Essays in Political Science*. New York: Pantheon.

Evans, Sara. 1979. *Personal Politics: The Roots of Women's Liberation in the Civil Rights Movement and the New Left*. New York: Knopf.

Farr, James. 1988a. "Political Science and the Enlightenment of Enthusiasm." *American Political Science Review* 82:51–69.

———. 1988b. "The History of Political Science." *American Journal of Political Science* 32:1175–95.

Gunnell, John G. 1986. *Between Philosophy and Politics: The Alienation of Political Theory*. Amherst: University of Massachusetts Press.

———. 1988. "American Political Science, Liberalism, and the Invention of Political Theory." *American Political Science Review* 82:71–87.

Hegel, G.W.F. 1967. *Philosophy of Right*, trans. T. M. Knox. Oxford: Oxford University Press.

Laslett, Peter. 1956. Introduction to *Philosophy, Politics and Society*, first series. Oxford: Blackwell.

———, W.G. Runciman, and Quentin Skinner. 1972. Introduction to *Philosophy, Politics and Society*, fourth series. Oxford: Blackwell.

Leonard, Stephen, and John Dryzek. 1988. "The History and Discipline of Political Science." *American Political Science Review* 82:1245–60.

MacIntyre, Alasdair. 1966. *A Short History of Ethics*. New York: Macmillan.

———. 1971. *Against the Self-Images of the Age*. Notre Dame: University of Notre Dame Press.

———. 1981. *After Virtue*. Notre Dame: Notre Dame University Press.

———. 1983. "The Indispensability of Political Theory." In David Miller and Larry Siedentop, eds., *The Nature of Political Theory*. Oxford: Clarendon Press.

Magee, Brian, ed. 1978. *Men of Ideas*. New York: Viking Press.

Miller, James. 1987. *Democracy is in the Streets: From Port Huron to the Siege of Chicago*. New York: Simon and Schuster.

Noble, David W. 1989. "The Reconstruction of Progress: Charles Beard, Richard Hofstadter, and Postwar Historical Thought." In Lary May, ed., *Recasting America*. Chicago: University of Chicago Press.

Nozick, Robert. 1974. *Anarchy, State and Utopia*. New York: Basic Books.

Oakeshott, Michael. 1962. *Rationalism in Politics*. London: Methuen.

Partridge, Ernest, ed. 1981. *Responsibilities to Future Generations*. Buffalo: Prometheus Press.

Plamenatz, John. 1960. "The Use of Political Theory." *Political Studies* 8: 37–47.

Searle, John R. 1969. *Speech Acts*. Cambridge, England: University Press, ch. 8, "Deriving 'Ought' from 'is'."

Seidelman, Raymond. 1985. *Disenchanted Realists: Political Science and the American Crisis, 1884–1984*. Albany: SUNY Press.

Shils, Edward. 1955. "The End of Ideology?" *Encounter*, 5:52–58.

Sikora, R.I., and Brian Barry. 1978. *Obligations to Future Generations*. Philadelphia: Temple University Press.

Strauss, Leo. 1962. "Epilogue." In Herbert J. Storing, ed., *Essays on the Scientific Study of Politics*. New York: Holt, Rinehart and Winston.

Tinder, Glenn. 1979. *Political Thinking: The Perennial Questions*, third edition. Boston: Little, Brown.

Tully, James, and Quentin Skinner, eds. 1989. *Meaning and Context: Quentin Skinner and His Critics*. Princeton: Princeton University Press.

Walzer, Michael. 1970. *Obligations: Essays on Disobedience, War, and Citizenship*. Cambridge: Harvard University Press.

———. 1977. *Just and Unjust Wars: A Moral Argument with Historical Illustrations*. New York: Basic Books.

Wolin, Sheldon S. 1960. *Politics and Vision*. Boston: Little, Brown.

———. 1969. "Political Theory as a Vocation." *American Political Science Review* 63: 1062–82.

4

The Theory of Rational Action: What Is It? How Useful Is It for Political Science?

Kristen Renwick Monroe

What is the theory of rational action? What are the main criticisms of this theory? How useful is the theory for political science? And what should be the focus of research in this area during the next ten years? Answering these questions is my charge in this chapter. To respond to this charge, I begin by presenting the key assumptions of the rational actor theory, a theory that originated in classical economics. I then note how the theory was modified via Simon's theory of bounded rationality, a modification that altered only three of the minor assumptions of the general theory while retaining the four core assumptions. I next summarize the general critiques of the theory. These critiques emanate from a wide range of disciplines but cluster in four areas: (1) strong disagree-

I should like to thank the Earhart Foundation and the Academic Senate Committee on Faculty Research at the University of California for their generous support. The University of California Inter-Campus Activity Fund provided funds to organize a conference on rational actor theory. Many of the chapters cited here as part of my edited volume (1991b) were presented originally at this conference. My thanks to the participants of the conference, especially Bernard Grofman, and to David Easton and Wil Lampros for their encouragement and support. Howard Margolis, Jane Mansbridge, Walter Mebane, and Eric Uslaner provided thoughtful comments on an early draft of this paper. An expanded version of this chapter appears in *The Economic Approach to Politics*, ed. Kristen R. Monroe (New York: HarperCollins, 1991).

ments with cultural theory, (2) technical modifications or corrections within economics and cognitive psychology, (3) empirical challenges within experimental psychology, and (4) failures to explain collective political behavior and altruism.

To summarize the main points from these critiques within space constraints and to stimulate future research, I focus discussion on specific questions and make reference to particular works only in passing. I conclude by suggesting the three particular areas that I believe will be most central in modifying the economic theory of rational action so it can be applied more successfully to political phenomena.

KEY ASSUMPTIONS OF RATIONAL ACTOR THEORY

There are seven assumptions of the economic theory of rational action as it developed in classical economics. The first four are foundation assumptions, so widely held in our post-Enlightenment world that they are seldom discussed explicitly. The last three are less basic and often stated explicitly. These assumptions are:

1. Actors pursue goals.[1]
2. These goals reflect the actor's perceived self-interest.[2]
3. Behavior results from conscious choice.[3]
4. The individual is the basic actor in society.[4]
5. Actors have preference orderings that are consistent and stable.
6. If given options, actors choose the alternative with the highest expected utility.
7. Actors possess extensive information on both the available alternatives and the likely consequences of their choices.

The traditional rational actor is thus an individual whose behavior springs from individual self-interest and conscious choice. He or she is credited with extensive and clear knowledge of the environment, a well-organized and stable system of preferences, and computational skills that allow the actor to calculate the best choice (given his or her preferences) of the alternatives available to him or her. The importance of this model is demonstrated by the fact that "practically the whole of classical economic theory is constructed within the framework of this [rational] model" (Simon 1982:213).

Rational actor theory contains no discussion about the nature of actors' particular preferences. It assumes little about the way in which actors make probability estimates of uncertain events. It assumes actors choose the alternative with the highest expected utility, defined as the

average of the utilities of all alternatives, each weighted by the probability that the outcome will ensue if the alternative in question is chosen
(Simon 1984:296). The traditional economic theory of rational action
ignores the limitations inherent within the actor. It considers only those
constraints that arise from the external situation. Once we know an actor's preferences, we can make objective judgments about the extent to
which the actor optimally adapts to the situation.

Bounded or Procedural Rationality: Modification of Assumptions 5–7

Bounded rationality shared the same initial intellectual heritage of traditional economic rationality. Perhaps because of this, it thus also accepts the first four critical foundation assumptions—that is, that
behavior results from individual actors consciously choosing to pursue
their perceived self-interest. Its actual birth, however, occurred in reaction to the behavioral movement in psychology. The cognitivists' deemphasis on culture, history, and context meant their conceptualization of
rational action minimized the external situation surrounding an actor
(Gardner 1985). Its emphasis on mental representations or schema
makes rational choice as a method only as effective as the actor's decision-making and problem-solving means permit. To judge whether an
act is rational according to bounded rationality, we need to know the
chooser's goals, his or her conceptualization of the situation, and his or
her abilities to draw inferences from the information he or she possesses.

Because of its origin in cognitive psychology, bounded rationality is
more concerned with the mental process of decision-making itself than
with behavior. This contrast with the traditional economic theory of
rational action probably accounts for some of the current confusion
over whether rational action refers to behavior or to a decision-making
process within the actor. Bounded rationality's emphasis on process—
not outcome—makes it analogous to the legal concept of procedural
due process, which asks whether the procedure that led to the result was
fair, rather than the outcome itself. This stands in contrast to the traditional economic concept, which stresses rational outcomes—that is,
outcomes occurring not necessarily from a rational process but as if they
had resulted from that process (see Friedman 1953 or Wittmann 1991).
In practice, we often use the terms "rational actor theory" and "rational
choice theory" to capture this important distinction between the traditional economic theory of rational action and bounded rationality's emphasis on decision-making. Unfortunately, this distinction, while one
of common practice, is not universally followed and confusions in ter-
minology often occur.

Bounded Rationality Assumptions: Key Points of Difference from the Traditional Economic Concept

While it retained the four foundation assumptions (individual action, pursuit of goals, conscious choice, and self-interest), bounded rationality differs from the traditional economic concept of rationality at several critical junctures. These can be noted briefly by stating the assumptions of bounded rationality. (When necessary, I also draw attention to the subtle way in which these assumptions differ from the analogous assumptions of traditional economic rationality.)

1. Computational Limitations. Actors possess limited computational abilities. For bounded rationality theorists, rational behavior is adaptive within the constraints imposed both by the external situation and by the capacities of the decision-maker.

2. Uncertain and Limited Information. Actors search for alternatives, consequences, and information selectively and incompletely. This search is based on limited and uncertain information.

3. Satisficing. Decisions are reached once a satisfactory alternative is found; this alternative need not be the optimal one, merely one that satisfies some minimum.

4. Cognitive Maps Relevant. Predicting behavior requires extensive supplemental knowledge of the actor, particularly the actor's goals and conceptual orientation to the world.

5. Process Key, Not Outcome. Emphasis on the decision-making process of the unit analyzed (e.g., person, firm, government) means that the process of decision-making itself, rather than the outcome of that process, is the hallmark of bounded rationality.

GENERAL CRITIQUES

Despite its widespread use, the theory of rational action has nonetheless received severe criticism, primarily from four different sources. (1) Cultural theorists attack its limited nature (e.g., Eckstein, Almond). They argue that the theory ignores the limitations on free choice imposed by culture, such as habit, tradition, and societally imposed norms. Furthermore, because values are always exogenous to the model, revealed only through behavior, the theory produces tautological explanations in which any behavior can be deemed "rational" in pursuit of exogenous goals simply unknown to or misunderstood by the outside observer.[5] Cultural critics are particularly concerned with the difficulties involved in cross-cultural analysis and fear that the theory's claims to scientific objectivity masks a Western individualistic bias (see Mansbridge 1990; Barber 1984). (2) The second stream of criticism comes from work at the intersection of economics and cognitive psychology. This critique is best represented by Simon's previously described work on bounded rationality. Simon argues that the human decision-making process is not one that maximizes utility but rather one that satisfices—that is, actors seek a certain minimum level of satisfaction and thereafter are indifferent among choices.[6] (3) More recent critiques emanate from experimental work in cognitive psychology (see Kahnemann, Tversky, and Slovic 1982). This careful empirical work presents striking evidence that neither the existence of preferences, the process by which preferences are pursued, nor the evaluation of information in the basic decision-making process is as consistent or efficient as the rational actor theory posits.[7] (4) And, finally, even scholars working within the rational actor framework admit the theory has difficulties explaining altruism and collective behavior, both important deviations from the key assumption of the rational actor theory: the belief that individuals pursue their self-interest (Olson 1965; Margolis 1982). Let me discuss the more important questions raised by these critiques in greater detail, focusing discussion on the theory's viability for political science.

Questions for Future Research

1. How appropriate is the market metaphor for political action? The rational actor theory adopts the rational maximizing actors from economics and transforms them into utility-maximizing voters and politicians who trade in votes and policies just as the economic individual trades in apples or shoes.[8] This market metaphor—as Almond (1991) refers to it— has a long and legitimate tradition in politics, with V. O. Key (1942) and Schattschneider (1975) utilizing it to explain American politics. But the market is only one metaphor we should utilize. Politics as religion, stressing "conversion, prayer, and worship rather than buying and selling as the defining activity," has been utilized widely in comparative politics, very effectively in the Middle Eastern or Latin American context (Almond 1991:36). Politics as warfare has been widely used to explain authoritarian movements, such as Fascism and Nazism. Politics as symbolic affirmation of the actors' position, power, or the roles played in society (Geertz 1953), and politics as a game played for the fun rather than the winning of a particular goal, are two other widely utilized metaphors (Almond 1991). By their insistence that rational models are the only truly scientific models of politics, hard-core rational actor theorists have seriously limited and isolated themselves.[9]

On this point, it is interesting that both Almond—a critic—and Simon—a proponent—agree that much of the explanatory power of rational models actually comes from the auxiliary assumptions, assumptions about specific motivations, preferences, and aims of agents in specific contexts:

Actors in the political drama do appear to behave in a rational manner—they have reasons for what they do, and a clever researcher can
usually obtain data that give good clues as to what those reasons are.
But this is very different from claiming that we can predict the behavior of these rational actors by application of the objective rationality
principle to the situations in which they find themselves. Such prediction is impossible . . . because it depends on their representation of
the world in which they live, what they attend to in that world, and
what beliefs they have about its nature. [Simon, *American Political Science Review* 79: 2 (1985) 300, cited in Almond 1991:47]

All of this suggests that rational models have great heuristic value but
may best be used in conjunction with other approaches and certainly
with more humility than is too often the case.

2. *Do people pursue goals?* The rational actor theory assumes people
pursue goals. Indeed, Downs defines rational action as action "reason-
ably directed toward the attainment of conscious goals" (1957:4; see
also Riker 1962). Simon's bounded rationality substitutes satisficing for
maximizing, thereby substituting any good outcome for the best outcome. But Simon still assumes that "almost all human behavior consists
of sequences of goal-oriented actions" (1984:297).

In a wide-ranging examination of this, Eckstein (1991) disagrees.
He cites extensive evidence, ranging from experimental work with rats
(Maier 1961) to work on Appalachian mountaineers (Gaventa 1980;
Toynbee 1946; Caudill 1962; Weller 1965; Ball 1968), inner-city blacks
(Frazier 1966) and Puerto Ricans (Moynihan and Glazer 1966), poverty in Trinidad (Rodman 1971), and lower-class schools in Britain and
the U.S.A. (Eckstein 1984). Eckstein argues that the idea of goal-directed behavior is too limited to work well outside the confines of up-
per-middle-class post-Enlightenment Western societies. The rest of the
world, Eckstein argues, exists not in a goal-directed culture but in an
analgesic culture. In analgesic cultures actors wish only to avoid pain,
decrease precariousness, limit the emotional stress of surviving in a hostile world, and establish some predictability in an environment in which
it is better to have the predictability of frustration than the bitter disap-
pointment of failing to achieve goals. This results in the frustrated behavior we see in cultures of poverty or aggression. Eckstein argues that
this behavior is not mere risk-aversion, although it is certainly that.
Rather, he argues that action known from its inception to be destined to
fail "involves acting beyond all consideration of risk. It is not really
possible to divorce risks from goals . . . . It is so high a degree of risk-
aversion that the difference in degree becomes a difference in kind, at
least for theory" (Eckstein 1991:84).

3. *Does the individual pursuit of self-interest result in collective political
welfare?* As formulated originally by Adam Smith, human action ema-

nates in the emotions, not reason, and the driving passion was self-inter-est (Myers 1983). For Smith, some regulation was required for the pursuit of individual self-interest to result in the common good. This could come through self-regulation, governmental regulation, or through some natural force, such as the market (see Myers 1983 or Whitehead 1991). In the economic realm, Smith located the critical emotion as self-interest and the market as the natural regulatory force. But Smith found neither "a dependable set of emotions or a reliable natural regulatory" mechanism in the political sphere (Whitehead 1991:54). Whitehead demonstrates that it was the marginalists who ar-gued the feasibility, indeed the desirability, of extending the economic metaphor to the political arena. The marginalists treated individual preferences as assumptions of the model. The marginalists did not try—as Smith did—to explain the preferences themselves. The origin and nature of these preferences became exogenous to the model. Individuals became autonomous actors:

> [Their] diverse emotional motivations for behavior and their need for regulation became masked behind the new static theory of rational choice. . . . The problem is that if there are no clearly defined collec-tive goals in the political world or if there is no regulatory mechanism to harmonize self-interested maximizing behavior with such goals, then it is not clear that self-interested maximizing behavior should be considered rational or that unconstrained individual preferences should be granted sovereignty as they are in the rational actor model. [Whitehead 1991:55]

Thus, rational actor theorists assume that individual desires will re-sult in (or at least be compatible with) collective political goals and wel-fare. Such a relationship is central to the theory. And yet we do not know that individual preferences will result in the collective good or the collective goals of a society or group (see Whitehead 1991). Nor do we know *how* these individual drives to pursue self-interest should be regu-lated if and when they are not compatible with the collective good. It is ironic that the question that compelled Smith to found economics was this very question on which the political theory of rational action now founders: if it is a scientific given that people are self-interested, how do we achieve the common good without resorting to unacceptable levels of governmental regulation?

4. *Do political actors actually behave in the self-interested way described by the rational actor theory?* My own research with rescuers of Jews in Nazi Europe, heroes, and philanthropists suggests they do not (Monroe 1991a and Monroe, Barton, and Klingemann 1990). Even when con-fronted with the systematic state torture of the Nazi regime, the rescuers risked their lives and those of their families to save strangers. They did not pursue their own self-interest. Nor did psychic gratification serve to

disguise a thinly veiled self-interest. Honor or praise were not sought, and despite the fact that their actions were well documented by others, all the rescuers minimized their actions, even as they told us of being arrested many times or being persecuted for their rescue activities. The existence of such altruistic behavior, no matter how rare empirically, poses a significant theoretical challenge to any theory founded on self-interest. (For the most extreme statement of the all-encompassing aspect of rational actor theory, see Becker 1976.)

   5. *Is self-interest the same thing as utility maximization? Does the use of utility maximization locate the theory's drive in the intellect rather than the emotions and thus rob the theory of its vitality?* If utility maximization is not self-interest, which drives the theory? Economists and rational choice theorists like to explain behavior that violates the self-interest assumption by arguing that the theory is based on utility maximization, not self-interest. The few eccentrics like Mother Teresa are then explained as simply having strange utility functions, or a preference for altruism. I believe this sleight of hand masks an important intellectual break. Whitehead's (1991) work is important in documenting how the marginalist revolution shifted the theoretical emphasis from Smith's self-interest to contemporary utility maximization, a process that also accompanied the above-discussed deemphasis on the importance of the emotions as motivating action and focused instead on the action itself.

   Both Whitehead and Myers identify Smith's genius and the power of his theory as lying in the fact that he rooted behavior in the emotions rather than in a conscious calculus. In contrast, the marginalists reduced rationality to a mental process. In attempting to develop a mathematical science, the marginalist revolution thus robbed economic theory of its emotional vitality. This process was completed by Simon's work, which further located rational action in a mental process. Instead of Smith's *desires*, we now have *preferences*. The *value* of a good is now *utility*. And the way we transform preferences (Smith's desires) into utility (values) is no longer through pursuing self-interested desires but rather through making formulated choices among alternate (usually transitively ordered) goods. Self-interest thus becomes separated from any emotional impetus and becomes instead a rational product of choice.

   While this contemporary version of the rational actor model has heuristic value, it also carries clear limitations for the model as applied to political contexts:[10]

> The rational actor model can be extracted from the economic context and applied in other contexts as an empirical devise to explore if individuals do act in a self-interested and maximizing way in these other contexts. And, the collective consequences of such behavior can be analyzed. But, unless it is assumed that individuals should be able to follow their self-interested desires regardless of the social conse-

quences, then the basic question of how the individual should relate to society again becomes the framework for analysis. This was Smith's basic question and it is not surprising that it is the question underlying many current critical analyses of economic theories of politics. . . . Economic analysis became isolated from the historical and political context in which it previously had been considered. Since government was not an integral part of the market process, it was omitted from the model and was no longer considered explicitly except as part of public finance. Questions of power and coercion within the private economy, which were of concern to classical economists as they looked at the changing distribution of income, were also no longer considered. Nor were societal questions of morality and justice issues of concern. And, perhaps most importantly, the emphasis shifted to the individual and away from either analytical or normative concern with collective needs and outcomes. But, in political analysis, it is just such a concern with collective needs and outcomes that is required. [Whitehead 1991:67]

6. *Do real people make decisions the way the theory postulates?* I have already mentioned the difficulties in translating the market metaphor to political situations. This leaves open a broader critique. Do real people make decisions as the theory specifies? Experimental psychologists from Bartlett (1932) to Kahneman, Tversky, and Slovic (1974, 1982 inter alia) have offered convincing evidence on the individual's limited or bounded capacity to perceive, recall, interpret, and calculate. Happily, this criticism is now being incorporated into economic theory. But let me mention just a few of these criticisms briefly, paying close attention to the political arena. (See Rosenberg 1991 or Nisbett and Ross 1980 for a more thorough review, or Wittmann 1991 for a criticism of this body of work, often referred to as prospect theory.)

(1) Feedback is not as direct in politics as it is in the marketplace. If I buy a new pair of shoes, I soon know if they fit properly. If I vote for a senator because I want someone who is tough on crime, it is more difficult to ascertain whether I have made the right choice. (2) An actor's search for information is incomplete. We know this; Simon addressed it early in his career. But the search for information is also biased by an actor's preconceptions. (3) Actors weigh particular kinds of information (e.g., vivid, personally relevant) more heavily than others (e.g., pallid, statistical data). (4) Actors' abilities to recognize correlational relationships and make causal attributions are severely limited (see Rosenberg 1991 or Nisbett and Borgida 1975). This can result from human desires to be consistent (Heider 1958 or Abelson et al. 1968). (5) Actors use shortcuts or heuristics in making mental calculations (Tversky and Kahneman 1974). (6) Actors also are extremely sensitive to the way in which choices are framed (Quattrone and Tversky 1988).

What does all of this mean for political analysis?[11] I believe it suggests the need to determine the actor's view of the world, and in particular the actor's view of him or herself in relation to others. One promising area might be script or schema theory. This might be the kind that focuses on the definitional computational qualities of the mind itself, apart from any influence of social environments (Heider 1958; Festinger 1957; Koffka 1935; Kahneman and Tversky 1972) or that which emphasizes how the mind's organization of incoming data reflects cultural influences (see Fiske and Taylor 1984 or Rosenberg 1991). Such work could provide links to key psychological theories of human development and to cultural theory.

7. *Do political actions and decisions emanate from a conscious calculus?* The original theory of rational action propounded by Adam Smith required only that decisions proceed *as if* they had originated in a rational calculus. In point 5 I noted that contemporary theories of rational choice—as opposed to rational action—require a conscious calculus. Yet how much of political action, even political choice, is driven by a conscious process? Consider voting. The original Downsian formulation of voting stresses a conscious calculation of costs and benefits weighted by the voter's expected probability that his or her vote will actually affect the outcome. The problem for analysts was that fewer voters participate in local than in national elections, even though it is in such local contests where their votes are more likely to affect the outcome. Faced with this empirical reality, analysts have introduced auxiliary assumptions, such as civic duty, to explain this phenomenon. Let me suggest an alternative explanation, based on years of close observations of my mother, a story about Austin Ranney, and my empirical analysis of rescuers of Jews in Nazi Europe.

My mother always votes. But seldom is her party or her candidate elected. Still, she continues to vote. Why? "Well, it's important to vote. What kind of a person would I be if I didn't vote?" This is her standard explanation. Perhaps this is civic duty; I would characterize it more as basic identity, a perception of self that defines and limits the options seen as available to the actor.

Anecdote #2. Long a Democrat, Austin Ranney tells of becoming disgruntled with the Democrats and going into the voting booth determined to send them a clear and direct message by voting Republican. Once in the booth, however, his hand would start to shake as it approached the Republican lever and it would slowly move—as if compelled by a force of its own—back to the Democratic lever. Civic duty? No. Basic identity or self-perception? More likely. Now, I have no doubt that Ranney eventually was able to vote Republican. And I imagine there has been—or will be—an occasional election in which my mother fails to vote. I offer these anecdotes only as thought-provoking, certainly not definitive, evidence on the nonconscious extent to which people "decide" to actually vote and on how they reach their particular vote choice.

8. *How much political behavior results from decisions and how much results from an actor's identity perception?* More systematic evidence from in-depth interviews with both rescuers and nonrescuers of Jews in Nazi Europe (Monroe, Barton, and Klingemann 1990 or Monroe 1990) suggested to me that certain political acts may be less the result of conscious choice and that our identity constructs effectively limit the perceived choice options available to actors. For both the rescuers and the unrescuers identity was so strong that there was no conscious choice for them to make in the traditional sense of assessing options and choosing the best one for them. Instead, their perception of themselves in relation to others limited the options available *to them*. Rescuers certainly knew most people did *not* risk their lives to save Jews, and so they knew that theoretically this choice was available. But they did not see this choice as an option that existed for them. We asked rescuers how they began their activities, how they made their decision to risk their lives for strangers:

Interviewer: You started out . . . talking about making conscious choices. And you said you didn't think you operate that way. Was there really a conscious choice that you made?

Margot: I don't make a choice. It comes, and it's there.

Interviewer: It just comes. Where does it come from?

Margot: I don't know. I don't think so much because I don't have that much to think with. . . .

Interviewer: It was just totally nonconscious?

Margot: Yes. You don't think about these things. You can't think about these things. It happened so quickly.

Interviewer: But it isn't really totally quickly, is it? There's a tremendous amount of strategic planning that has to be done [to do what you did].

Margot: Well, I was young. I could do it. Today I don't know. I'd have to try it. But I was thirty-two years old. That was pretty young.

Interviewer: You didn't sit down and weigh the alternatives?

Margot: God, no. There was not time for these things. It's impossible.

Interviewer: So it's totally spontaneous? It comes from your emotions?

Margot: Yes. It's pretty near impossible not to help. You couldn't do that. You wouldn't understand what it means—suppose somebody falls in the water as I said before. You want to think "Should I help or should I not?" The guy would drown! You know, that's no way.

Interviewer: How about the repercussions of your actions. Did you think about what might happen because you were doing this?

Margot: You don't think about it. No way.

Interviewer: You didn't worry about possible consequences for you? For your family?

Margot: No. No way. [Monroe 1991a]

For me, these findings suggest certain political behaviors—and these may well entail the most significant personal and political acts we all make—are not the result of choice at all. This implies that work that increases our understanding of how we view ourselves again becomes critical. Understanding how we view ourselves in relation to others should be extremely useful in understanding political behavior, behavior that by its very nature involves others (see Hauptmann 1980 or Monroe 1990). Since cognitive frameworks may be the link between the theory of rational action and cultural theory, this area should be a major focus for scholars interested in constructing future empirical political theory. Such work may also provide a clue to understanding which metaphor will be most useful in explaining particular political actions and in determining the extent to which political conflict results from mixed metaphors and when there truly are conflicts of interest.

9. *Can political calculus be put in cost/benefit terms?* Rational choice theory assumes political behavior results from an economic cost/benefit calculus. But is this so? To what extent do other, less tangible, more symbolic factors drive political actions, even those that do result from choice? Again, our research on rescuers of Nazi victims is instructive. For the rescuers, saving someone's life was not something to be subjected to a calculation of cost or benefit. Since these were significant political acts, we need to know whether other, similar political acts exist. And we need to determine more carefully which political acts can be explained by an economic cost/benefit calculus and which political acts cannot. Even political acts that are the product of conscious decision-making (e.g., sending troops into the Bay of Pigs or dropping the atomic bomb on Hiroshima) may be better explained by another model, for example, the deliberation model proposed by Johnston (1991), which expressly allows for ambiguity and the conflicts arising from an individual actor's multiple roles and the values they impose on human beings (see Elster 1986 or Nussbaum 1986).

10. *Is the theory value-free? Does its methodological individualism mask a preservation of the status quo?* Rational actor theory explains political behavior through reference to individual action (Goldfield and Gilbert 1990). This method of analysis, often referred to as methodological individualism, stands in contrast to other approaches to politics, such as Marxism's stress on class structures and membership or sociobiology's emphasis on inherited nature. Critics of methodological individualism argue that such emphasis on the individual causes analysts to neglect deeper sources of political change in favor of superficial ones. Norma-

tive theorists have argued further that this emphasis on the individual—
and on a particular concept of the individual as a competitive, self-interested optimizer—actually conserves and protects a liberal, self-interested status quo. They argue that insofar as rational actor theorists
assume self-interest as a scientifically established part of human nature,
rational actor theory has perpetuated normative and empirical consequences that support the prevailing system of political power and privi-
lege. This argument is clearly evidenced in discussions of American
democracy. Scholars as different as Pateman (1970) and Wattenberg
(1988) have noted that the rational actor approach to American politics
gained strength just as democratic theorists were disconcerted by increasing empirical evidence of voting suggesting that the United States
was not a sound democracy in the eighteenth- and nineteenth-century
sense. Pateman suggests this led to revisionist theories of democracy
(i.e., Dahl, Downs, or Sartori), designed to bring normative theory
more into line with empirical reality. As described by Barber (1984) and
Mansbridge (1980), democratic theory à la rational choice shifted its
emphasis from explaining political change to justifying political stability. The empirical effect of this shift, Petracca (1991) suggests, is that we
focus too much on voters and pay too little attention to what a vote
means. We ask how elections are won but not what elections mean in
terms of empowerment. We view citizens only as vote-traders and ignore what it means to be a citizen, what citizen obligations entail, and
what citizens can expect to achieve in a political system that makes individual self-interest the norm.

So far, there has been too little dialogue between rational actor theorists and normative political theorists over methodological individualism, liberalism, and the ideological/scientific nature of rational actor
theory. These critical questions remain unanswered.

   11. Which is more important for political action: economics or politics?
Does the rational actor theory necessitate the primacy of the economic? As
contemporary rational choice theory is increasingly classified as a normative rather than as a positive formal theory, we are returned to the
debate between scholars who study normative and ancient political theory and those who do contemporary political science: What is human
nature and what is its relation to the political? On this point, we might
recall early work by Cropsey (1977), an economist turned political phi-
losopher, who argues that it is only modern political theorists (after
Hobbes and Locke) who believed civil law—and social science—
should reflect a law of nature. The ancients held no such view, demonstrating a quite different idea of the proper realm of the political as they
argued that the polity must shape human nature:

   In confining itself to making explicit what is implicit in man's primitive state, political philosophy caused itself to be supplanted primarily

by economics, the discipline that systematically enlarges upon the self-preserving motives of pre-civil man. Political science inherited as its content the ministerial questions pertaining to the support of the essentially economic order of society. In this way, and in the indicated order of rank, economics and political science arose out of the self-limitation of political philosophy. [Cropsey 1977:43]

Current attempts to introduce the political—through civic duty or other-directed behavior—into rational models are a first step in correcting this, but most of the actual models (Margolis 1982) do not go far enough. A recent piece by Downs (1991), which argues that democracy cannot be adequately explained without reference to social values, should be quite significant in legitimizing a paradigm shift in this direction and in encouraging analysts to introduce values directly into their rational models. Such a concern with values might encourage a more civil dialogue between normative and positive political theorists, to the enrichment of the discipline.

CONCLUSION

I have outlined the essentials of the theory of rational action. I then summarized the wide-ranging critiques of the theory and tried to suggest questions on which future research in this area might profitably focus. Let me conclude by noting the three central problem areas that I believe are most critical to address in modifying the economic theory of rational action so it can be applied successfully to political phenomena. These center on (1) self-interest, (2) conscious choice, and (3) identity perception.

Self-Interest. As a student of altruism, it seems clear to me that self-interest does explain much of human behavior. I would not argue that we should discard this as part of our theory of rational political behavior. I would, however, claim that the theory's limits are exceeded when it is applied to situations where individual self-interest is not the dominant force behind behavior and that many significant political acts fall into this domain. While self-interest can remain a basic part of our political theories, it should be balanced by human needs for sociability, defined as a feeling of belonging to a group or collectivity.[12]

To understand when and why we pursue self-interested behavior and when we exhibit more public-spirited behavior—surely a question of some concern to political scientists—we must understand the complex linkages between optimization of an actor's self-interest and an actor's perception of himself or herself in relation to others. Why is individual self-interest sometimes pursued and group interest pursued at other times? The answer may depend on which of the actor's identities is made most relevant by external conditions. This is where we could introduce the importance of framing, of social contexts, and the role of culture, thereby responding positively to both the cultural critiques and the cognitive critiques of the rational actor theory.

Conscious Choice. Another limitation in the theory results from its overemphasis on conscious choice; one solution here is to focus more on learned strategies that result in optimal outcomes. Choices may well be less important than strategies that lead to successful outcomes. Furthermore, choices do not have to be conscious. A successful strategy can originate in unconscious choices, emotions, or chance. The conscious element may enter when the success of a strategy is recognized or learned. Even learning does not require consciousness, however, although in many cases (perhaps even most) consciousness will exist ex poste in recognition of the strategy's successful outcome. This recognition may be conscious, but it need not be; it must be conscious only insofar as it is reproducible in the future, either by the same actor or by another. This posits a close relationship between outcomes and strategies, and emphasizes both of these instead of individual choice. Such a treatment would allow for nonconscious forces in behavior, such as emotions and intuition, factors that now have to be introduced exogenously in both traditional and bounded rational models. And it would also revitalize the theory by reinstating the theoretical impetus for political behavior in the emotions.

If we design a theory of political rationality in which the concern is with learned strategies that further particular choice *outcomes* rather than with the *process* of choice, we allow a role for culture in replicating the strategy that led to optimization. The critical variables would then not be the actual decisions and choices taken by an actor, but would instead be the outcomes, intended or fortuitous. The crucial component of rational behavior would thus be the *process* of evolving toward some stationary optimal point, not an actual decision itself. In this process, critical distinctions should be made between the long and the short term. Strategies need not be the best (optimal) at any one particular moment, but they must be good enough to allow the individuals following them to survive. Behavior thus need not maximize in the short term, although over the long term it must optimize and do better than all other existing possibilities in order to survive. Optimal strategies, not individual choices, would thus be key. If the emphasis could just as well be on strategies instead of choices, then rationality can be defined (in part) as a strategy that leads through adaptation to survival. This would incorporate the famous "muddling through" we all know so well.

In the short term, all of this would suggest satisficing rather than maximizing behavior. An emphasis on constant movement and local adaptation, however, would set a theory of political rationality apart from bounded rationality's satisficing, which still emphasizes the process of choice instead of the outcome of a process.

Identities: Individuals and Groups. Finally, we should assume actors have multiple identities, whose importance varies in response to cultural and situational contexts (see Elster 1986). The key to understanding political behavior would then lie in delineating the actor's constant shift between these identities, and the manner in which the actor's perception of his or her own identity in relation to others defines the domain of relevant options. To determine when an actor pursues strategies to further individual self-interest and when an agent will act to further interests as a member of a group, we must understand how the perception of a critical identity will affect action.

Traditional economists concerned with collective action have argued that individuals join groups because the group mediates resources for that individual or provides side benefits (Olson 1965). But other forces also determine group memberships—for example, parental-offspring bonds or socialization. The logic of social (as well as economic) competition is often mediated by a group; and the group to which you give allegiance at a particular moment may be determined by the problem you confront at the time and the way you view yourself in relation to others in the group.[13] The marital relationship offers an instructive example. Husband and wife are a couple, a single unit to deal with mutual problems. But during a fight, each conceives of himself or herself as an individual with conflicting interests. Political negotiation may resolve many marital arguments, but just as many may be resolved by each actor simply deciding whether to remain a part of the marital group. While an economic calculus may explain part of this group behavior, understanding why the group forms and exists is certainly more complex. To understand group formation, we must focus on how groups mediate interests and act to replicate successful strategies.[14] In all of this, the perception of one's central identity and how actors shift between their individual and their group identities is crucial.

Parsing out the relevant part of the process by which actors shift from individual to group identity necessarily involves our understanding the cognitive frameworks of different actors. This allows for both internal stability and for changing conditions. It again allows for cultural variations, especially in that most critical variable: the actor's view of the relationship between the individual and society. Both traditional and bounded concepts of rationality reflect a post-Enlightenment framework, which separates the individual from the collectivity.[15] Interests are not identified this way in many non-Western societies, however; and even in Western society, individuals conceptualized their relationship with society quite differently in other historical eras.[16] (This may explain why so many Western decision models, based on individualistic assumptions, often fail to accurately predict behavior outside the Western market system.) A successful theory of political rationality should allow for the complex ties between individuals, groups, and society in general. How this can be done is unclear, but the focus on identity perception seems the right route to pursue, not the least because it will reduce the existing theory's individualistic bias and will allow us to focus on the polity's role in shaping both public and private identities.

NOTES

1. See Harry Eckstein (1991) for an excellent consideration of this assumption.

2. See Smith (1937:14) or Myers (1983) on the extent to which "the first principle of economics is that every agent is actuated only by self interest" (Edgeworth, quoted in Sen 1977:317). The twentieth-century specialization of rational choice theory also assumes self-interest as the norm (Harsanyi 1969; Buchanan and Tullock 1962; Downs 1957; Olson 1965).

3. Traditional economic rationality actually adopts an outcome rather than a process view by use of the "as if" assumption (Friedman 1953 or Wittmann 1991).

4. See Mansbridge (1980) or Myers (1983) for evidence of this.

5. See Barry (1970) or Harsanyi (1969) on the distinction between cultural and rational actor theories.

6. See Simon (1983) or (1984), inter alia.

7. See Kahneman and Tversky (1972) or Kahneman, Slovic, and Tversky (1982)

8. Riker's politician as fiduciary agent exemplifies this. Votes are traded for policies. Politicians act as entrepreneurs trying to increase their share of the political market by trading issue positions to put together winning coalitions.

9. "Since politics can take on aspects of a market, a game, a war, a church, a dramatic performance—and the history of the politics of individual societies shows how the explanation of politics over time may require some or all of them—opting for one of them as the realistic or the most realistic model is bound to have costs, to exaggerate some of the potentialities of politics at the expense of others, and at the expense of the dynamic developmental perspective. [Thus] . . . rational choice analysis may lead to empirical and normative distortions, unless it is used in combination with the historical, sociological, anthropological, and psychological sciences which deal with the values and utilities of people, cross-culturally, cross-nationally, across the social strata, and over time" (Almond 1991:36; see also Turner [1987] on group formation). All page numbers referring to selections from *The Economic Theory of Politics* are pages within the cited chapter itself, not the final volume, which is in press.

10. In a closely related though less critical assessment, Kavka (1991) agrees that "the central idea of the economic theories of politics is that we can best explain the behavior of political actors (e.g., voters, office seekers, bureaucracy) by assuming that they are rational utility maximizers" (Kavka 1991:abstract). Kavka also agrees with Simon (1984) and with Almond (1991) that much of the real explanation in such theories comes from the auxiliary assumptions about human motivation. But Kavka argues that utility maximization acts as the "idea-generator" to produce "(without logically implying) these assumptions" (Kavka 1991:abstract).

11. Rosenberg (1991) concludes that taken as a whole, the research in cognitive, social, and experimental psychology suggests "people do not have the information gathering, interpretive or computational skills required to properly recognize, comprehend, and evaluate the circumstances and consequences of choices made under conditions typical of political life" (Rosenberg 1991:14).

12. While these two needs vary innately among individuals, both an individual's average position over time and the particular fluctuations along his or her individual continuum are determined by cultural conditions. Specifying how culture (in a general way) and context (in a more immediate way) affect identity will be difficult; but it will do much to specify how an actor's need to advance individual self-interest is balanced by his or her need to identify with a group or a collectivity.

13. The importance of multiple roles has long been recognized in social science; see Rossiter's (1956) analysis of the presidency. How these roles are a function of societal conditions, or aspects of the problem confronted, has been a concern of anthropologists. See Evans-Pritchard's work on the Nuer (1962).

14. For biologists, traits enabling survival are transmitted genetically. In social science the transmission mechanism is not so clearly identified. Replication of strategies is an evolutionary process, with evolution traditionally said to occur in one of three ways. (1) The more effective individuals survive and reproduce. (2) Trial and error learning occurs, either by actors pursuing their more effective strategies and altering the strategies that were less effective in the past. Or (3) actors observe and imitate strategies of more successful actors. In this process, it is the particular strategy followed that is the key to understanding behavior, not the action of any one individual. Understanding how these strategies are replicated would emphasize both the role of evolutionary change and how cultural constraints directly affect rational behavior.

15. Ironically, the Enlightenment's passion for individualism has made it difficult for traditional economic concepts of rationality to explain collective and group behavior (Arnhart 1987). Kolm (1983:62) also notes the extent to which the individualization of society is a legacy of the eighteenth century, one from which contemporary social theory must free itself.

16. A less individualistic, more organic view argues that individual self-fulfillment results from taking part in the life of the polis or society. (As the child grows into the woman or man, so the individual grows into the citizen.) Individual and group happiness cannot be separated. The good life is the life spent in civic duties. This organic view corresponds to ideas expressed by Plato

and certain other classical Greek or Roman theorists. An organismic view of the relationship between the individual's ties to a collectivity is exemplified by medieval theorists such as Aquinas. (As the heart is an organ independent within but meaningless without the entire body, so the individual is a separate yet integral part of society.) Each individual has his or her function to play within society; at the same time, each maintains an identity distinct within (but not separate from) society.

REFERENCES

Abelson, Robert et al. 1968. *Theory of Cognitive Consistency: A Source Book*. Chicago: Rand-McNally.

Almond, G. 1991. "Rational Choice Theory and the Social Sciences." In *The Economic Approach to Politics*, Kristen R. Monroe, ed. New York: HarperCollins.

Arnhart, L. 1987. *Political Questions*. New York: Macmillan.

Ball, Richard A. 1968. "A Poverty Case: The Analgesic Subculture of the Southern Appalachians." *American Sociological Review* 33:885–95.

Banfield, Edward C. 1950. *The Moral Basis of a Backward Society*. Chicago: University of Chicago Press.

Barber, B. 1984. *Strong Democracy*. Berkeley: University of California Press.

Barry, B. 1970. *Economists, Sociologists and Democracy*. Chicago: University of Chicago Press.

Bartlett, F.A. 1932. *Remembering*. Cambridge: Cambridge University Press.

Becker, G. 1976. *The Economic Approach to Human Behavior*. Chicago: University of Chicago Press.

Buchanan, J., and G. Tullock. 1962. *The Calculus of Consent*. Ann Arbor: University of Michigan Press.

Caudill, Harry M. 1962. *Night Comes to the Cumberlands*. Boston: Little, Brown.

Cropsey, J. 1977. *Political Philosophy and the Issues of Politics*. Chicago: University of Chicago Press.

Downs, A. 1957. *An Economic Theory of Democracy*. New York: Harper and Row.

———. 1991. "Social Values and Democracy." In *The Economic Approach to Politics*, Kristen R. Monroe, ed. New York: HarperCollins.

Eckstein, H. 1984. "Civic Inclusion and Its Discontents." *Daedalus* 113: 107–46.

———. 1991. "Rationality and Frustration in Political Behavior." In *The Economic Approach to Politics*, Kristen R. Monroe, ed. New York: HarperCollins.

Elster, J. 1986. *The Multiple Self*. Cambridge: Cambridge University Press.

Evans-Pritchard. 1962. *The Nuer Religion*. Oxford: Clarendon Press.

Festinger, L. 1957. *A Theory of Cognitive Dissonance*. Stanford: Stanford University Press.

Fiske, S.T., and S.E. Taylor. 1984. *Social Cognition*. Reading, Mass.: Addison-Wesley.

Frazier, E. Franklin. 1966. *The Negro Family in the United States*. Revised and abridged edition. Chicago: University of Chicago Press (originally 1939).

Friedman, M. 1953. *Essays in Positive Economics*. Chicago: University of Chicago Press.

Gardner, H. 1985. *The Mind's New Science*. New York: Basic Books.

Gaventa, John. 1980. *Power and Powerlessness: Quiescence and Rebellion in an Appalachian Valley*. Urbana: University of Illinois Press.

Geertz, C. 1953. *Interpretation of Cultures*. New York: Basic Books.

Goldfield, Michael, and Alan Gilbert. 1990. "The Limits of Rational Choice." Paper presented at the annual meeting of the American Political Science Association, August 30–Sept. 2, 1990.

Harsanyi, J. 1969. "Rational Choice Models of Political Behavior vs. Functional and Conformist Theories." *World Politics* 21, 4 (July): 513.

Heider, F. 1958. *The Psychology of Interpersonal Relations*. New York: John Wiley.

Hauptmann, Emily. 1990. "When Politics Make Choices Disappear: Rational Choice Theory's America and Marcel Ophul's France." Paper presented at the annual meeting of the Western Political Science Association, March 21–25, 1990.

Johnston, D. 1991. "Human Agency and Rational Action." In *The Economic Approach to Politics*, Kristen R. Monroe, ed. New York: HarperCollins.

Kahneman, D., P. Slovic, and D. Tversky, eds. 1982. *Judgment Under Uncertainty: Heuristics and Biases*. New York: Cambridge University Press.

Kahneman, D., and A. Tyersky. 1972. "A Subjective Probability: A Judgment of Representativeness." *Cognitive Psychology* 3:430–54.

Kavka, G. 1991. "Rational Maximizing in Economic Theories of Politics." In *The Economic Approach to Politics*, Kristen R. Monroe, ed. New York: HarperCollins.

Key, V.O. 1942. *Southern Politics in State and Nation*. New York: Knopf.

Koffka, K. 1935. *Principles of Gestalt Psychology*. New York: Harcourt, Brace and World.

Kolm, S.C. 1983. "Altruism and Efficiency." *Ethics* 94, 1:18–65.

Maier, Norman. 1961. *Frustration: The Study of Behavior Without a Goal*. Ann Arbor: University of Michigan Press (first ed., 1949).

Mansbridge, J. 1980. *Beyond Adversarial Democracy*. New York: Basic Books.

———. 1990. *Beyond Self-Interest*. Chicago: University of Chicago Press.

Margolis, H. 1982. *Selfishness, Altruism and Rationality*. Cambridge: Cambridge University Press.

Monroe, Kristen R. 1990. " 'What Else Could I Do?' The Role of Conscious Choice and Identity in Political Action." Paper presented at the annual meeting of the American Political Science Association, August 30–September 2, 1990.

————. 1991a. "John Donne's People: Explaining Differences between Rational Actors and Altruists through Cognitive Frameworks." *The Journal of Politics* 53:2.

————, editor. 1991b. *The Economic Approach to Politics*. New York: HarperCollins.

Monroe, Kristen R., M.C. Barton, and U. Klingeman, 1990. "Altruism and the Theory of Rational Action: Rescues of Jews in Nazi-Europe." *Ethics* 101: 103–22.

Moynihan, D.P., and Nathan Glazer. 1966. *Beyond the Melting Pot*. Cambridge: MIT Press and Harvard University Press.

Myers, M. 1983. *The Soul of Economic Man*. Chicago: University of Chicago Press.

Nisbett, R.E., and E. Borgida. 1975. "Attribution and the Psychology of Prediction." *Journal of Personality and Social Psychology* 32:932–43.

Nisbett, R.E., and L. Ross. 1980. *Human Inference: Strategies and Shortcomings of Social Judgment*. Englewood Cliffs, N.J.: Prentice-Hall.

Nussbaum, Martha. 1986. *The Fragility of Goodness*. Cambridge: Cambridge University Press.

Olson, M. 1965. *The Logic of Collective Action*. Cambridge: Harvard University Press.

Pateman, C. 1970. *Participation and Democratic Theory*. Cambridge: Cambridge University Press.

Petracca, Mark P. 1991. "The Rational Actor Approach to Politics: Science, Self Interest and Normative Democratic Theory." In *The Economic Approach to Politics*, Kristen R. Monroe, ed. New York: HarperCollins.

Quattrone, G.A., and A. Tversky. 1988. "Contrasting Rational and Psychological Analyses of Political Choice." *American Political Science Review* 82: 719–37.

Riker, William. 1962. *Theory of Political Coalitions*. New Haven: Yale University Press.

Rodman, Hyman. 1971. *Lower Class Families: The Culture of Poverty in Negro Trinidad*. London: Oxford University Press.

Rosenberg, S. 1988. *Reason, Ideology, and Politics*. Princeton: Princeton University Press.

————. 1991. "Rationality, Markets and Political Analysis: A Social Psychological Critique of Neoclassical Political Economy." In *The Economic Approach to Politics*, Kristen R. Monroe, ed. New York: HarperCollins.

Rossiter, Clinton. 1956. *The American Presidency*. New York: Harcourt Brace.

Scalia, Laura. 1991. "Self-Interest and Democracy." In *The Economic Approach to Politics*, Kristen R. Monroe, ed. New York: HarperCollins.

Schattschneider, E.E. 1975. *The Semi-Sovereign People: A Realist's View of Democracy in America*. Hinsdale, Ill.: Dryden Press.

Sen, A. 1977. "Rational Fools: A Critique of the Behavioral Foundations of Economic Theory." *Philosophy and Public Affairs* 6, 4 (Summer): 317–44.

Simon, Herbert A. 1982. *Models of Bounded Rationality*, vols. 1 and 2. Cambridge: MIT Press.

———. 1983. *Reasons in Human Affairs*. Stanford: Stanford University Press.

———. 1984. "Human Nature in Politics: The Dialogue of Psychology with Political Science." *The American Political Science Review* 79, 2:293–304.

Smith, A. 1937. *The Wealth of Nations*. New York: Modern Library.

Taylor, S.E., and S.T. Fiske. 1975. "Point-of-View and Perceptions of Causality." *Journal of Personality and Social Psychology* 32:439–45.

Toynbee, A. 1946. *A Study of History*. New York: Oxford University Press.

Turner, J. 1987. *The Reemergence of the Social Group: A Self-Categorization Theory*. New York: Basil Blackwell.

Tversky, A., and D. Kahneman. 1974. "Judgment Under Uncertainty: Heuristics and Biases." *Science* 185:1124–31.

Wattenberg, M. 1988. "Economic, Psychological and Sociological Theories of Voting." Paper presented at the University of California conference in honor of Anthony Downs. University of California, Irvine, October 28–29.

Weller, J.E. 1965. *Yesterday's People: Life in Contemporary Appalachia*. Lexington: University of Kentucky Press.

Whitehead, J. 1991. "Reason and Regulation in Economic Theory." In *The Economic Approach to Politics*, Kristen R. Monroe, ed. New York: Harper-Collins.

Wittmann, D. 1991. "Contrasting Rational and Psychological Analyses of Political Choice: An Economist's Perspective on Why Cognitive Psychology Does Not Explain Democratic Politics." In *The Economic Approach to Politics*, Kristen R. Monroe, ed. New York: HarperCollins.

5

Analytic Theory
and Methodology

Paul E. Johnson and Philip A. Schrodt

Mathematical modeling of political behavior is a relatively recent phenomenon, largely confined to the post–World War II era. While the field began by borrowing most of its methods and concepts from economics, demography, and applied mathematics, it has subsequently identified a series of problems that are uniquely political in nature and has developed its own literature and techniques to supplement those acquired earlier. In this process, modeling has acquired the usual manifestations of an academic subdiscipline, including journals, conferences, and a jargon virtually incomprehensible to the uninitiated.

The purpose of this paper is to survey both the literature and theoretical issues in analytic theory and methodology as it stands on the verge of the last decade of the twentieth century. The field is unusual in being defined both by substantive foci and by mathematical techniques. Because of the technical difficulties involved in mastering (or even reading) the methodology employed in a modeling approach such as game theory or differential equations, researchers in the field have tended to begin with a focus on technique. However, as a technique becomes widely known and applied, the focus shifts from the method to the application—for example, to committee voting or arms races.

This topic is also unusual in covering behaviors ranging from the decisions of the individual American voter to the global structure of

For helpful, if contradictory, advice, we would like to thank Christopher Achen, Randall Calvert, Raymond Duvall, and Dina Zinnes.

nuclear deterrence, sometimes with the same model. The generality of modeling techniques allows the researcher to cross substantive boundaries that have traditionally separated subdisciplines. For example, rational choice models, which use the techniques of decision and game theory, can be applied to substantive areas ranging from voter participation (Riker and Ordeshook 1968; Ferejohn and Fiorina 1974; Palfrey and Rosenthal 1985) to balance of power and war initiation in international relations (Niou and Ordeshook 1986, 1987, 1989; Bueno de Mesquita 1985). Optimal control theory has found applications in such substantively diverse areas as arms races (Gillespie et al. 1976) and class conflict (Przeworski and Wallerstein 1982; Lancaster 1973; Roemer 1982, 1986). As the length of our less-than-comprehensive bibliography indicates, this encompasses a lot of territory.

We are not dealing with "methodology" in a vacuum, nor do we feel that it should be treated that way. As we note below in the section on stochastic models, the choice of methodology should be dictated by the formal model or theory underlying the research hypothesis. While there have been some recent developments in methodology per se—for example, the increased use of time series and logit techniques—methods should ultimately be determined by models. Therefore analytic theory should guide the development of new methodology.

While a variety of techniques are used in formal modeling, all models of political behavior should be abstract, explicit, deductive, and empirically applicable:

Abstract. A model simplifies reality in order to find behaviors and generalizations that are not apparent when the system is studied in its full complexity. As Ross Ashby notes:

> Every model of a real system is in one sense second rate. Nothing can exceed, or even equal, the truth and accuracy of the real system itself. Every model is inferior, a distortion, a lie. No electronic model of a cat's brain can possibly be as true as that provided by another cat, yet of what *use* is the latter as a model? Its very closeness means that it also presents all the technical features that make the first so difficult [to study]. ([Quoted in Fiorina 1975])

Models simplify: that is their purpose, not their weakness. If a system can be completely understood without simplification (for example, the game of tic-tac-toe) there is nothing to be gained from modeling it. Most political behavior is far too complex to be easily understood, and so models have a role to play.

Explicit. The assumptions of a model are presented openly, either in the specification of the model itself or in combination with the assumptions of the language (e.g., linear algebra, probability theory) in which it is specified. Because natural languages are inherently ambiguous, most models are specified in formal languages, usually logic, mathematics, or computer code.

Deductive. A model is used deductively to discover things that were not immediately obvious from the assumptions of the model. Deduction is usually logical, following the standards of a mathematical proof, but deduction can also be numerical, as in computing the predictions of a simulation, or procedural, as in determining the behavior of a complex algorithm by running in on a computer.

Empirically relevant. The objective of a model of politics is to mirror, in some sense, actual political behavior. Models do not necessarily have to be formally tested, but they must at least be plausible. As Simon (1954:388) notes:

> Mathematical social science is first and foremost social science. If it is bad social science (empirically false), the fact that it is good mathematics (i.e., logically consistent) should provide little comfort.

In particular, before something is accepted as a universal law of human behavior, it is helpful to know that it applies in at least one case.

In writing this survey we were torn by the conflicting objectives of comprehensively surveying the literature and focusing in detail on the issues we felt to be most important. In the end, we have done some of each. Included in our study are models that satisfied any of three criteria. First, models that are currently subjects of active research; these comprise the bulk of the discussion. Second, we provide some bibliographic information on earlier, but now inactive, research foci such as zero sum games and the Richardson arms race model. Finally, we briefly discuss some models that occupy only small niches in political science but are common elsewhere in the mathematical literature—for example, stochastic models. Our survey is still short of comprehensive—for example, we do not discuss applications of graph theory (e.g., Harary 1977; Miller 1977) or catastrophe theory (e.g., Holt, Job, and Markus 1978; Oliva, Peters, and Murthy 1981)—but does cover most of the major research concentrations.

A BRIEF HISTORY OF MODELS IN POLITICAL SCIENCE

Mathematical models first became popular in political science in the 1950s, when inferential statistics came into common usage. The 1950s and 60s are referred to as the "behavioral era," because most effort was focused on the detection of empirical patterns in voting behavior and public opinion data. During this period, considerable infrastructure was developed to administer and make available national surveys on a regular basis, which made sufficient data available that serious statistical work could be done in the academic community. Also during the 1950s, however, the roots of modern mathematical modeling were established. Though there is still a great deal of interest in empirical results, there has been a substantial growth in emphasis on mathematical theory as a technique for the derivation of testable hypotheses.

There are three major mathematical approaches, called political economy, systems modeling, and artificial intelligence. The fundamental axioms of the political economy approach are that individuals in a political system are rational actors (they have well-defined preferences and behave in accordance with them) and that social outcomes (equilibria) result from the interaction of these individuals within the constraints imposed by social institutions. Models in this tradition have three technical components: individual behavioral principles, institutional structures, and an equilibrium (or, more generally, solution) concept. An equilibrium is a situation that exists when none of the actors with power to effectuate change choose to do so. Observably stable or repetitive political events are explained by equilibrium concepts.

This approach, which is also called public choice or rational choice, has thrived on the healthy interaction of political scientists and economists. Though the early research mainly concerned legislatures and elections, the field speaks to a much larger set of topics, including bureaucratic-legislative relations, international alliances and war, interest groups, and presidential power. Game theory is the mode of investigation that unifies these studies.

The second approach, which we call "systems modeling," examines properties of systems and their changes over time. In contrast to the emphasis on individual behavior in the political economy tradition, these approaches theorize about aggregates or systemic variables. There are two branches of inquiry in this area. Dynamic modeling is the name used to refer to a genre of studies in which a system's states are hypothesized to follow a set of differential equations. The existence and stability of equilibria are examined. This field has benefited substantially from interaction with biologists and other natural scientists. The second systems approach may be called stochastic modeling. Standard techniques for the analysis of random or stochastic processes are applied to political processes.

The third, and newest, field, is artificial intelligence or computational modeling. These models also involve explicit specifications of the mechanisms of political reasoning, but the assumptions tend to be closer to those of cognitive psychology than to economics. The models are usually specified as computer programs and solved procedurally rather than algebraically. The potential scope of this method of research is quite broad and, in many ways, it offers a potential bridge between political economy and systems models, in that systems too complex to manage analytically might yield to computer analysis.

VOTING MODELS: LEGISLATURES AND ELECTIONS

The basic assumption of research on voting models is that democratic decisions should be studied as aggregation procedures: systems that combine the individual tastes of the voters into a social outcome. The set of alternatives from which the voters choose may take one of three forms. It may be a simple list of alternatives, $X^1 = \{x, y, z\}$, or it may be a set of some sort, such as an interval in the real number line or a point in Euclidean n-space R^n. Interestingly enough, one of the major results in this line of research is that there are fundamental differences in the nature of voting procedures in the three kinds of choice spaces.

Voter/participants are hypothesized to be rational, in the sense that they have transitive preference orderings over the alternatives from which they choose. That is, if P_i is a binary "preferred to" relation for a voter $i \varepsilon N$ (where $N = \{1, 2, \ldots n\}$) and the alternatives include x, y, and z, then transitivity means that xP_iy and yP_iz imply xP_iz. Sometimes articles, instead of assuming that a voter i has preferences, will simply say that i has a "utility function $U_i(x)$," but this is just another way of saying the same thing. That is, if xP_iy then $U_i(x) > U_i(y)$. In no serious sense do voting models assume that voters actually calculate their utilities; rather, voters know what they like from the outset and attempt to bring it about.

Early social choice research was concerned with preference aggregation on a discrete space, X^1. Suppose that we are given the preferences of three voters over the alternatives x, y, and z. Suppose, for simplicity, that the voting procedure is majority rule, the most frequently investigated method of social choice. Majority rule generates a binary social preference relation, M. This relation[1] is xMy, meaning x is preferred by a majority to y, if the following more than half of the voters prefer x to y: $| \{i \varepsilon N: xP_iy\} | > n/2$. Early research was inspired, in part, by a widely noted "paradox of voting":[2] given transitive preferences for three voters,

$$xP_1y \text{ and } yP_1z \quad yP_2z \text{ and } zP_2x \quad zP_3x \text{ and } xP_3y$$

under majority rule, x beats y, z beats x, but, surprisingly, y beats z. When the social order is intransitive (there is a cycle yMzMxMy), the social decision is indeterminate—there is no meaningful way to infer the "will of the people" from the voting process, because every proposal can be defeated by another one. In the terms of the trade, there is no "Condorcet winner." Kenneth Arrow's "impossibility theorem" showed that intransitivity of this sort is generic to all nondictatorial social choice rules that meet certain minimal criteria of democratic government (1951, 1963). The theorem does not mean that all voting procedures go wrong all the time, but it does mean that there is always a set of rationally structured individual preferences that causes a binary social preference relation to be irrational or incoherent. Excellent introductory discussions of the theorem can be found in Ordeshook (1986) and Riker (1982).

For some time, it was believed that the intransitivity problem could be minimized by giving the policy alternatives some geometric structure. The first wave of research concerned voting in a space on the real line: the unidimensional model of voting (Black 1948, 1958). In this model, for convenience, we work with a utility function rather than a preference relation. A voter's preferences are said to be single-peaked if $U_i(x)$ is quasiconcave in x. Duncan Black found one solution to the paradox of voting, which is called the Median Voter Theorem: if the number of voters is odd, the choice space is unidimensional, and voter preferences are single-peaked, then under majority rule the median of the voters' ideal points is a Condorcet winner (it defeats all other proposals) and, furthermore, majority rule generates a transitive binary social preference relation. The single-peakedness requirement is thought to be reasonable—people generally have a favorite policy alternative and movements along a line going away from the favorite policy are not preferred.

Black's theory dealt with committee voting in which the members could propose alternatives to the winner of the previous vote. The only unbeatable proposal, the Condorcet winner, was the median voter's ideal point. Essentially the same result was reached in Downs's classic discussion of candidate position-taking, in *An Economic Theory of Democracy* (1957). In a unidimensional model of two-candidate competition for votes, Downs found that an equilibrium exists in which both candidates announce positions that are equal to the median of the voters' ideal points. Voting models for committees and elections thus have essentially the same logic; the major difference is in the voting agenda: the set of alternatives available to the voters and the rules of agenda access. The candidate positions set the agenda in an electoral model, while committee models may have considerably more complicated agendas.

The main limitation on the Median Voter Theorem is that it applies only to unidimensional social choice spaces and is relevant only to majority rule systems. Most voting processes in reality seem to range over spaces of considerably higher dimensionality (see Stokes 1963). The typical multidimensional spatial model pictures voters choosing from a convex subset of Euclidean n-space. The desirability of a point $x \varepsilon X$ to voter i depends on the distance between x and the voter's most preferred point, $x_i^* \varepsilon X$, according to a function $U_i(x;x_i^*)$.

The literature appearing in the 1970s and 1980s on cycles and multidimensional models is immense and mathematically sophisticated. Cycling in higher dimensions usually cannot be avoided unless much stronger assumptions than single-peakedness are imposed (see Plott 1967; Kramer 1973). Since these much stronger conditions are not thought to prevail in reality, the result implies that majority rule decisions are generally intransitive (see the caveat of Enelow and Hinich 1983a). More surprisingly, if preferences are single-peaked (quasiconcave) in the multidimensional space, the so-called chaos theorems indicate that, if no point exists that is majority preferred to all other points, then a cycle exists between any two points in the space. As McKelvey put it, "when transitivity breaks down, it *completely* breaks down, engulfing the whole space in a single cycle set" (McKelvey 1976:475). It is now known that, in spaces of sufficiently high dimension, a continuous trajectory of proposals exists leading from one point to any other, along which each point defeats the immediately preceding point (Schofield 1978, 1989). Later research convincingly demonstrates that equilibria generically (in the measure theoretic sense: almost always) do not exist (McKelvey and Schofield 1986, 1987; for an unusually readable explanation of these results, see Feld and Grofman 1987). To summarize, it has been shown that the Median Voter Theorem cannot be extended to a multidimensional setting.

The pervasiveness and severity of voting cycles is considered to be one of the most important problems in the field. Are observable social decisions, either in legislatures or elections, as chaotic as the theorems seem to imply? Gordon Tullock said no. "If we look at the real world, . . . we observe not only is there no endless cycling, but acts are passed with reasonable dispatch and then remain unchanged for very long periods of time" (1981:190). Tullock asked "Why so much stability?," a question with which we have been perplexed for some time. There are essentially two approaches. The first, called "the new institutionalism" or structure-induced equilibrium, adds a richer, more empirically relevant model of political institutions and diagnoses the stabilizing impact of these institutions. The second approach minimizes emphasis on institutions and instead investigates alternative models of voter or candidate behavior.

Institutional Models

The new institutionalism is associated with an important article by Shepsle (1979). The viewpoint is that emphasis on the institution-free properties of a majority preference relation overlooks critical structural variables that guide social choices. Emphasis on the impact of institutions on decisions comes up in a variety of contexts, such as the theory of constitutional design (Hammond and Miller 1987), presidential-congressional relations (Kiewiet and McCubbins 1988), fund raising through referenda and the effects of agenda-setting (Romer and Rosenthal 1978), but most of the research is concentrated on decision-making in legislatures. A legislature has committees and agendas, and following Shepsle a great deal of research has been done on the equilibrium-inducing power of these congressional structures. Krehbiel (1988) provides an exhaustive, up-to-date survey of spatial models of legislatures that lists more than sixty articles on the subject written in the past ten years. Among the most interesting developments in this field:

Supramajority rules. If, rather than pure majority rule, a legislature requires majorities of $2/3$ or more, the likelihood of cycles can be considerably reduced (Schofield, Grofman, and Feld 1988, and many studies cited therein). Given some mild "regularity" conditions (i.e., assumptions about the distribution of preferences), one study has recently shown that the stability-inducing majority requirement is 64 percent (Caplin and Nalebuff 1988).

Dimension-at-a-time voting. Shepsle's (1979) original model of a legislature treated it as a body in which the dimensions of the choice space were decided one at a time. Legislators were treated as *myopic* voters who considered the dimensions in isolation. The effect of *foresight* on voting in dimension-at-a-time voting has been examined (Denzau and Mackay 1981; Enelow and Hinich 1983b). Depending on the model of foresight chosen, majority rule may or may not converge to a stable outcome.

Committee systems and the "power to propose." A subset of the members, a committee, might propose on the floor a policy change from the status quo. The freedom of the legislature to amend the committee's proposal has a fundamental effect on the nature of equilibria that we should expect to observe. Several studies have looked at the power of committees and their ability to get their way, against the wishes of the parent chamber, by exploiting the rules (Denzau and Mackay 1983; Shepsle and Weingast 1987; Krehbiel 1987a, 1987b). Committee power varies systematically with the amount of "sophistication" that the actors (in committee and on the floor) are presumed to possess, and the agenda-setting rules that forbid or limit the ability of members on the floor to propose amendments to the committee's proposal. Sophistication, a term coined by Farquharson 1969 is the ability of the voters to foresee the impact of contemporary decisions on decisions to be made later on. Methods of measuring these effects empirically have recently been developed and applied to actual decisions in Congress (Gilligan and Krehbiel 1988a; Krehbiel and Rivers 1988a).

Recognition of the effects of committees and the rules that protect their bills on the floor of the legislature leads to the consideration of *endogenous* rules and committee systems. Typically, the members of Congress recognize the value of committee expertise and specialization, but might worry that the committee will take advantage of its expertise to steer the body away from its median. Gilligan and Krehbiel have offered several very insightful models of the relationship between the parent body and its committees that explain the conditions under which committees will be created and allowed to bring their proposals to the floor under restrictive amendment rules (1987, 1988b).

Agendas and sophisticated voting. In his original presentation of what is now called the "chaos theorem," McKelvey (1976) felt the result was really important because of the power that it gave the agenda setter in the legislature. Theoretically, the agenda setter should be able to design a sequence of votes that leads to the agenda setter's ideal point. This result hinges on the hypothesis that the voters are *sincere*: when presented with a choice between two alternatives, voters express their true preferences. How likely is it that the members of a legislature would let their agenda setter lead them down the garden path?

To answer this question, many studies have considered what happens if the voters are sophisticated and vote strategically (misrepresent their preferences to "steer" the voting process in directions that they prefer). The classic method of analyzing sophisticated voting is presented in McKelvey and Niemi (1978). The agenda is modeled as a game tree and the sophisticated voters are able to look to the end of game tree and anticipate where the early votes are going to lead.

Miller (1980) proposed a very influential solution concept called "the uncovered set." Technical definitions of the uncovered set vary among articles, but the essential idea is that an outcome x covers y if 1) x is majority-preferred to y and 2) any alternative z that is majority-preferred to x is also majority-preferred to y. Intuitively, a covered alternative y should be excluded from the set of "reasonable outcomes" because it can be defeated by x, *and* y cannot defeat any points that can defeat x. Hence the emphasis on the uncovered set. Miller observed that sophisticated voters can never be led out of the uncovered set by an "amendment agenda": a vote is held between the first two alternatives in a list, and the winner is paired against the next proposal, and so on. Furthermore, it was shown that anywhere that an agenda setter can lead sophisticated voters can be reached in one or two steps, greatly diminishing the worry that an impossibly complicated agenda would be required for an agenda setter to do his or her damage (Miller 1980; Shepsle and Weingast 1984). This observation led to a more intuitive definition of the uncovered set: x is uncovered if it defeats all other alternatives either directly or in one step. That is, either 1) xMy or 2) if yMx, there is a third point z such that xMz and zMy. McKelvey (1986) showed that outcomes under three quite different institutional choice procedures are in the uncovered set, a fact that led him to emphasize the uncovered set as an "institution-free" solution concept.

Unfortunately, it was soon shown that outcomes outside the uncovered set can occur in more realistic models of the legislative process. The "institution-free uncovered set" solution holds only for amendment agendas, not more general agenda structures like the ones used in congress (Ordeshook and Schwartz 1987; see also Banks 1989). In addition, when the voters do not know each other's preferences with certainty (the voters are not "completely informed") even the worst can happen: if there is a Condorcet winner, it might not be chosen (Ordeshook and Palfrey 1988). On the encouraging side, the uncovered set does have an "attracting effect" on social choices. If an amendment procedure requires that the final vote be between the "perfected" alternative and the status quo, then the uncovered set (and a closely related set that McKelvey called the *yolk*, or "generalized median set" [1986:301]) sets limits on the power of an agenda setter to impose his will on the legislature. The uncovered set and the yolk both tend to be centrally located in the middle of the distribution of the voter ideal points. Feld, Grofman, and Miller (1989) have summarized the agenda control results. Essentially, an agenda setter has a much easier time leading majorities into the uncovered set than away from it.

Where does all this leave research on legislative voting models? The debate continues about the importance of institutions in determining social choices. On one side, we find the view that the institution-free social choice solutions are desirable. The variety of conceivable voting institutions is infinite, and unless we can make some general statements about their tendencies, we will be swamped in a series of disjointed observations about a potpourri of institutions. The possibility still exists that social choice outcomes might be more or less independent of particular legislative institutions or agendas (for an encouraging result along these lines, see Ferejohn, Fiorina, and McKelvey 1987).

On the other side, many scholars believe that institutions have a fundamental effect on social choices and that we are misguided to search for institution-free solutions. Since no general solution is likely to hold for a broad variety of institutions, it is argued that we should follow two main research strategies. First, we need models of endogenously created institutions. Since institutions do matter, we want to know why they are created and maintained, and if we understand the circumstances under which certain institutions are created, we will get a handle on the kinds of institutions that deserve most study. Thus, there is a premium on results that can demonstrate the endogeneity and effect of voter behavior of legislative institutions, be they agendas (Austen-

Smith 1987; Koehler 1987) or rules governing committee systems (Gilligan and Krehbiel 1987). One of the major goals along these lines, of course, is explaining why institutions are not in a state of perpetual chaos, as a believer in the chaos theorems might suspect (for an influential discussion, see Riker 1980).

Second, we need to do more careful case studies and empirical analysis of particular institutions and the effects of these institutions on the behavior of rational actors. We are learning more about the Powell amendment in 1956 than most of us wanted to know, but in the process we are learning more about the tendencies of voters to behave with sophistication and the circumstances under which we should expect sincerity to diverge from sophistication (most recently, see Denzau, Riker, and Shepsle 1985; Krehbiel and Rivers 1988b; Austen-Smith 1987).

Electoral Models

The major structural difference between the models of legislative and electoral decisions is the agenda-setting process: legislatures allow the members to propose alternatives on an agenda, while election models constrain voters to choose between the offerings of the candidates. Thus, in many ways, elections are simpler institutions than legislatures. The research questions that drive candidate position-taking studies concern electoral equilibrium and "candidate convergence." Are there stable candidate positions? However, candidates, like legislatures, do not seem to be frantically changing their positions from moment to moment as the chaos theorems would lead us to suspect. Why so much stability? Research on electoral models is driven by an additional question. In equilibrium (if it exists), do the candidate positions "converge" to identical points in the policy space? The early unidimensional models supported the convergence hypothesis (Hotelling 1929; Downs 1957), but empirically most observers agree that candidates do not take identical positions, though they do tend to be in the center. Hence, there must be factors that keep candidate positions apart, but also in the center of the electorate.

Recent electoral research examines the effect of variations in assumptions about candidate and voter incentives and information, as well as the effect of variations in electoral rules. Cox argues quite persuasively that the uncovered set is a viable solution set for candidate position-taking. "If one accepts the extremely mild assumption that candidates will not adopt a spatial strategy y if there is another available strategy x which is at least as good as y against any strategy the opponent might take and is better against some of the opponent's possible strategies, then one can conclude that candidates will confine themselves to strategies in the uncovered set" (Cox 1987a:420; for discussions of candidate strategies in other kinds of electoral systems, see Cox 1987b, 1989). This important result implies that candidate positions are likely to be found within a relatively small and centrally located uncovered set. The power of the uncovered set as a solution in electoral position-taking models results from the difference between electoral and legislative institutions. The institutional features—especially complicated agendas—which can steer the social choice out of the uncovered set in legislative voting models are not present in electoral models.

A variety of other approaches to candidate competition have been taken. One stream of research abandons the assumption that candidates are merely office seekers and allows the possibility that they have preferences about the policies that they will implement while in office. There are variations among the time frames of the models and the sophistication attributed to voters, but the results generally indicate that candidates will take positions close or identical to each other (Wittman 1983; Calvert 1985; Alesina 1987, 1988). Differing policy objectives may cause them to take different stands, but under a variety of hypotheses these differences seem rather minor. Policy oriented candidates do take separate positions when the effects of political party support are taken into account (see Aldrich and McGinnis 1989, and sources cited therein). By taking into account the relationship between candidates and their partisan followers, the stability of nonmedian, nonconvergent candidate positions can be explained. Even if the candidates are solely interested in winning elections, Palfrey has shown that two major party candidates take distinct positions if they take into account the possibility that third parties might form in the extreme regions of the policy space and siphon off major party support (1984).

Another stream of research investigates the effect of voter and candidate uncertainty. Voter uncertainty arises because voters cannot be sure of the policies that the candidates will adopt if elected. These models, which travel under the label "probabilistic voting," generally show that candidates take similar (or identical) positions in equilibrium that appeal to centrist, though not necessarily median, voters (Hinich, Ledyard, and Ordeshook 1972a, 1972b; Coughlin and Nitzan 1981; Coughlin 1982, 1984; Enelow and Hinich 1984a, 1984b; Hinich 1977). A good deal of extremely rigorous empirical analysis has been done that bears out the centrist tendencies of the probabilistic voting models (see Enelow and Hinich 1989, and sources mentioned therein). When the voters are unsure of the policy impact of their choice between candidates, it has been shown that incumbency and reputation can play critical roles in influencing candidate position-taking. Challengers are seen as more risky than incumbents, and incumbents are limited in spatial mobility by their reputations (Bernhardt and Ingberman 1985; Ingberman 1989). If, on the other hand, candidates are unsure of the voters' preferences but the voters take the candidates' promises at face value and one candidate (presumably the incumbent) announces his or her position first, the opponent seems sure to imitate that strategy, regardless of whether it is in the center of the electorate (Glazer, Grofman, and Owen 1989).

GAME AND DECISION THEORY

Legislatures and elections have been the dominant fields of inquiry in political economy and the models increasingly use the concepts and tools of game theory. The methods of game and decision theory, however, can be applied more generally to situations that involve strategy choice or multiperson decision-making. Decision theory is the study of individual choice behavior when the behavior of others is taken to be exogenous. Game theory is the study of N decision makers whose payoffs are jointly determined by their choices. The field began with the monumental accomplishment of Von Neumann and Morgenstern (1944). Their book made many lasting contributions, including results for zero sum games, n-person cooperative games, and simple games. In addition, they provided a utility theory for decision-making in risky situations (which are represented by lotteries).[3] The second edition (1947) presents a proof of the expected utility theorem, which states that under some general conditions, a person's utility for a lottery may be represented by the probability-weighted sum of the utilities of the prizes that are offered in the lottery. The most widely read introductory text in game theory has been Luce and Raiffa (1957), though as it has become dated, a number of other helpful texts have become available (Hamburger 1979; Davis 1983; Friedman 1986; Owen 1982; and Ordeshook 1986).

Since the genesis of game theory was in the analytical problems of World War II, it is not surprising that it has seen extensive use in the study of military problems in international relations. Military problems tend to be zero-sum and two-person, which are the type of game where complete results exist; cooperative and N-person games have been extensively applied to the problem of negotiation (e.g., arms control: Saaty 1968) though with less success due to the ambiguity of the results in this field. Most books on game theory provide examples of military/diplomatic applications: Luce and Raiffa (1957) is still an excellent survey; Schelling (1960) specifically addresses conflict issues; Snyder and Deising (1977) provide extensive examples of game theory as a descriptive tool in studying international conflict, and Brams (1975, 1985) provides good text-level introductions on the formal application of game theory in that field. Brewer and Shubik (1979) provide a survey of the use of these techniques (and models generally) in the Department of Defense; Kugler and Zagare (1987) provide some typical examples of the use of game theory in contemporary studies of nuclear deterrence.

Variations on the expected utility decision model have had some applications in the field of international relations. An excellent survey of these models with respect to related modeling approaches is found in Intriligator (1982): this article covers differential equation models, decision and control theory, game theory, bargaining theory, theories of uncertainty, stability and equilibrium theories, action-reaction models, and organizational theory as applied to the problems of quantitative arms races, war initiation, termination and timing, military strategy, threats and escalation, qualitative arms races, alliances, nuclear proliferation, and defense budgeting

The most notable and ambitious recent work using expected utility decision-making is Bueno de Mesquita (1981); the approach has been extended by others (e.g., Berkowitz 1983; Altfeld and Bueno de Mesquita 1979; Morrow 1985, 1986, 1987; Bueno de Mesquita and Lalman 1990; Lalman 1988). The Bueno de Mesquita approach has, however, been criticized on a number of grounds—conceptual, theoretical, and empirical—Mitchel and Nicholson (1983) and Majeski and Sylvan (1984) are among the more extensive criticisms of the approach. Brito and Intriligator (1985), O'Neill (1986) and Niou and Ordeshook (1986, 1987, 1989) provide other decision-making approaches to international politics issues such as war and balance of power.

The Variety of Games

Games differ along several dimensions: cooperative versus noncooperative games, normal versus extensive form, complete versus incomplete information. We briefly consider each of these dimensions. All game theory models are mainly concerned with finding equilibria—stable patterns of strategy choice—which presumably can be used to predict outcomes of social interaction.

A *noncooperative game* is one in which the players are not allowed to make binding agreements, while in a *cooperative* game they can. Cooperative game theory tends to focus on bargaining and contracting, agreements that (in real life) may necessitate exogenous enforcement. In a noncooperative game, the players cannot be bound to comply with agreements that are not in their interest. Noncooperative games may allow communication among the players, but there are no enforceable agreements.

Second, representations of games vary according to the sequencing of play. Games are represented either in normal or extensive forms. First, consider games in *normal form*, also called *strategic form*, which have no sequencing at all. If each player chooses simultaneously from a finite list of possible strategies, the game can be represented as a "matrix" game that indicates each player's payoff, which results from a given set of actions. More generally, a game in normal form has three elements: a list of players $i = \{1, \ldots, N\}$, the strategy set S_i, from which each player chooses an action, and each player's payoff, $U_i(s)$, that results from the N-tuple of strategy choices $s = (s_i, \ldots s_N)$. A zero sum game is one in which all the player's payoffs sum to zero. In N-person cooperative games, we are often interested in coalition formation, and a *characteristic function* is derived to represent the payoffs that a subgroup of the players can enforce (see Owen 1982:145).

At the other end of the sequencing dimension are games in *extensive form*, which are represented by the familiar "game tree": a set of "nodes" at which the players make choices along with lines (called paths) that connect the nodes to denote the sequence of play. The play of the game travels down the game tree, from the initial node to one of the terminal nodes. The payoffs to the game are attached to the terminal nodes of the game. If a player is ever in a situation of not knowing an opponent's choice at a previous node, the game is said to be one of *imperfect information*. Imperfect information is represented by the dotted line that encircles two or more nodes, and the player who is choosing a strategy does not know which node he or she is "really at," since she or he does not know the previous player's move. Extensive form games are often the starting point for representing realistic interactions that have an element of "sequencing" to them. Extensive form games can be translated into normal form, noting that the play of a game tree essentially amounts to each player deciding what to do at each decision point. In fact, some authors define extensive games first and then introduce the normal form as a representation of the extensive form game (Owen 1982:4).

The transition in representation from extensive form to normal form imposes complications, however, which as yet remain unresolved. If the play of a normal form game is repeated, it can be represented by an extensive form game. If the time interval between the moves in an extensive form game becomes arbitrarily small, so that the moves are continuous and the "state" of the game changes smoothly, we have what is called a *differential game*. These kinds of games have not cropped up very often in political science (though they have been applied to arms race modeling; e.g., Zinnes et al. 1978; Simaan and Cruz 1975) but they have much potential.

Finally, games may be played under conditions of complete or incomplete information. In a game of complete information, each player knows all the players' payoffs and their possible moves. In this paper, we reserve the term "incomplete information game" for ones in which the players are uncertain about each others' payoffs (equivalently, preferences), strategy sets (i.e., capabilities), or knowledge about the game itself or about the other players.

For the most part, our discussion explores progress in noncooperative game theory, focusing on two important lines of research that explore the meaning of equilibrium and its application. Game theoretic reasoning has been applied in such a broad range of fields that a comprehensive review of the substantive applications even in political science is beyond the scope of this paper. This discussion will highlight some important methodological developments and give an indication of trends in game theory.

The Struggle over Equilibrium Concepts

There are many different equilibrium concepts that come up in game theory and unifying them under a single theoretical rubric has been a leading preoccupation. In noncooperative normal form game theory, the most influential concept is Nash equilibrium (Nash 1950). A Nash equilibrium is a set of player actions that are self-reinforcing—no player will unilaterally alter his or her choice if the others remain in equilibrium.[4] This concept has been extended to incomplete information games by Harsanyi (1967, 1968a, 1968b) using an approach that is now often called Bayesian Nash equilibrium.[5]

Many normal form games have a multiplicity of equilibria, as in the well-known "battle of the sexes game" (Luce and Raiffa 1957; Banks and Calvert 1988). Multiple equilibria may be a central feature of a game, but in an important class of games they arise more or less as a result of a technical quirk in normal form representations of extensive form games. About the same time that Nash offered his solution of normal form games, Kuhn (1953) offered a solution for extensive form games, which is often called "backwards induction." Our discussion of sophisticated voting in legislative agenda games used this logic. The last player's choices are anticipated by the second to last player, and her or his choices are anticipated by the third to last player, and so on, back to the initial node of the game tree. Interestingly enough, the Nash equilibria of the normal form game do not necessarily parallel the intuitively attractive "backwards induction" equilibrium.

To illustrate why the difference between these equilibrium concepts is extremely important, we have borrowed an example from Kohlberg and Mertens (1986), which is presented in Table 5.1. The extensive form game is easily solved by backwards induction. Player II will choose "L" at the second node, and anticipating this, Player I will choose M, and the payoffs for the players will be (3,3). In the same figure, we present the normal form representation of the game. There are two Nash equilibria:

Table 5.1
Nash Equilibria in Extensive Form and Normal Form Games

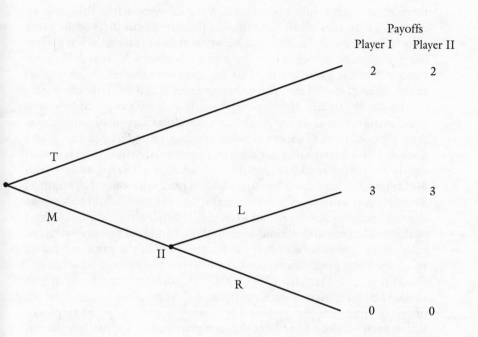

Payoffs

	Player I	Player II
2	2	

	Player II	
	L	R
T	2,2	2,2
M	3,3	0,0

the "backwards induction" equilibrium (M,L) as well as (T,R). The outcome (T,R) is an equilibrium only because player II is indifferent between L and R when player I chooses T—the second node is never reached. Generally, in translating from an extensive form to a normal form game, seemingly nonsensical Nash equilibria like this tend to emerge. Often they result from the fact that choices in parts of the game tree "off the equilibrium path" (ones that are not reached when players use equilibrium strategies) can be arbitrarily chosen, as player II might choose R in the game above. This outcome is considered unstable because, if the game did ever reach that node, then II would not choose R.

In the 1970s and 1980s, several methods were proposed by which these unstable (and distracting) Nash equilibria can be discarded. Acceptable outcomes have been limited to subgame perfect equilibria (and a variant called trembling-hand perfect equilibria, Selten 1975), proper equilibria (Myerson 1978), sequential equilibria (Kreps and Wilson 1982a), and others. Each has some advantages, but none of them offers a completely satisfactory way to sort through the Nash equilibria, as was demonstrated by Kohlberg and Mertens (1986). As they argue, the goal of this kind of research should be to find the equilibria that are "strategically stable," ones such that "in any actual play of the game, no player will ever have an incentive to deviate from his prescribed strategy" (Kohlberg and Mertens 1986:1004). In addition, stable equilibria should be insensitive to irrelevant changes in the game tree and the addition of strategies that players would never see fit to use. Examples in which each of the extant "equilibrium reduction" approaches do not yield the intended result are demonstrated, and some hints about the stability of equilibria are offered.

On the theoretical side of the research agenda in game theory, then, one of the top issues is whether or not there is a workable criterion of stability that can be applied to all games. Harsanyi and Selten (1988) have recently proposed an approach to equilibrium selection. They lay out many possible properties of a solution, dismiss some as impossible or undesirable, and then show that their approach, applied to a representation they call the *standard form*, satisfies the important criteria.

What does all this mean for applied research in political science? Consider the problem of deterrence and reputation building in international relations. Brams and Kilgour (1987) offer a complete information game model of deterrence and find a multiplicity of Nash equilibria. They choose to emphasize one, the so-called deterrence equilibrium, because it has substantive implications that they find interesting. However, the strategies in this equilibrium require that the players make threats that they would never carry out if the situation arose in which their threats were ignored. Rational players would, of course, anticipate that their opponents would not carry out their threats, so the deterrence equilibrium is not strategically stable. As Brams and Kilgour admit, the solution "is neither perfect nor subgame perfect" (839). To circumvent the imperfection problem, they assume that "the players can irrevocably precommit themselves to carry out their threats" (839). Tacitly, they have assumed that the originally noncooperative game is transformed into a cooperative game—one in which binding preplay commitments can be made.

This solution seems rather heavy handed. Alternative game models have recently been offered that provide a more reasonable approach. By representing interactions as incomplete information games—ones in which the players do not know each other's "resolve" or willingness to carry out their threats—recent work by Powell (1987, 1988) and Alt, Calvert, and Humes (1988) has shown that reputation and deterrence can be meaningfully addressed. These studies restrict attention to sequential equilibria that are rational throughout the whole game tree and the players' beliefs are consistent with the available information. Without making any strong assumptions about precommitment, these models provide a number of interesting results about reputation and deterrence.

Incomplete information game theory adds a realistic element—as critics of game theory are fond of pointing out, players in the real world do not know each other's payoffs with certainty. We hesitate to say that the available incomplete information models have completely solved the problem, however. Incomplete information models tend to be mathematically intractable. To solve them, certain simplifications must be imposed. In Powell (1988) the incomplete information takes a very particular form: each player may have either of two levels of "resolve," and the probability that a player is strongly or weakly resolved is "common knowledge" among the players. Alt, Calvert, and Humes (1988) follow the same approach, though they allow for a bit more realism by allowing one of the player's types to be drawn from a continuum according to a given probability distribution (which is common knowledge). Hipel, Wang, and Fraser (1988) and Shupe et al. (1980) use a "hypergame" approach, defined as a situation "in which one or more players have misperceptions about the true nature of the dispute" to analyze the Falklands/Malvinas and Suez crises, respectively.

The intractability problem has arisen in most incomplete information games (e.g., incomplete information bargaining: Chatterjee and Samuelson 1983). Greenberg (1982) extends the incomplete information further to deal with situations where one actor is deliberately trying to mislead another about the payoffs of the game, using the Normandy invasion in 1944 as an example. Solutions to games in which the types of all players can be drawn from a continuum or a more complicated space have been rare (for exceptions, see Palfrey and Rosenthal 1985;

Lien 1987a). In addition, although the theory of incomplete information games is quite highly advanced and leaves room for the possibility that the players are uncertain about each other's knowledge (Mertins and Zamir 1985), almost all workable applications invoke the common knowledge assumption. Whether or not these technical barriers will be overcome remains to be seen. Since analytical solutions are so difficult to obtain, numerical or algorithmic approaches may be called for.

Repeated Games

The strengths and weaknesses of equilibrium analysis are clearly seen in studies of the prisoner's dilemma (PD) game, the most extensively studied two-person noncooperative game. Axelrod's (1984) heralded study firmly implanted it in the mainstream research agenda. The research is driven by the following problem. In a single play of a complete information PD game, both players have dominant strategies to defect—both receive higher payoffs if they do not adopt cooperative strategies, regardless of what the opponent does. Mutual noncooperation is thus a Nash equilibrium. The perplexing thing about the game is that both players would be better off if they cooperated with each other—the Nash equilibrium is Pareto inefficient.

This observation has been used in many fields to explain why suboptimal outcomes occur. Two of the most widely recognized applications are models of collective action and interest group formation (Hardin 1982) and arms races in international relations (for example, Brams 1985). The unsavory conclusion seems to be that some kind of dictator or enforcement mechanism must be created (Hardin 1971 showed that majority rule voting would lead a group to create such a leader). Noting that the creation of a powerful leader might be undesirable either because of the threat to liberty that it would impose (see also Taylor 1976, 1987) or because leadership cannot necessarily induce the desired amount of cooperation (see Holmstrom 1982), an enormous amount of research has been devoted to finding out "under which conditions will cooperation emerge in a world of egoists without central authority?" (Axelrod 1981:306). Or, perhaps more fittingly, when will the players in a noncooperative game behave as if they were playing a cooperative game?

Along these lines, the iterated or repeated prisoner's dilemma game (IPD) has been investigated. The player's payoff in the "supergame," as the repeated game is called, is a sum of the payoffs of the individual plays of the game, usually with some discounting rule applied to reduce the weight attached to payoffs in the future. Even when the game is repeated for a sufficiently long period, the players do not discount future payoffs too heavily, and neither player knows exactly when the game will end, *permanent noncooperation is still a Nash equilibrium*.

However, there are other Nash equilibria as well, some of which are quite cooperative. For example, if both players say "I will cooperate until you defect, and I will defect thereafter," cooperation may arise if both players place enough weight on the benefits of long-term cooperation to outweigh the short-run benefit of exploiting the opponent on the first play of the game. This assumes some kind of communication mechanism is in place, but even without communication it seems that cooperative strategies might emerge. Axelrod's (1984) computer tournament of IPD strategies showed that a strategy called tit-for-tat, which cooperates on the first move and then mimics the opponent's move on the previous play, did quite well. On the basis of this result, Axelrod observed that successful strategies seem to be nice (never the first to defect), quick to retaliate, and forgiving. Axelrod also adapted the concepts of evolutionary stability of Maynard Smith (1982) and discussed the evolution of cooperation from a biological/evolutionary perspective. He observed that a small cluster of players using tit-for-tat can "invade" a community of uncooperative strategies because the cooperative strategies meet each other and build up big "surpluses" that end up with higher scores than aggressive strategies, which accumulate slight profits against tit-for-tat but never build up any surpluses when they play each other. This leads to the conjecture that norms of reciprocal cooperation will evolve when individuals interact repeatedly under certain conditions.

Recent research has cast a great deal of doubt over the evolutionary part of Axelrod's analysis. Contrary to Axelrod's conjecture, no non-randomized strategy is evolutionarily stable and the tendency of cooperation to emerge is dramatically reduced as the size of the community is increased (Boyd and Lorberbaum 1987). Dacey and Pendegraft (1988), Hirschleifer and Martinez-Coll (1988) and McGinnis (1986) all explore a variety of ways in which relatively minor changes in the original Axelrod experiment leads to situations where tit-for-tat does not emerge from evolutionary competition.

Many suspect that the unlikelihood of the emergence of cooperation results from the weaknesses of the IPD game as a representation of social interaction. The game has only minimal internal structure and incentives for cooperation. Moreover, if the effect of imperfect information is included—the players cannot monitor each other's moves with complete certainty—cooperation is even less likely to emerge (Bendor 1987). These observations, like the chaos theorems in social choice research, have inspired new emphasis on institutions and their tendency to induce stable, cooperative outcomes. Bendor and Mookherjee, for example, have considered hierarchical institutions and the tendency of reciprocal cooperation to emerge in n-person IPD games when the players are grouped into subunits (1987) and the effect of adding a third player to the game who can punish the players for defecting on their agreements (1988). Hechter (1989b) recently argued that social institutions that promote visibility and monitoring are relatively easy to construct and can enhance cooperative interaction. Hence, by changing the game slightly, more cooperation can be induced. Another strategy has been to change the game to include the effects of incomplete information. When the players do not know each other's preferences with certainty, and each believes it is possible that the other might adopt a cooperative strategy like tit-for-tat, it has been shown that cooperation can emerge (Kreps, Milgrom, Roberts, and Wilson 1982).

The approach of the IPD literature—which observes that the Nash equilibrium of a game is either unpalatable or unrealistic, and tinkers with the assumptions of the game to change the predicted outcome—is being used in research on several other games. Most similar are oligopoly (cartel) games. In a single play of the game, the firms are tempted to cheat on a cartel agreement by producing above their quotas and thus cooperation breaks down. Repetition of the game, however, can encourage cooperation, as in the PD (see Friedman 1983; for an imperfect information iterated oligopoly game, see Abreau, Pearce, and Stacchetti 1986). This research is relevant to a wealth of political phenomena—for example, competition among political parties (see Alesina 1988) or interest groups.

Also in this genre are principal-agent games. The principal wants to hire an agent to do some work, but for whatever reason is unable to monitor with precision the agent's effort. Recognizing that the agent is likely to "slack off," the principal designs an employment contract different from the Pareto optimal (first-best) contract, which would have been imposed if monitoring were perfect (Holmstrom 1979). This research, closely tied to the new economic theory of the firm that analyzes strategic relationships between employees and employers, has found many interesting applications in political models of bureaucratic behavior (e.g., Bendor, Taylor, and van Gaalen 1987; Moe 1984) and legislative/executive relations (Niskanen 1971; Miller and Moe 1983). The new wave of game theory research explores the effect of iteration of the principal-agent game and shows the possibility that stable outcomes in the repeated game may approach the optimal contract (see Spear and Srivastava 1987, and sources therein).

Despite these advances, one cannot say conclusively that repeated interaction leads to cooperation. Repetition may allow for rational cooperation, mainly because reciprocating strategies are made feasible (see Lien 1987b), but it also allows a wealth of other Nash equilibrium outcomes. This is the major point of the so-called folk theorem.[6] An individually rational outcome is one that is better than permanent mutual defection, in the PD game's terms. In a widely read article, Fudenberg and Maskin (1986) formalized and proved several versions of the folk theorem: "Any individually rational outcome can arise as a Nash equilibrium in infinitely repeated games with sufficiently little discounting" (533). Mutual cooperation and noncooperation can be equilibria, but so can asymmetric outcomes, such as the pattern induced in the PD when one player says "I will defect on the first three moves of the game, and unless you cooperate each time, I will defect for eternity." As Gary Miller recently pointed out, the folk theorem has at least two implications. First, "we can't predict what will happen in repeated social interactions using game theory alone," and second, "there is nothing inevitable about the emergence of cooperation in any given organizational setting" (1989:26).

Recognizing the existence of multiple equilibria, a new wave of research has concentrated on the effects of communication and leadership as mechanisms that can coordinate individual expectations and enhance cooperation. Given the multiplicity of equilibria, the players face a game of "coordination" or noncooperative "bargaining" through which they choose one of the many equilibria. Research on the effect of leadership, especially in Congress, outlines the benefits that the members can reap by cooperating and explains why they might give some power to leaders who can punish members who fail to go along (Calvert 1987a, 1987b). In addition, the role of leaders in psychologically motivating workers—creating expectations—is leading to a new emphasis on leadership in the theory of organizations (Miller 1989).

In nonhierarchical interactions, the coordinating effect of preplay communication in incomplete information games is being investigated (Banks and Calvert 1988, 1989). This ties in to the "signaling" literature in information economics. These models are close cousins of incomplete information models of legislative decision-making, in which the legislators have some private information and selectively reveal it in the hope of influencing the social choice (see Austen-Smith and Riker 1987). The discouraging results of Austen-Smith and Riker, which imply that nonhierarchical, decentralized information revelation may lead to Pareto inferior results, seem to open the door to models that include leadership or other kinds of structures that can induce more favorable outcomes. Though some authors seem to have become impatient with game theory as a result of the many twists and turns in this stream of research (Hechter, forthcoming), we see the recognition of multiple equilibria and coordination games as a promising path for research.

DYNAMIC MODELS

The unifying concepts of the systems modeling approach are drawn from the methodology of dynamic systems (see Cortes, Przeworski, and Sprague 1974; Hanneman 1988), which drew much of its inspiration from the successes of mathematical models of dynamic physical systems and the movement in "general systems theory" (Bertalanffy 1975) to construct similar models of complex social and biological systems. Research in this field typically emphasizes process more than equilibrium, and aggregates more than individuals. The emphasis on aggregates is mainly due to the research questions that inspire these studies. Proponents of the systems' perspective generally believe that static (rational choice) models cannot explain change except with reference to exogenous variables. Systems modelers believe that change is endogenous, a result of adjustment processes that can be explicitly represented.

The emphasis on aggregation is often seen as a rejection of individual level analysis approach of political economy, though this is not necessarily so. The macro/micro controversy has not yet been settled. Some scholars believe that individual behavior is not sufficiently well understood or regularized to be the primitive concept of social science research. In this view, aggregated analysis is the only option. A second school of thought is ambivalent. Aggregate patterns may, but need not, have a basis in individual behavior. In the same way that the physics of large bodies can be studied apart from the movement of the atomic particles of which they are composed, meaningful statements can be made about systems without regard to individual behaviors. There is reason for hope that the micro/macro gap will be bridged. Schelling (1971, 1978), Kramer (1983), and Goodman (1957) provide some discussion of how to deal with aggregation problems.

Dynamic models have been used more extensively in international relations than in other subfields, so this section is organized on the basis of the IR modeling literature. Differential equation models of arms races developed out of the Richardson arms race model tradition and became a substantial, if specialized, literature. Computer simulation developed jointly out of a human-machine simulation tradition (e.g., RAND Corporation war and crisis simulations, and Harold Guetzkow's INS simulation work) and DYNAMO-like all-computer simulations, particularly "world models" coming out of the Forrester tradition (see Ward 1985). Finally, there is a sizeable literature on stochastic modeling, which, again, grew out of Richardson's early work in *Statistics of Deadly Quarrels* (1960b) but has been extended substantially.

Arms Race Models

Lewis Richardson's model of an arms race between two nations, first drafted in 1918 (Richardson 1919), was posthumously brought to the forefront of political science by Anatol Rapoport (1957) and by the publication of Richardson's *Arms and Insecurity* (1960a). Richardson hypothesized that two countries' armament levels, x and y, change in a way that is represented by a system of differential equations:

$$dx/dt = ky - ax + g$$
$$dy/dt = mx - by + h$$

The terms dx/dt and dy/dt are derivatives with respect to time that represent changes in armament levels. The constants a, b, k, and m are assumed positive, while g and h, which represent "grievances," may be positive or negative. Richardson's analysis of stability and the time paths of the armament levels drew attention to the power of this kind of analysis.

The Richardson arms race model is the most widely studied dynamic model in international relations and, with the possible exception of the incremental budgeting model, the whole of political science. It is, for example, the only political science dynamic model that one is likely to encounter in general texts on mathematical modeling (e.g., Olinick 1978; Luenberger 1979). The model has all the characteristics of a good mathematical model: it is simple, provides commonsense results while also revealing some deeper insights, and it can be incorporated into other models.

Richardson's pioneering work spawned an entire genre of arms race models, which has flourished in the post-1960 period. For example, Anderton's (1985) bibliography on arms race modeling contains 224 entries and new models are still being proposed (e.g., Intriligator and Brito 1984; Mayer 1986; Marra 1985; Saperstein and Mayer-Kress 1988), though arms race modeling is not the active research area it was twenty years ago. Differential equations have subsequently been extensively used to model not only arms races but other types of international behavior such as protracted conflict and event interactions; Zinnes (1976), Zinnes and Gillespie (1976), Zinnes (1984), and Luterbacher and Ward (1985) provide a variety of examples; Isard and Anderton (1985), Anderton (1985), and Cioffi-Revilla (1979) provide extensive bibliographies. Differential equations use a variety of well-understood, previously obtained, analytical results from mathematics. Frequently one can construct parsimonious models that capture the general characteristics of the behavior in question. At the same time, differential equations are relatively inflexible, they are difficult to estimate accurately, and it is easy to construct simple models for which no analytical solutions exist. These problems are compounded when one switches to finite difference equations, which are more appropriate to the annual budget cycles found in defense spending.

The Richardson model has been extensively tested, with mixed results. An assortment of empirical problems exist with the model—the estimates of the coefficients are frequently very strange, interaction between pairs of nations is frequently statistically insignificant, and there are numerous measurement and statistical problems involved in working with the model (see discussions by Stoll 1982; Majeski and Jones 1981; Majeski 1985; Schrodt and Ward 1981). The problem of empirically verifying the model is further complicated by the presence of nuclear weapons or alliances in many of the arms races on which the model is being tested: Richardson's original two-nation model was not intended to deal with either of those complicating factors. Even if the Richardson model is rarely completely correct, it is also rarely completely wrong—most arms races do look a lot like the Richardson model would predict (as opposed, say, to being spiked or cyclical), and no models that fit consistently better have emerged. The statistical record of the Richardson model is also mixed in part because it has been very extensively tested—probably on fifty or more arms races—and has a known record; most other models have been seldom tested.

While arms races are most commonly modeled using dynamic equations, there is also a substantial arms race literature using expected utility modeling and game theory. The possible convergence between the competition of the marketplace and the competition among nations has been a theme of international relations theory for centuries (see Parkinson 1977). It is not surprising that the extensive formal theory of economic competition and the results of that competition—some sort of optimized allocation of benefits based on resources—should be applied to international affairs. The bulk of this work has been concerned with arms races and two-nation competition, but more detailed work in the "balance of power" framework also exists (e.g., Niou and Ordeshook, 1986, 1987, 1989). Intriligator (1971) provides a survey of the techniques, and Intriligator has been one of the more prolific scholars in applying the methods (e.g. Intriligator 1964; Brito and Intriligator 1974; Intriligator and Brito 1984); Busch (1970) and McGuire (1965) also take this approach.

Computer Simulation

Large-scale computer simulations, growing out of the two traditions of Guetzkow's INS work and the Forrester/Meadows global dynamics models, have proliferated extensively in the past decade and a half; for a review see Deutsch et al. (1977), Guetzkow and Valdez (1981), Ward (1985), and Hughes (1984). Hughes (1985) provides a good analysis of the similarities and differences of the various models, and the extent to which those differences are accounted for by parameters as opposed to structure. The most extensive recent effort in political simulation has been the GLOBUS project (Bremer 1987) directed by Stuart Bremer and Karl Deutsch. At the heart of most simulations is a set of difference equations, but the simulations emphasize complexity and numerical results, where the differential equations emphasize parsimony and analytical results. Since the simulation is freed from the constraint of having to be workable algebraically, vastly more complicated systems can be studied. As a consequence, the simulation literature is far richer than the differential equation literature. At the same time, the problems of estimation remain, and simulations tend to be so complex that their behavior is not fully explored.

The publication in the early 1970s of *Limits to Growth* led to an explosion of large-scale computer models of global systems. These have become a standard research technique in international relations, and several dozen major models now exist. This simulation work initially incorporated few political components and thoroughly ignored the extensive earlier international relations simulation work of the 1960s, but more recently has incorporated political and political-economic factors. These models have in all likelihood had greater impact on policy—or at least on the popular wisdom—than any differential equation models, even though the underlying mathematical assumptions of the techniques are virtually identical. The simulation models also show far more variety: the differential equation models have seldom gone far from their roots in Richardson, whereas simulations have gone way beyond the original models of INS or *Limits to Growth*, both in terms of ideological assumptions, relevant variables, and levels of disaggregation.

The complexity of simulations makes them very difficult to test, and here they have no empirical track record comparable to the Richardson model. This problem is further complicated by the fact that many models are designed to make predictions several decades into the future and it is impossible to test such models until a significant period of time has passed. There is considerable current research directed along these lines and the related problem of trying to get some sort of convergence in the predictions of the models, so this situation may improve in the future.

An additional challenge to the underlying assumptions of simulation has emerged with discoveries in the field of dynamic chaos theory (not to be confused with the majority voting chaos theorems discussed above). Devaney (1986) discusses the mathematical issues in detail; the issue has also been thoroughly covered in the popular press (e.g., Gleick 1987). In the early 1970s, Robert May (1976) and others noted that some simple nonlinear difference equations such as the logistic equation for population growth under resource constraints

$$x_{t+1} = r \, x_t \, (1 - x_t/K)$$

would exhibit seemingly random behavior under plausible choices of parameter values. Such equations also exhibited extreme sensitivity to initial values: arbitrarily small changes in the initial conditions would lead to arbitrarily large deviations in the predicted value of the equations after relatively short periods of time. This is true *even if the underlying system is deterministic*. Since models of social processes inevitably involve measurement error of the initial conditions—and probably random variables in the equation as well—the long-term predictions of such models are meaningless even as approximations. Chaotic behavior does not affect all models—for example, systems of linear equations are not chaotic—but the potential for chaos substantially restricts the types of processes that can be realistically modeled. Chaos models are not completely unpredictable—they still restrict the likely behavior of a system to "orbits" of points that are encountered repeatedly—but these predictions are quite different from the smooth curves and error bounds that one usually associates with dynamic models.

Other Dynamic Models

The use of dynamic models has slowly expanded beyond international relations to a range of fields. A host of dynamic studies of mass behavior appeared in the 1960s. William McPhee made a substantial contribution with the publication of a general volume of dynamic models (1963) and some essays on dynamics of voting behavior (in McPhee and Glaser 1962). By that time, the links between this kind of model and biological models were recognized (for example, Kemeny and Snell 1962; Coleman 1964; May 1974). Some classic studies of aggregate patterns in voting behavior used the dynamic logic, though the flavor of dynamic models was used without most of the formalism (Key 1949; Converse 1969; Stokes and Iverson 1966). Considerably more advanced approaches to mass behavior and public opinion phenomena have recently appeared (see MacKuen 1981; Przeworski and Sprague 1986; Brown 1987); Banaszak (1986) applies models of biological competition to third-party politics with an empirical test using Great Britain. One indicator of the progress in the field is the high quality of available textbooks (Huckfeldt, Kohfeld, and Likens 1982; Boynton 1980; Hanneman 1988).

Dynamic models of territorial behavior are found in the "coop models" of the aggregation of territorial states and alliances. These models were named after the hexagonal territories used in Bremer and Mihalka (1977), which create a pattern resembling chicken wire but have been developed independently in a number of articles; variations include Schelling (1971), Schrodt (1981), Cusack and Zimmer (1986), and Stoll (1987). Coop models start with a random distribution of small states that aggregate to form larger, spatially organized entities through the conquest of their neighbors. The process is very robust with respect to the initial conditions and reproduces a variety of characteristics found in actual political geography.

STOCHASTIC MODELS

In stochastic models, the dependent variable is random and is explicitly studied as such. The predictions of stochastic models are probability distributions rather than individual points, and the mathematical techniques come primarily from probability theory rather than deterministic calculus or linear algebra. While the concept of randomness is found in many of the other models in political science, it is usually considered as "error," "imperfect information," or some other undesirable characteristic, whereas in stochastic modeling randomness is the primary focus. Because stochastic models deal with distributions rather than points, they are more difficult to work with analytically and empirically, but there is still a substantial literature dealing with them. Bartholomew (1971) provides a general introduction to the models commonly used in the social sciences; Feller (1968) provides an extensive mathematical development of these models; Schrodt (1985) surveys the models with respect to international relations research.

Statistical Models

The most common class of stochastic models in political science are statistical models. Any statistical model containing a random variable on the right-hand side of the equation specifying the dependent variable is a stochastic model. Unfortunately, this aspect of statistical analysis is poorly appreciated in political science, and a side effect of the increased availability of standardized statistical software has been the near disappearance of serious discussion of the implications of specific statistical tests in most empirical political analysis.

For example, the use of the chi-square test in the cross-tabulation of nominal variables and the use of stepwise regression on interval-level variables are probably the two most common statistical techniques used in political science research. However, the null hypothesis underlying the chi-square test throws out considerable useful information (see King 1989, ch. 6) and stepwise least-squares is a risky technique in many situations (notably the all but inevitable presence of colinearity) and for that reason was infrequently recommended prior to its becoming the default in SPSS.

It is instructive to look at the early work in agricultural and demographic statistics, psychometrics, and econometrics—for example the work of Kendall, Yule, Savage, Gossett,[7] and Pearson—to see how statistical analysis was originally intimately connected with model specification. Richardson (1960b), who learned statistics from Pearson, also provides numerous examples of how statistical models can be explicitly developed for political behavior. For early researchers, *how* one looked for a statistical relationship depended entirely on *what* one was looking for: theoretically justified models came first, the method of estimating parameters came second. This is a far cry from the "cookbook" approach of too much of contemporary political methodology, where techniques are applied with little understanding of either their origins or consequences. To use but one of many potential examples, political scientists working with time series data are usually admonished to account for trend and remove autocorrelated error: in fact a linear temporal trend can account for 44 percent of the variance in a random walk (Nelson and Kang 1984) and removing autocorrelated error frequently deletes precisely the causal linkages one should be looking for (King 1989, ch. 4).

There are a number of indications that this situation is improving. Political methodology is now a separate section in the APSA with an annual, NSF-sponsored conference and an annual yearbook, the "workshop" section of the *American Journal of Political Science* has an excellent record of introducing new methods explicitly designed for political science problems, and recent graduate-level texts such as King (1989) are introducing new conceptual approaches and techniques specifically for political research. As King has noted, the discipline is gradually coming to realize that "econometrics for political science" is an oxymoron. In addition, the shift in the professional statistics community away from simple hypothesis testing toward exploratory data analysis is encouraging greater experimentation with alternative models, and the massive increase in computing power available to the average researcher makes it possible to employ robust methods such as general maximum likelihood estimators and nonlinear models, which were previously computationally prohibitive. Methodological advances are allowing us to dispense with some of the restrictive assumptions that previously called into question applications of econometric methods to individual voting behavior (Rivers 1988).

Poisson Models

The Poisson model and its variants are the focus of a number of studies, particularly in international and comparative politics. The Poisson provides a basic definition of "randomness" across time or space: an event shows a Poisson distribution if its probability of occurrence in an interval of time is proportional only to the length of the interval. This eliminates processes dependent on prior events, cycles, contagion, saturation effects, or other variables. The classic application of the model was Bortkiewicz's (1898) demonstration that the Poisson distribution modeled the distribution of the number of Prussian cavalry officers kicked to death by horses; as Williams (1954:10) notes, the Poisson should fit equally well the number of horses kicked to death by Prussian cavalry officers. While the Poisson is generally a null model rather than an explanatory model, and it is possible to design processes that are not Poisson but still generate events matching a Poisson distribution (Houweling and Kune 1984), the distribution has been shown to fit a variety of political behaviors. The Poisson is also frequently used as the starting point for models that introduce elements of contagion, saturation, or diffusion, so many studies use both the Poisson and minor variants of it.

Richardson (1960b) originally experimented with the pure Poisson as a model for the outbreak of war; this work was replicated by Singer and Small (1972) on a larger data set. Variations on the Poisson have been used to study war initiation by Horvath (1968), Davis, Duncan, and Siverson (1978), Li and Thompson (1975), Most and Starr (1980), Bremer (1982), and a variety of works by Midlarksy (1970, 1978, 1986). Poissonlike models are used to study alliance behavior by Mc-Gowan and Rood (1975), Siverson and Duncan (1976), Job (1976), Chan (1978), and Midlarksy (1981); the Poisson was used as the basis for studying networks of international events by Mintz and Schrodt (1987a, 1987b). The model has also been widely used to model legislative and executive turnover, for example in the supreme court (Wallis 1936; Ulmer 1982), the Soviet central committee (Casstevens and Ozinga 1980), the Canadian house of commons (Casstevens and Denham 1970) and Italian governments (Cioffi-Revilla 1984); Casstevens (1989) reviews this literature.

Markov Chains

Markov chain models are a thoroughly studied stochastic process that has seen a number of applications in international relations, though few in other subfields of political science. In a Markov chain the random variable is the "state" of the process at a given time. For example, in studying the relations between two nations over time, the state of the relationship might be "hostile," "neutral," or "friendly"; the model would track the probability of the relationship being in a particular state over time. In a Markov chain, the probability of a transition from one state to another is known, constant over time, and dependent only on the current state of the process. Markov models have been used to study various aspects of international behavior by Wilkenfeld (1972), Leavitt (1972), Zinnes, Zinnes, and McClure (1972), Duncan and Siverson (1975, 1982), and Midlarsky (1983). The model is also commonly used to study social mobility (Bartholomew 1973; Leik and Meeker 1975) and has been extended by Dobson and Meeter (1974) to model change in party identification.

ARTIFICIAL INTELLIGENCE

The term "artificial intelligence" (AI) refers to a very large set of problems and techniques ranging from formal linguistic analysis to walking robots. AI models differ from the existing modeling efforts in the specification of models as algorithms rather than equations, the emphasis on nonnumerical data (usually categorical data and sometimes natural language text), and the use of larger, less regularized data than those used in statistical studies. As Yale AI guru Roger Schank (1987) notes:

> Most practitioners would agree on two main goals in AI. The primary goal is to build an intelligent machine. The second goal is to find out about the nature of intelligence. . . . [However,] when it comes down to it, there is very little agreement about what exactly constitutes intelligence. It follows that little agreement exists in the AI community about exactly what AI is and what it should be. [60]

Research in AI has always proceeded in parallel, rather than serially, with dozens of different approaches being tried on any given problem. As such, AI tends to progress through the incremental accumulation of partial solutions to existing problems, rather than through dramatic breakthroughs. Nonetheless, from the standpoint of applying AI to political behavior, there were two major changes in AI research in the late 1970s that were important.

First, "expert systems," which used a large number of *if-then* rules specific to their problem-solving domain, were shown to be able to solve nontrivial, messy, real-world problems such as medical diagnosis, credit approval, and mechanical repair at the same level of competency as human experts (see Coombs 1984; Hayes-Roth, Waterman, and Lenat 1984; Klahr and Waterman 1986). Expert systems research broke away from the classic emphasis in AI on generic problem-solving, as embodied in chess-playing and theorem-solving programs, toward an emphasis on knowledge representation: they use simple logical inference on complex sets of knowledge, rather than complex inference on simple sets of knowledge. The commercial success of expert systems led to an increase in new research in AI generally—the influx of funding helped—and spun off a series of additional developments such as memory-based reasoning, scripts, schemas, and other complex knowledge representation structures as well as renewed interest in machine learning systems such as classification generators and genetic algorithms.

Second, the personal computer, and exponential increase in the capabilities of computers more generally, brought the capabilities of a 1960s mainframe onto the researcher's desk. While most AI techniques require extensive computing power, an equally important consequence of the small computers was freeing researchers from dependence on the slow and idiosyncratic software development on centralized main-frames. In the personal computer environment new compilers for LISP, Prolog, and other languages could be purchased for several hundred dollars, and software could be easily exchanged across standardized UNIX or MS-DOS operating systems. In addition, the "AI-style" of programming led to a generation of programmers and programming environments sufficiently powerful to construct complicated programs that would have been virtually impossible using older languages and techniques.

As with other types of formal modeling, AI provides a set of general and proven techniques for problem solving. Just as a statistical modeler approaches a problem knowing the strengths and weaknesses of a variety of standard methodologies (e.g., cross-tabulation, regression, factor analysis, logit, and so forth), AI modeling usually involves general methods such as searching, expert systems, neural networks, genetic algorithms, knowledge representation techniques, and so forth (for introductions, see Charnick and McDermott 1985; Winston 1984). In contrast to contemporary statistical modeling, where most computation is done with commercial software such as SAS and SPSS, most existing AI applications use custom-written software, a situation similar to statistical computing in the 1950s. Generalized AI software is becoming increasingly common, particularly for expert systems development (Brent 1988), which will make the techniques substantially easier to apply.

At the present time, most of the theoretical applications of AI to political behavior are in the fields of foreign policy and international relations, though applied AI, usually in the form of expert system, is also increasingly common in public administration. Most of the key ideas needed to apply AI to international relations (AI/IR) had been proposed and formulated long before the AI hype of the 1980s in the work of Hayward Alker and his students at MIT (e.g., Alker and Christensen 1972; Alker and Greenberg 1976; Alker, Bennett, and Mefford 1980) and by 1987 about a dozen major IR/AI projects were underway across the country.

Generally, IR/AI models derive from three sources:

(a) psychological models of individual and group decision-making, particularly those models emphasizing bounded rationality rather than optimization;

(b) artificial intelligence models of knowledge representation and processing, particularly rule-based models and machine learning techniques;

(c) behavioralist IR concepts of data, particularly events data, case-based foreign policy studies, and increasingly textual analysis.

Stated slightly differently, in IR/AI the questions come from IR, the process theories come from cognitive psychology, and the concrete techniques come from computer science.

This apparently chimerical fusion of theory and technique is providing numerous insights into international behavior. While superficially these models differ dramatically from the traditional political science literature because of their formal specifications, in fact such models frequently have much in common with these theories because of a common basis in human psychology and the peculiarities of human decision-making in situations of limited information, risk, and multiple objectives. As such, the assumptions of AI models are often far closer to traditional political theories than models using statistical or dynamic approaches.

There are three major research foci in IR/AI today: rule-based models, precedent-based models, and natural language analysis. This discussion will, necessarily, be simplifying the details of the implementations in each of these approaches, and there is no clear-cut division between the three approaches: for example, a natural language or rule-based model can also invoke precedent.

Rule-Based Systems

The expert systems research of the late 1970s showed that large numbers of *if-then* rules could be used to solve many problems at the same level of performance as humans. While in retrospect this approach appears obvious, it goes against at least two very strong trends in scientific modeling. First, it sacrifices a great deal of parsimony—there is nothing elegant about bludgeoning a problem into submission with hundreds of rules. Second, and more subtly, it abandons the statistical modeling principle of modeling on the basis of average behavior in large samples, substituting a principle of modal (most common) behavior in small samples. Most rule-based systems effectively partition the universe of cases into small subsets determined by the independent variables, and then predict the dependent variable using the modal value within each of those subsets.

In exchange for embracing these two scientific heresies, the rule-based systems achieve two things. First, they have a great deal of empirical accuracy—rule-based systems have been applied in hundreds of knowledge domains and consistently show a level of problem-solving accuracy comparable to that of human experts. Successful applications of expert systems have now become so common that they are frequently considered AI "engineering" rather than "research." Second, rule-based systems provide an alternative to the statistical and axiomatic approaches that had heretofore dominated the modeling of human decision-making. AI models are able to implement many of the characteristics observed in actual human problem-solving (Newell and Simon 1972), which are virtually impossible to model systematically using algebraic techniques.

The simpler and more common rule-based models in IR use fairly small sets of *if-then* rules. The recent models are usually based in the expert systems literature; the older models usually use the "production system" vocabulary (see Nilsson 1980). Rule-based applications in political science include Chinese foreign policy (Tanaka 1984), the political decision-making of President Jimmy Carter (Lane 1986), Soviet foreign policy on interventions (Kaw 1986), supreme court decisions on discrimination (Grunbaum 1986), Morton Kaplan's balance of power models (Mefford 1986a), authoritarian political structures (Banerjee 1986), the India-China dispute of 1962 (Hudson 1987), and U.S. military expenditure decision-making (Majeski 1989).

In the early expert systems literature, rules are derived by "knowledge engineers" who study the situation and interview human experts. This is the approach used in most of the existing studies, but it is a time-consuming process and results in a model that contains only the knowledge already available to the human experts. It is also possible to use machine learning methods to induce sets of rules directly from the data, bypassing the human experts. Schrodt (1987b) demonstrates a machine learning technique called the CLS/ID3 algorithm in developing rules to predict the outcome of international disputes. In commercial AI systems there has also been a shift away from labor-intensive human-based learning toward greater use of machine learning; a variety of machine learning systems are now available.

Rule-based systems are especially attractive when one is modeling the behavior of organizations, for organizational behavior is frequently openly and explicitly rule-following. One of the definitive characteristics of bureaucracies is their use of formal rules; these formal rules are supplemented by informal "standard operating procedures" and institutional norms of behavior. To the extent that formal, fixed rules actually guide behavior, and the informal rules are followed consistently over time, it is possible to model a great deal of the behavior of the organization through rules.[8]

Rule-based systems can be extended substantially beyond the *if-then* rules of expert system, particularly when complicated data structures are introduced that approximate the wealth of information available to a decision maker. Several AI models have tried to replicate, in part, the actual rules used by actors in an international system. These systems attempt to capture the process of decision-making as well as the outcome. Situations that have been modeled using this approach include Saudi Arabian foreign policy (Anderson and Thorson 1982), the Cuban

Missile Crisis (Thorson and Sylvan 1982), U.S. policy toward Central America (Job, Johnson, and Selbin 1987), U.S. policy toward the Dominican Republic (Job and Johnson 1986), Japanese energy policy (Bobrow, Sylvan, and Ripley 1986; Sylvan, Goel, and Chandresekaran 1988), and Middle East international politics (Phillips 1987).

Fuzzy sets are another concept borrowed from AI and applied to foreign policy decision-making. They were introduced by Lotfi Zadeh in the 1960s to deal with the problem of decision-making under uncertainty and provide an alternative to expected value calculations in this regard. Kickert (1978) and Cioffi-Revilla (1981) provide surveys of the approach. Unlike a conventional set, where an element either belongs to a set or does not belong to it, elements of fuzzy sets have a probability of membership. This allows one to formally model the uncertainty that human decision makers apply to judgments. For example, if an analyst says that a coup is "unlikely" in country X and "very likely" in country Y, we could model this by stating that X's membership in the fuzzy set (countries that will have coups) is 0.15, whereas Y's membership is 0.95. Sanjian (1988a, 1988b) has provided an extensive application of this approach to the problem of arms transfers.

Precedent-Based Systems

One of the distinguishing characteristics of most IR/AI research is the assumption that decision-making in foreign policy is heavily based on historical precedent. The arguments for precedent are reviewed in Mallery and Hurwitz (1987), Anderson (1981), and various papers employing precedent-based modeling. The general concept of precedent-based models was developed in a series of papers by Alker and others during the 1970s. The models also are closely related theoretically, though not necessary in technique, to an extensive body of AI research on analogical reasoning (Prieditis 1987) and "case-based reasoning" (Kolodner 1988).

The basic argument for precedent is summarized in Mefford (1989):

> People make extensive use of memory in their effort to reach decisions, interpret messages, or solve problems. While in any given task . . . there may be several steps of inference, some of which may be deductive or syllogismlike, [many important steps] depend on the ability to recognize similarities and differences. The assumption is, broadly, that because new problems or new situations remind us of problems or situations we have encountered [or learned about] in the past, we intuitively entertain the possibility that what we know of prior cases may apply to the current one. [11]

More generally, as Mefford notes, Polya's (1962) classic work on mathematical problem-solving noted that the most common human problem-solving strategy was to take solutions that worked on earlier problems and modify them to attack new problems. Recollection, which humans do quickly and very easily, is substituted for deductive reasoning, which humans do slowly and rather painfully.

Precedent is particularly important in international behavior because little other information is available. For example, a market may have thousands of transactions daily and prices subject to open bargaining; in a legislature members interact on a prolonged basis and hence get a general idea of each other's preferences. In contrast, the international environment is characterized by long periods of inactivity punctuated by surprise, uncertainty, and risk. Between the lack of information and the complexity of the system, the international system is virtually impossible to analyze deductively, and so precedent—often distant precedent—is invoked instead. For example, in trying to comprehend the events following the Islamic revolution in Iran in 1979–80, commentators frequently, and fairly accurately, invoked the precedent of the French revolution, an event occurring two centuries earlier.

While generally accepted as a modeling principle, the actual implementation of a precedent-based system is a substantial undertaking. Modeling reasoning by precedent involves a data base of precedents, a metric for comparing an existing situation to potential precedents, and an explicit model of how learning and error correction occur. Acquiring the precedent data base presents two problems. The first is the sheer size of human memory. Political analysts probably use thousands of potential precedents in addition to heuristic knowledge about basic political motives. Mefford (1986b) proposes a system for acquiring precedents using machine-expert collaboration; Schrodt (1989) does this inductively using the COPDAB international events data set and the Holland classifier (see Holland 1975, 1986) machine learning system.

Comparing precedents is complicated by the fact that precedents involve complex data structures with elements of varying importance rather than simple numbers or vectors. The case-based reasoning literature (see Kolodner 1988) proposes a variety of comparison techniques, usually based on the concept of "schema," which deals with composite data structures. Levenshtein metrics, a technique developed to compare DNA sequences (see Mefford 1984, 1987b; Sankoff and Kruskal 1983), are an alternative approach for precedent matching specific to international relations, where precedents usually take the form of sequences of events (e.g., the Cuban missile crisis). Schrodt (1990) develops a machine learning algorithm for using Levenshtein metrics to distinguish between war and nonwar crises.

Finally, a precedent-driven decision structure must be able to learn and to correct errors in its knowledge base. Empirically, one of the problems with modeling precedent learning is the very slow rate of change in the actual international system. A particular precedent may be invoked only once or twice each decade and therefore evidence that the decision-makers have changed their precedent matching criterion is difficult to accumulate. Beyond this there are additional theoretical problems involving representation and reasoning. Mallery and Hurwitz (1987) discuss a number of facets of this issue in the context of using the Relatus system (see below) in a precedent-based reasoning mode; Mefford's papers (1985b, 1986b) also deal with the issue.

Natural-Language Based Systems

An attractive feature of AI is the relative ease with which natural language in limited domains (e.g., restricted vocabulary and syntax) can be handled. Natural language is particularly attractive in IR because virtually all data concerning the external international environment reaches the decision-makers in the form of natural language text, and virtually all information available to the researcher is in the form of text. Direct experience in international affairs is left to relatively low-level minions—soldiers, embassy clerks, reporters, spies—who transmit information through dispatches, diplomatic cable traffic, memoranda, analyses, and so forth, often processed through several layers of bureaucracy. The debate within the bureaucracy is witnessed firsthand, but even this is often formally conducted through written memoranda and becomes partially accessible in public documents such as budgets and legislative debate. In other words, in contrast to many fields of human enterprise, where decision-makers have direct experience with the physical and social world that they are affecting, the decision-maker in international affairs almost always has indirect contact mediated through text. While some of this text has been classified or destroyed, a formidable amount remains available, particularly when one begins dealing with declassified files in the United States. Added to these official records are the contemporary journalistic sources, diaries, and memoirs, and other historical sources.

Textual resources are easily processed by human readers. In general, a knowledgeable human reader is able to absorb the information available to the bureaucracy, and thereby be able to answer questions about the belief systems and assumptions of that bureaucracy at any point in time. Ideally, a natural language system would be able to do the same thing, with the additional advantage of having the ability to access very large amounts of text with perfect fidelity. However, unlimited natural language comprehension is still a formidable computational problem and as a consequence two different approaches, almost at polar extremes, have been taken on this issue.

At one extreme, sophisticated programs have been developed that attempt to understand the text through linguistic analysis and the application of domain-specific knowledge. The Relatus project (Duffy and Mallery 1986; Hurwitz et al. 1986) uses a huge LISP program running on a Symbolics 3600 LISP machine. The design objectives are described as:

> The Relatus system is an implemented artificial intelligence system for representing and analyzing English texts. The capability to construct "word models" from texts prepares the development not only of analysis of the structure of political discourses but also for simulating cognitive processing (such as learning and reasoning) based on the semantic contents of those texts. . . . It can incrementally construct knowledge representations of text by parsing sentences and performing intrasentential and intersentential reference. [Duffy and Mallery 1986:1]

Relatus is thus a general purpose system for building knowledge structures directly from text. The advantages of this approach are obvious; the disadvantage is that the feasibility of the project in dealing with the diverse quantities of text generated in the foreign policy process has yet to be demonstrated. To date, Relatus has been demonstrated only on a few problems. For example, it can answer simple questions concerning the Soviet invasion of Hungary, and it has been used by Hurwitz to analyze transcripts of player motivations in sequential prisoners' dilemma experiments, but is still far from complete.

At the other extreme, the computer can be used primarily as a very sophisticated tool for indexing and processing text, with the comprehension of that text being left to the human analyst. One can argue that such applications are statistical rather than "AI," but they accomplish tasks that could otherwise only be done by an intelligent human such as a research assistant or reference librarian. This approach allows one to access quantities of text that could not be mastered by the unaided researcher with a very limited programming investment; the disadvantage is that humans are still doing much of the processing.

In an ongoing project, Majeski and Sylvan (1983, 1985) are analyzing early Vietnam decision-making as viewed from the position of Walt W. Rostow. They have accumulated thousands of pages of machine-readable text on the Vietnam decision and originally intended to analyze this using sophisticated AI techniques, but over the past several years have decided that direct machine comprehension of that material was beyond available technical capabilities. Instead, they are using a set of simpler, keyword-based tools to provide sophisticated access to the textual data. Fan (1985, 1989) has developed a series of techniques for analyzing wire service data and has applied them to the study of public opinion. Bennett (1987) and Boynton (1987) also have been using relatively simple text manipulation techniques to analyze political debate.

This bifurcated approach to natural language is reflected in AI generally. Clearly, the objective of complete machine "understanding" of natural language text is both intellectually challenging and stimulating. However, it is also extraordinarily difficult: a slow, complex program running on an expensive machine may still have little more functionality than a sophomore work-study student. In contrast, cruder techniques operating on very large amounts of text may provide rapid and reliable access to a large body of material, even if the comprehension is left to the researcher. In principle, a sophisticated approach such as Relatus has far more capabilities than crude keyword-proximity searching; in practice, the crude techniques are in active use on data bases containing thousands of pages of text whereas the sophisticated systems are used only on much smaller and limited problems. As both hardware and software are still rapidly improving, only time will tell which approach ultimately shows greater utility.

DIRECTIONS FOR THE FUTURE

The field of analytic theory and methodology is alive, well, and thriving. Over a period of three decades, it has been able to attack a series of problems dealing with political behavior in a relatively coherent fashion, accumulate a core set of results that have survived empirical challenges and shifts in intellectual interests. While the field initially borrowed most of its techniques from economics and engineering, in the past decade or so it has begun it create its own intellectual puzzles, which have attracted attention from outside the discipline and has begun to develop a distinct set of statistical and modeling methodologies.

We close this paper with some suggestions on some general issues we feel are critical in analytic theory and methodology today. These are not necessarily the most active research fields, but they are basic issues that are likely to receive considerable attention in the future.

What Impact Do Institutions Have on Social Choice and Why?

A variety of results indicate that institutional details can have a significant impact on social choices. A variety of special cases have been explored to demonstrate this fact. As yet, however, we do not have a workable general theory of political institutions. And possibly more troublesome, the need to explain why institutions are created and maintained is just now beginning to receive serious concern.

What is the Relationship between Micro and Macro in Political Science?

The rational choice tradition, couched in the principles of methodological individualism, holds that macrolevel outcomes should be explained with respect to microlevel behavior. The tendency of decentralized individual choices to have unintended aggregate consequences has been noted in many fields, from collective action (interest group formation) to voting theory (the paradox of not voting and the majority voting chaos theorems). Hence, as a general rule of thumb, system behavior need not follow the logics of individual behavior. The real question is whether this result should discourage system-level research based on aggregate principles that are not derived from individual-level behavior.

Many systems-level modelers point to the fact that their models often yield more powerful and accurate empirical predictions than individual-level studies. They argue that the assumptions of the individual choice models are so tenuous—empirically inaccurate—that there is no reason for them to wait for aggregation principles. Whether one agrees with the rational choice or the systems view, one can see that we face major problems: individual-level models often do not lead to workable *if-then* statements of the sort needed for macrolevel research, while macrolevel research is often guided by assumptions that have no firm footing in individual behavior and often seem rather ad hoc and noncumulative.

A related but more subtle problem can be found in some of the results of the individual-level models themselves. Both the majority voting chaos theorems and folk theorem deduce indeterminancy as the result of modeling collective action based on the assumption of individual preference. This is problematic in two regards. First, most political actors do not perceive their world as particularly chaotic: a variety of political structures are maintained for very long periods of time. Second, indeterminant predictions, while mathematically interesting, have little empirical utility in describing political behavior. In other words, the upshot of these results may be that preference alone is insufficient for modeling most political behavior and that additional information— for example, the constraints imposed by institutions, memory, or rules—is a necessary supplement.

An analogy to the role of the analysis of groups in a world where behavior is known to be produced by individuals is found in the field of organic chemistry. As Brodbeck notes:

The reduction of chemistry to physics is by now a fairly well-accomplished fact. . . . Once [the laws of quantum physics] were known, it turned out that the (chemical) laws by which molecules combine could be derived from them. Yet, organic chemistry appears to be here to stay. In principle, the interactions of the complex molecules can be derived from the laws of physics about the fundamental particles. However, the mathematics of the relevant composition laws is so involved that it is much simpler to study directly the behavior of these organic complexes. [Brodbeck 1968:302]

The untangling of operation of the hemoglobin molecule (Perutz 1978) provides an example of this: despite the fact that the function of the hemoglobin molecule was known (and fairly simple) and the relevant physical laws governing the atoms within that molecule were known, many years of experimentation with the *aggregate* of these atoms were necessary to ascertain how the molecule functioned. In this same fashion, it is likely that individual-level and systems-level models will continue to coexist.

How Much Long-Term Regularity Exists in Political Behavior?

The discoveries of dynamic chaos theory in the 1980s (see, e.g., May 1976; Devaney 1986) poses a major threat to the ability of dynamic simulations to realistically model political or economic behavior over long periods of time. While no one seriously claimed these models were a crystal ball, the dynamic modeling tradition implicitly assumes that the models are good approximations and the effects of errors on the predictions would be bounded and fairly well-behaved. If those models instead contain chaotic elements—which seems plausible on mathematical grounds—then those models are useless even as approximations: arbitrarily small errors in either the parameter or initial value estimates will lead to arbitrarily large errors in long-term predictions, even if the deterministic specification itself is correct.

What Accounts for the Emergence of Cooperation?

Axelrod's initial results on the emergence of cooperation from an anarchic system through the selective advantage gained by actors following a tit-for-tat strategy appeared to solve a very fundamental problem in political behavior. Subsequent work has indicated that Axelrod's results are not as robust as they first appeared, but the fundamental problem itself has not gone away. Political life is not nasty, brutish, and short for most individuals most of the time, and complex, long-lived, cooperative structures do emerge under circumstances where they would appear to be impossibly unstable. The basic roots of collective action still require more explanation than our present theories provide.

Is Expected Utility a Reasonable Approximation to Human Decision-Making?

The assumption of expected utility (EU) maximization, while apparently obvious and commonsensical, has fared poorly in empirical tests. The earliest challenges were the Allais paradox (1953), which dealt with the valuation of certain versus probable events, and the Ellsburg paradox (1961), which dealt with the assessment of unknown probabilities; the full-scale assault on EU came with the work of Kahneman, Tversky, Slovic, and others (see Kahneman, Slovic, and Tversky 1982; Hogarth and Reder 1986) during the 1980s. While there is considerable debate concerning the appropriate theory for accounting for these results, they have been replicated in thousands of experiments, no alternative experimental protocol has been developed that refutes those challenges, and thus their validity is seldom seriously questioned on empirical grounds.

In economics, these challenges to the fundamental assumptions about the nature of rationality under uncertainty have been taken quite seriously. For example, the Hogarth and Reder (1986) volume resulted from a conference of over sixty scholars, including three Nobel Prize winners, addressing this issue. In contrast, the formal modeling community in political science has tended to dismiss this research as irrelevant. For example, Ordeshook's otherwise excellent *Game Theory and Political Theory* associates the Allais paradox with the entirely unrelated paradox of not voting (Ordeshook 1986:49) and does not even mention the Ellsburg paradox or the Kahneman et al. opus, despite the central position of expected value decision-making in game theory.

Ironically, the impact of dropping EU from the legislative and voting models would be relatively minor. The experimental results do not challenge the core assumptions about the existence of preference (and by implication, self-interest); they only challenge some idiosyncratic and mathematically convenient assumptions about decision-making under uncertainty. Like a poisonous weed entangling an otherwise sound structure, the EU assumption has infiltrated voting models because it seemed innocuous. If those models were reconstructed without EU, most of the interesting results would remain intact. Dropping the EU assumption in favor of other types of decision-making—for example, decisions constrained primarily by institutions or precedent rather than uncertainty—may also clear up a variety of gross empirical inconsistencies (speciously referred to as "paradoxes") scattered through the literature.

The situation is quite different in international relations, where the EU assumption tends to be central and critical (for example, Brams 1985; Bueno de Mesquita 1981; Morrow 1985; Powell 1988). Furthermore, the environment of risk and uncertainty characterizing international politics provides precisely the circumstances that invoke the Allais and Ellsburg paradoxes. However mathematically elegant the EU formulations in IR may be, their advocates eventually need to confront the psychological evidence that indicates that EU is unlikely to accurately describe human behavior in the circumstances being modeled.

Where Will Game Theory Go from Here?

The recent flurry of research on equilibrium selection in noncooperative games is promising. We do not mean to imply that the research on noncooperative games is settling down to a clean, simple result comparable to the (minimax) theory of two-person, zero-sum games. The concepts are more cumbersome, the proposed solutions are not so elegant. However, it is safe to say that noncooperative game theory is settling down to focus on a few major problems and progress is being made.

There is an emerging consensus that noncooperative game theory will displace cooperative game theory as the method of dealing with bargaining and other traditional "cooperative games." Cooperative game theory has not converged to a single solution—if anything, the number of "solution concepts" expanded exponentially. Each approach has some intuitive merit, but "as a group they fail to provide a clear, coherent theory of cooperative games," as Harsanyi and Selten argue (1988:8). They contend the reason is that cooperative games overlook the negotiation process and other noncooperative aspects. They offer several illustrations of ways in which the conundrum of cooperative game theory can be avoided by taking a noncooperative approach. The development of noncooperative game theory, thus, offers the possibility of addressing one of the field's major trouble spots.

The theoretical progress is encouraging, but the problems of empirical application and testing have barely received attention. Given the misgivings of psychologists about expected utility analysis (as well as the computational limitation of humans) that we have just discussed, there are grounds for skepticism about the applicability of the advanced game theoretic models. Experimental studies have mainly focused on the prisoner's dilemma game and various solution concepts for cooperative game theory. We still await experimental evaluation of the "cutting edge" concepts (sequential or perfect equilibrium, for example). Nonexperimental tests usually consist of case studies as illustrations of a game's central notions. The applications are illuminating, but they hardly constitute tests of falsifiable hypotheses.

What Are the Appropriate Statistical Models for Political Behavior?

Most of the statistical models currently used in political science were borrowed from other disciplines, notably economics and psychology. As King and others have noted, many of these may be inappropriate for theoretical reasons. For example, in contrast to economics, most political behavior consists of phenomena measured nominally at irregular time periods; in contrast to psychology, our data are rarely generated under controlled experimental conditions and often deal with collectives rather than individuals. These features of our data make them more difficult to deal with, but that aspect of political behavior makes the development of appropriate techniques all the more important. With computational power now essentially unlimited, it may be possible to use techniques such as maximum likelihood estimation, bootstrapping, and nonlinear modeling, which were previously prohibitively expensive. We also need to address the problem of training graduate students to take model construction seriously rather than instinctively reaching for the SPSS manual.

NOTES

1. If voter indifference and abstention are taken into account, this definition must be modified, but not in a substantial way.

2. This paradox is attributed to the eighteenth-century writings of the Marquis de Condorcet (see Arrow 1963:93).

3. A lottery is a list of possible prizes with the probability of each prize attached.

4. The Nash equilibrium concept is based on the following mathematical observation. Given a list of the other player's actions, denoted s_{-i}, player i can choose an optimal response, which is called a best reply function, $s_i{}^* = r_i(s_{-i})$. Nash showed that finding an equilibrium, $s^* = (s_1{}^*, \ldots, s_N{}^*)$ is equivalent to finding a fixed point in vector-valued mapping $(s_1{}^*, \ldots, s_N{}^*) = (r_1(s_{-1}{}^*), \ldots, r_N(s_{-N}{}^*))$. I.e., each player's equilibrium strategy is a best reply to the other's equilibrium strategies. He also noted that existence of equilibrium could be proven with the fixed-point theorem of Kakutani in a class of noncooperative games (see Friedman 1986:30–47 for an exceptional exposition of this argument).

5. Each player's "private information," preferences, or beliefs is represented by a set $t_1 = \{t_{i1}, \ldots t_{im}\}$. A Bayesian, or expected value maximizing, player knows the probability distribution of each player's types and knows that the other players are uncertain of his own type. Each player is thinking, "if my type is t_{ij}, I will play a strategy $s_i(t_{ij})$," for all types j. A Bayesian Nash equilibrium is one that maximizes expected utility given the other player's strategies for each of their types: i.e., a list of actions that each player will take for each of his types,

$\{s_1*(t_1), s_2*(t_2), \ldots, s_N*(t_N)\}$. Each element is a function that maps the type set into the strategy set. For a much more complete and readable explanation, see Myerson (1985).

6. It is a "folk" theorem because, like a folk song, no one is quite sure who wrote it but many people are familiar with it.

7. Better known as "Student," as in "Student's t."

8. The parallels between rule-based systems and bureaucracy is sufficiently close that one of the more common commercial applications of AI is to replace middle-level bureaucracy in areas such as credit approval and inventory control (Feigenbaum, McCorduck, and Nii 1988).

REFERENCES

Abreu, Dilip, David Pearce, and Ennio Stachetti. 1986. "Optimal Cartel Equilibria with Imperfect Monitoring." *Journal of Economic Theory* 39:251–69.

Aldrich, John H., and Michael D. McGinnis. 1989. "A Model of Party Constraints on Optimal Candidate Positions." *Mathematical and Computer Modelling* 12:437–50.

Alesina, Alberto. 1987. "Macroeconomic Policy in a Two-Party System as a Repeated Game." *Quarterly Journal of Economics* 102:651–78.

———. 1988. "Credibility and Policy Convergence in a Two-Party System with Rational Voters." *American Economic Review* 78:796–805.

Alker, Hayward J., and Cheryl Christensen. 1972. "From Causal Modeling to Artificial Intelligence: The Evolving of a UN Peace-Making Simulation." In *Experimentation and Simulation in Political Science*, J.A. LaPonce and P. Smoker, eds. Toronto: University of Toronto Press.

Alker, Hayward J., and W. Greenberg. 1976. "On Simulating Collective Security Regime Alternatives." In *Thought and Action in Foreign Policy*, M. Bonham and M. Shapiro, eds. Basel: Birkhauser Verlag.

Alker, Hayward J., James P. Bennett, and Dwain Mefford. 1980. "Generalized Precedent Logics for Resolving Security Dilemmas." *International Interactions* 7:165–200.

Allan, Pierre. 1980. "Diplomatic Time and Climate: A Formal Model." *Journal of Peace Science* 4:133–50.

Allison, Graham T. 1971. *The Essence of Decision*. Boston: Little, Brown.

Alt, James E., Randall L. Calvert, and Brian D. Humes. 1988. "Reputation and Hegemonic Stability: A Game-Theoretic Analysis." *American Political Science Review* 82:423–44.

Altfeld, Michael F., and Bruce Bueno de Mesquita. 1979. "Choosing Sides in Wars." *International Studies Quarterly* 23:87–112.

Anderson, Paul A. 1981. "Justifications and Precedents as Constraints in Foreign Policy Decision-Making." *American Journal of Political Science* 25: 738–61.

Anderson, Paul, and Stuart Thorson. 1982. "Artificial Intelligence Based Simulations of Foreign Policy Decision-Making." *Behavioral Science* 27:176–93.

Anderton, Charles H. 1985. "Arms Race Modeling: Categorization and Systematic Analysis." Washington, D.C.: International Studies Association.

Arrow, Kenneth J. 1951, 1963. *Social Choice and Individual Values*. First and second editions. New Haven: Yale University Press.

Austen-Smith, David. 1987. "Sophisticated Sincerity: Voting over Endogenous Agendas." *American Political Science Review* 81:1323–29.

Austen-Smith, David, and William Riker. 1987. "Asymmetric Information and the Coherence of Legislation." *American Political Science Review* 81: 897–918.

Axelrod, Robert. 1981. "The Emergence of Cooperation among Egotists." *American Political Science Review* 75:306–18.

———. 1984. *The Evolution of Cooperation*. New York: Basic Books.

Banerjee, Sanjoy. 1986. "The Reproduction of Social Structures: An Artificial Intelligence Model." *Journal of Conflict Resolution* 30:22–252.

Banaszak, Lee Ann. 1986. "The Rise and Decline of Third Parties: A Difference Equations Model of Mobilization." Paper presented at the Midwest Political Science Association meetings, Chicago.

Banks, Jeffrey S. 1989. "Equilibrium Outcomes in Two-Stage Amendment Procedures." *American Journal of Political Science* 33:25–43.

Banks, Jeffrey S., and Randall L. Calvert. 1988. "Communication and Efficiency in Coordination Games with Incomplete Information." Dept. of Political Science, University of Rochester.

———. 1989. "Incentive Efficiency without an Arbitrator in Coordination Games." Dept. of Political Science, University of Rochester.

Barr, Aaron, Paul R. Cohen, and Edward A. Feigenbaum. 1982. *The Handbook of Artificial Intelligence*. Los Altos, Calif.: William Kaufmann.

Bartholomew, J.D. 1973. *Stochastic Models of Social Processes*. New York: John Wiley.

Bendor, Jonathan. 1987. "In Good Times and Bad: Reciprocity in an Uncertain World." *American Journal of Political Science* 31:531–58.

Bendor, Jonathan, and Dilip Mookherjee. 1987. "Institutional Structure and the Logic of Ongoing Collective Action." *American Political Science Review* 81:129–54.

———. 1988. "Norms, Cooperation, and Third Party Sanctions." Stanford University.

Bendor, Jonathan, Serge Taylor, and Roland van Gaalen. 1987. "Stacking the Deck: Bureaucratic Missions and Policy Design." *American Political Science Review* 81:873–96.

Bennett, James P. 1987. "Deterrence in Contemporary Policy Debates: The Expression of Strategic Doctrines in Political Arguments about SDI." Paper presented at the International Studies Association, Washington.

Berkowitz, Bruce. 1983. "Realignment in International Treaty Organizations." *International Studies Quarterly* 27:77–96.

Bernhardt, M. Daniel, and Daniel E. Ingberman. 1985. "Candidate Reputations and the 'Incumbency Effect.'" *Journal of Public Economics* 27:47–67.

Bertalanffy, Ludwig. 1975. *Perspectives on General Systems Theory*. New York: Braziller.

Black, Duncan. 1948. "On the Rationale of Group Decision Making." *Journal of Political Economy* 56:23–34.

———. 1958. *The Theory of Committees and Elections*. Cambridge: Cambridge University Press.

Bobrow, David S., Donald A. Sylvan, and Brian Ripley. 1986. "Japanese Supply Security: A Computational Model." Paper presented at the International Studies Association, Anaheim.

Bortkiewicz, L. 1898. *Das Gesetz der kleinen Zahlen*. Leipzig: Tuebner.

Boyd, Robert, and Jeffrey P. Lorberbaum. 1987. "No Pure Strategy is Evolutionarily Stable in the Repeated Prisoner's Dilemma Game." *Nature* 327: 58–59.

Boynton, G. Robert. 1980. *Mathematical Thinking about Politics*. New York: Longman.

———. 1987. "Committee Law Making." Paper presented at the American Political Science Association, Chicago.

Brams, Steven J. 1975. *Game Theory and Politics*. New York: Free Press.

———. 1985. *Superpower Games*. New Haven: Yale University Press.

Brams, Stephen, and Marc Kilgour. 1987. "Threat Escalation and Crisis Stability: A Game-theoretic Analysis." *American Political Science Review* 81: 833–50.

Bremer, Stuart, and Michael Mihalka. 1977. "Machiavelli and Machina: Or Politics among Hexagons." In *Problems of World Modeling*, Karl W. Deutsch et al., eds. Boston: Ballinger.

Bremer, Stuart A. 1982. "The Contagiousness of Coercion: The Spread of Serious International Disputes, 1900–1976." *International Interactions* 9: 29–55.

———, ed. 1987. *The GLOBUS Model*. Frankfurt: Campus/Westview.

Brent, Edward. 1988. "New Approaches to Expert Systems and Artificial Intelligence Programming." *Social Science Computer Review* 6(4): 569–78.

Brewer, Garry D., and Martin Shubik. 1979. *The War Game: A Critique of Military Problem-Solving*. Cambridge: Harvard University Press.

Brito, D.L., and Michael D. Intriligator. 1974. "Uncertainty and the Stability of the Armaments Race." *Annals of Economic and Social Measurement* 3: 279–92.

Brito, Dagobert, and Michael D. Intriligator. 1985. "Conflict, War and Redistribution." *American Political Science Review* 79, 4:943–57.

Brodbeck, May, ed. 1968. *Readings in the Philosophy of the Social Sciences.* London: Macmillan.

Brown, Courtney. 1987. "Voter Mobilization and Party Competition in a Volatile Electorate." *American Sociological Review* 52:59–73.

Bueno de Mesquita, Bruce. 1981. *The War Trap.* New Haven: Yale University Press.

———. 1985. "The War Trap Revisited: A Revised Expected Utility Model." *American Political Science Review* 79, 1:156–73.

Bueno de Mesquita, Bruce, and David Lalman. 1990. "Domestic Opposition and Foreign War." *American Political Science Review* 84:747–766.

Busch, Peter A. 1970. "Appendix on mathematical models of arms races." In *What Price Vigilance*, Bruce M. Russett. New Haven: Yale University Press.

Calvert, Randall. 1985. "Robustness of the Multidimensional Voting Model, Candidate Motivations, Uncertainty and Convergence." *American Journal of Political Science* 29:226–39.

———. 1987a. "Reputation and Legislative Leadership." *Public Choice* 55: 81–119.

———. 1987b. "Coordination and Power: The Foundation of Leadership among Rational Actors." Presented at the American Political Science Association meetings, Chicago.

Caplin, Andrew, and Barry Nalebuff. 1988. "On 64%-Majority Rule." *Econometrica* 56:787–814.

Casstevens, Thomas W. 1989. "The Circulation of Elites: A Review and Critique of a Class of Models." *American Journal of Political Science* 33: 294–317.

Casstevens, Thomas W., and W.A. Denham. 1970. "Turnover and Tenure in the Canadian House of Commons, 1867–1968." *Canadian Journal of Political Science*, 3, 3:655–61.

Casstevens, Thomas W., and J. R. Ozinga. 1980. "Exponential Survival on the Soviet Central Committee." *American Journal of Political Science* 24,1:175.

Chan, Steve. 1978. "Temporal Delineation of International Conflicts: Poisson Results from the Vietnam War, 1963–1965." *International Studies Quarterly* 22:237–66.

Charnick, Eugene, and Drew McDermott. 1985. *Introduction to Artificial Intelligence.* Reading, Mass.: Addison-Wesley.

Chase-Dunn, Christopher K. 1979. "Comparative Research on World-System Characteristics." *International Studies Quarterly* 23:601–23.

Chatterjee, Kalyan, and William Samuelson. 1983. "Bargaining under Incomplete Information." *Operations Research* 31:835–51.

Cimbala, Stephen. 1987. *Artificial Intelligence and National Security.* Lexington, Mass.: Lexington Books.

Cioffi-Revilla, Claudio A. 1979. *Mathematical Models in International Relations: A Bibliography.* Chapel Hill: Institute for Research in Social Science, University of North Carolina.

———. 1981. "Fuzzy Sets and Models of International Relations." *American Journal of Political Science* 25, 1:129–59.

———. 1984. "The Political Reliability of Italian Governments: An Exponential Survival Model." *American Political Science Review* 78, 2:318–37.

Coleman, James S. 1964. *Introduction to Mathematical Sociology*. Glencoe, Ill.: Free Press.

Converse, Phillip. 1969. "Of Time and Partisan Stability." *Comparative Political Studies* 2:139–71.

Coombs, M. J. 1984. *Development in Expert Systems*. Orlando: Academic Press.

Cortes, Fernando, Adam Przeworski, and John Sprague. 1974. *Systems Analysis for Social Scientists*. New York: John Wiley.

Coughlin, Peter J. 1982. "Pareto-optimality of Policy Proposals with Probabilistic Voting." *Public Choice* 39:427–33.

———. 1984. "Probabilistic Voter Models." In *Encyclopedia of Statistical Sciences*, vol. 6, S. Kotz, N. Johnson, and C. Read, eds. New York: John Wiley.

Coughlin, Peter J., and Shmuel Nitzan. 1981. "Directional and Local Electoral Equilibria with Probabilistic Voting." *Journal of Economic Theory* 24: 226–39.

Cox, Gary W. 1987a. "The Uncovered Set and the Core." *American Journal of Political Science* 31:408–22.

———. 1987b. "Electoral Equilibrium under Alternative Institutions." *American Journal of Political Science* 31:82–108.

———. 1989. "Undominated candidate strategies under alternative voting rules." *Mathematical and Computer Modelling* 12:451–559.

Cusack, Thomas, and U. Zimmer. 1986. "The Bases of Multistate System Endurance." Paper presented at the International Studies Association, Anaheim.

Dacey, Raymond, and Norman Pendegraft. 1988. "The Optimality of Tit-for-Tat." *International Interactions* 15, 1:45–64.

Davis, Morton D. 1983. *Game Theory: A Nontechnical Introduction*. New York: Basic Books.

Davis, William W., George T. Duncan, and R.W. Siverson. 1978. "The Dynamics of Warfare, 1816–1965." *American Journal of Political Science* 22: 772–92.

Denzau, Arthur T., and Robert J. Mackay. 1981. "Structure-Induced Equilibria and Perfect-Foresight Expectations." *American Journal of Political Science* 25:762–79.

———. 1983. "Gatekeeping and Monopoly Power of Committees: An Analysis of Sincere and Sophisticated Behavior." *American Journal of Political Science* 27:740–61.

Denzau, Arthur T., William Riker, and Kenneth Shepsle. 1985. "Farquharson and Fenno: Sophisticated Voting and Home Style." *American Political Science Review* 79:117–34.

Deutsch, Karl W., Bruno Fritsch, Helio Jaguaribe, and Andrei S. Markovits. 1977. *Problems of World Modeling*. Cambridge, Mass.: Ballinger.

Devaney, Robert L. 1986. *An Introduction to Chaotic Dynamical Systems*. Menlo Park: Benjamin/Cummings Publishing.

Dobson, Douglas, and Duana A. Meeter. 1974. "Alternative Markov Models for Describing Change in Party Identification." *American Journal of Political Science* 18, 3:487–500.

Dougherty, James E., and Robert L. Pfaltzgraff. 1981. *Contending Theories of International Relations*. New York: Harper and Row.

Downs, Anthony. 1957. *An Economic Theory of Democracy*. New York: Harper and Row.

Duffy, Gavan, and John C. Mallery. 1986. "RELATUS: An Artificial Intelligence Tool for Natural Language Modeling." Paper presented at the International Studies Association, Anaheim.

Duncan, George T., and Randolph M. Siverson. 1975. "Markov Chain Models for Conflict Analysis." *International Studies Quarterly* 19:344–74.

————. 1982. "Flexibility of Alliance Partner Choice in a Multipolar System." *International Studies Quarterly* 26:511–38.

Enelow, James M., and Melvin J. Hinich. 1983a. "On Plott's pairwise symmetry condition for majority rule equilibrium." *Public Choice* 40:317–21.

————. 1983b. "Voting One Issue at a Time: The Question of Voter Forecasts." *American Political Science Review* 77:435–45.

————. 1984a. *The Spatial Theory of Voting: An Introduction*. New York: Cambridge University Press.

————. 1984b. "Probabilistic Voting and the Importance of Centrist Ideologies in Democratic Elections." *Journal of Politics* 46:459–78.

————. 1989. "The Location of American Presidential Candidates: An Empirical Test of a New Spatial Model of Elections." *Mathematical and Computer Modelling* 12:461–70.

Fan, David. 1985. "Lebanon, 1983–1984: Influence of the Media on Public Opinion." Mimeo, University of Minnesota.

————. 1989. *Predictions of Public Opinion*. Westport, Conn.: Greenwood Press.

Feigenbaum, Edward A. 1983. "Knowledge Engineering: The Applied Side." In *Intelligent Systems*, J. E. Hayes and D. Michie, eds. Chichester: Ellis Horwood.

Feigenbaum, Edward A., Pamela McCorduck, and H. Nii. 1988. *The Rise of the Expert Company*. New York: Times Books.

Feld, Scott L., and Bernard Grofman. 1987. "Necessary and Sufficient Conditions for a Majority Winner in n-Dimensional Spatial Voting Games: An Intuitive Geometric Approach." *American Journal of Political Science* 31: 709–28.

Feld, Scott L., Bernard Grofman, and Nicholas R. Miller. 1989. "Limits on agenda control in spatial voting games." *Mathematical and Computer Modelling* 12:405–16.

Feller, William. 1968. *An Introduction to Probability Theory and Its Applications*. New York: John Wiley.

Ferejohn, John, and Morris P. Fiorina. 1974. "The Paradox of Not Voting: A Decision Theoretic Analysis." *American Political Science Review* 69: 525–36.

Ferejohn, John A., Morris P. Fiorina, and Richard D. McKelvey. 1987. "Sophisticated Voting and Agenda Independence in the Distributive Politics Setting." *American Journal of Political Science* 31:169–93.

Fiorina, Morris P. 1975. "Formal Models in Political Science." *American Journal of Political Science* 19,1:133–59.

Forrester, Jay W. 1971 *World Dynamics*. Cambridge: Wright-Allen.

Friedman, James W. 1983. *Oligopoly Theory*. New York: Cambridge University Press.

———. 1986. *Game Theory with Applications to Economics*. New York: Oxford University Press.

Fudenberg, D., and E. Maskin. 1986. "Folk Theorems for Repeated Games with Discounting or with Incomplete Information." *Econometrica* 54:533–54.

Gillespie, John V., Dina A. Zinnes, G.S. Tahim, Philip A. Schrodt, and R. Michael Rubison. 1976. "An Optimal Control Model of Arms Races." *American Political Science Review* 71:226–44.

Gilligan, Thomas W., and Keith Krehbiel. 1987. "Collective Decision-Making and Standing Committees: An Informational Rationale for Restrictive Amendment Procedures." *Journal of Law, Economics, and Organization* 3: 287–335.

———. 1988a. "Complex Rules and Congressional Outcomes." *Journal of Politics* 50:625–54.

———. 1988b. "Organization of Informative Committees by a Rational Legislature." Presented at the annual meeting of the Midwest Political Science Association, Chicago.

Glazer, Amihai, Bernard Grofman, and Guillermo Owen. 1989. "A Model of Candidate Convergence Under Uncertainty About Voter Preferences." *Mathematical and Computer Modelling* 12:471–78.

Gleick, James. 1987. *Chaos: Making a New Science*. New York: Viking.

Gochman, Charles S. 1976. "Studies of International Violence." *Journal of Conflict Resolution* 20:539–60.

Goodman, Leo. 1957. "Some Alternatives to Ecological Correlation." *American Journal of Sociology* 64:610–25.

Greenberg, Irwin. 1982. "The Role of Deception in Decision Theory." *Journal of Conflict Resolution* 26,1:139–56.

Grunbaum, Werner, 1986. "Using Artificial Intelligence Techniques to Predict

Supreme Court Decision Making." Paper presented at the American Political Science Association.

Guetzkow, Harold, and Joseph J. Valdez, eds. 1981. *Simulated International Processes: Theories and Research in Global Modeling*. Beverly Hills: Sage.

Hamburger, Henry. 1979. *Games as Models of Social Phenomena*. San Francisco: Freeman.

Hammond, Thomas H., and Gary J. Miller, 1987. "The Core of the Constitution." *American Political Science Review* 81:1155–74.

Hanneman, Robert A. 1988. *Computer-assisted Theory Building: Modeling Dynamic Social Systems*. Beverly Hills: Sage.

Harary, Frank. 1977. "Graphing Conflict in International Relations." *Papers, Peace Science Society (International)* 27.

Hardin, Russell. 1971. "Collective Action as an Agreeable N-Prisoner's Dilemma." *Behavioral Science* 15:472–79.

———. 1982. *Collective Action*. Baltimore: Johns Hopkins University Press.

Harsanyi, John C. 1967, 1968a, 1968b. "Games with Incomplete Information Played by 'Bayesian' Players, Part I: The Basic Model." *Management Science* 14:159–82; Part II, 14:320–34; Part III, 14:486–502.

———. 1988. *A General Theory of Equilibrium Selection in Games*. Cambridge: MIT Press.

Hayes-Roth, Frederick, Donald Waterman, and Douglas Lenat. 1984. *Building Expert Systems*. Reading, Mass.: Addison-Wesley.

Hechter, Michael. 1989a. "The Emergence of Cooperative Social Institutions." In *Social Institutions: Their Emergence, Maintenance, and Effects*, Michael Hechter, Karl-Dieter Opp, and Reinhard Wippler, eds. New York: Aldine de Gruyter.

———. 1989b. "On the Inadequacy of Game Theory for the Solution of Real-World Collective Action Problems." In *The Limits of Rationality*, Margaret Levi and Karen Cook, eds. Chicago: University of Chicago Press.

Hinich, Melvin J., John O. Ledyard Peter, and C. Ordeshook. 1972a. "A Theory of Electoral Equilibrium: A Spatial Analysis Based on the Theory of Games." *Journal of Politics* 35:154–93.

———. 1972b. "Nonvoting and the existence of equilibrium under majority rule." *Journal of Economic Theory* 4:144–53.

Hinich, Melvin J. 1977. "Equilibrium in Spatial Voting: The Median Voter Result is an Artifact." *Journal of Economic Theory* 16:208–18.

Hipel, Keith W., Muhong Wang, and Niall M. Fraser. 1988. "Hypergame Analysis of the Falklands/Malvinas Conflict." *International Studies Quarterly* 32,3:335–58.

Hirschleifer, Jack, and Juan Carlos Martinez-Coll. 1988. "What Strategies Can Support the Evolutionary Emergence of Cooperation." *Journal of Conflict Resolution* 32,2:367–98.

Hogarth, Robin M., and Melvin W. Reder. 1986. *Rational Choice: The Contrast between Economics and Psychology*. Chicago: University of Chicago Press.

Holland, John H. 1975. *Adaptation in Natural and Artificial Systems*. Ann Arbor: University of Michigan Press.

———. 1986. "Escaping Brittleness: The Possibilities of General Purpose Algorithms Applied to Parallel Rule-Based Systems." In *Machine Learning* 2, R. S. Michelski, J. G. Carbonell, and T. M. Mitchell, eds. Los Altos, Calif.: Kaufman.

Holmstrom, Bengt. 1979. "Moral Hazard and Observability." *Bell Journal of Economics* 10:74–91.

———. 1982. "Moral Hazard in Teams." *Bell Journal of Economics* 13:324–40.

Holt, Robert T., Brian L. Job, and Lawrence Markus. 1978. "Catastrophe Theory and the Study of War." *Journal of Conflict Resolution* 22,2:171–209.

Horvath, William J. 1968. "A Statistical Model for the Duration of Wars and Strikes." *Behavioral Science* 13:18–28.

Hotelling, Harold. 1929. "Stability in Competition." *Economic Journal* 39: 41–57.

Houweling, Henk W., and J. B. Kune. 1984. "Do Outbreaks of War Follow a Poisson-Process?" *Journal of Conflict Resolution* 28,1:51–62.

Houweling, Henk W., and Jan G. Siccama. 1985. "The Epidemeology of War, 1816–1980." *Journal of Conflict Resolution* 29,4:641–64.

Huckfeldt, R. Robert, C.W. Kohfeld, and Thomas W. Likens. 1982. *Dynamic Modelling: An Introduction*. Beverly Hills: Sage.

Hudson, Valerie M. 1987. "Using a Rule-Based Production System to Estimate Foreign Policy Behavior." In *Artificial Intelligence and National Security*, Stephen Cimbala, ed. Lexington, Mass.: Lexington Books.

Hughes, Barry B. 1984. *World Futures: A Critical Analysis of Alternatives*. Baltimore: Johns Hopkins University Press.

———. 1985. "World Models: The Bases of Difference." *International Studies Quarterly* 29:77–101.

Hurwitz, Roger, John C. Mallery, Hayward R. Alker, and Gavan Duffy. 1986. "Anarchy or Community: A Study of Developmental Patterns in Sequential Prisoner's Dilemma Games." Paper presented at the International Studies Association, Anaheim.

Ingberman, Daniel E. 1989. "Reputational Dynamics in Spatial Competition." *Mathematical and Computer Modelling* 12:479–96.

Intriligator, Michael D. 1964. "Some Simple Models of Arms Races." *General Systems Yearbook* 9:143–47.

———. 1971. *Mathematical Optimization and Economic Theory*. Engelwood Cliffs: Prentice-Hall.

———. 1982. "Research on Conflict Theory: Analytic Approaches and Areas of Application." *Journal of Conflict Resolution* 26, 2:307–27.

Intriligator, Michael D., and D.L. Brito. 1984. "Can Arms Races Lead to the Outbreak of War?" *Journal of Conflict Resolution* 28:63–84.

Isard, Walter, and Charles H. Anderton. 1985. "Arms Race Models: A Survey and Synthesis." *Conflict Management and Peace Science* 8, 2:27–108.

Janis, Irving. 1982. *Groupthink*. Boston: Houghton Mifflin.

Job, Brian L., and Douglas Johnson. 1986. "A Model of US Foreign Policy Decision Making: The US and the Dominican Republic, 1961–1965." International Studies Association, Anaheim.

Job, Brian L., Douglas Johnson, and Eric Selbin. 1987. "A Multi-Agent, Script-based Model of U.S. Foreign Policy Towards Central America." Paper presented at the American Political Science Association, Chicago.

Kahneman, Daniel, Paul Slovic, and Amos Tversky. 1982. *Judgement Under Uncertainty: Heuristics and Biases*. Cambridge: Cambridge University Press.

Kaw, Marita. 1986. "Testing a Model of Soviet Conflict Involvement Behavior." Paper presented at the Midwest Political Science Association, Chicago.

Kemeny, John G., and J. Laurie Snell. 1962. *Mathematical Models in the Social Sciences*. New York: Blaisdell.

Key, V.O. 1949. *Southern Politics*. New York: Knopf.

Kickert, Walter J. M. 1978. *Fuzzy Theories on Decision-Making: A Critical Review*. Leiden: Martinus Nijhoff Social Science Division.

Kiewiet, D. Roderick, and Mathew D. McCubbins. 1988. "Presidential Influence on Congressional Appropriations Decisions." *American Journal of Political Science* 32:713–36.

King, Gary. 1989. *Unifying Political Methodology: The Likelihood Theory of Statistical Inference*. New York: Cambridge University Press.

Klahr, Philip, and Donald A. Waterman. 1986. *Expert Systems: Techniques, Tools and Applications*. Reading, Mass.: Addison-Wesley.

Koehler, David H. 1987. "The P-Set: A Structure-Induced Equilibrium for Sequential Legislative Voting." *American Journal of Political Science* 31: 940–64.

Kohlberg, Elon, and Jean-François Mertens. 1986. "On the Strategic Stability of Equilibria." *Econometrica* 54:1003–37.

Kolodner, Janet, ed. 1988. *Proceedings of the DARPA Workshop on Case-Based Reasoning*. Palo Alto, Calif.: Morgan Kaufmann.

Kramer, Gerald H. 1973. "On a Class of Equilibrium Conditions for Majority Rule." *Econometrica* 41:285–87.

———. 1983. "The Ecological Fallacy Revisited: Aggregate versus Individual-Level Findings on Economics and Elections and Sociotropic Voting." *American Political Science Review* 77:92–111.

Krehbiel, Keith. 1987a. "Sophisticated Committees and Structure-Induced Equilibria in Congress." In *Congress: Structure and Policy*, Mathew McCubbins and Terry Sullivan, eds. New York: Cambridge University Press.

———. 1987b. "Institutional Erosion of Committee Power." *American Political Science Review* 81:929–35.

———. 1988. "Spatial Models of Legislative Choice." *Legislative Studies Quarterly* 13:259–319.

Krehbiel, Keith, and Douglas Rivers. 1988a. "The Analysis of Committee Power: An Application to Senate Voting on the Minimum Wage." *American Journal of Political Science* 32:1151–74.

———. 1988b. "Sophisticated Voting in Congress: A Reconsideration." Working Papers in Political Science P-88-9. Hoover Institution, Stanford University.

Kreps, D., P. Milgrom, J. Roberts, and R. Wilson. 1982. "Rational Cooperation in the Finitely-Repeated Prisoner's Dilemma." *Journal of Economic Theory* 27:245–52.

Kreps, David, and Robert Wilson. 1982a. "Sequential Equilibria." *Econometrica* 50:863–94.

———. 1982b. "Reputation and Imperfect Information." *Journal of Economic Theory* 27:253–79.

Kugler, Jacek, and Frank Zagare. 1987. *Exploring the Stability of Deterrence.* Boulder: Rienner.

Kuhn, Harold W. 1953. "Extensive Games and the Problem of Information." In *Contributions to the Theory of Games II*, H.W. Kuhn and A.W. Tucker, eds. Princeton: Princeton University Press.

Lalman, David. 1988. "Conflict Resolution and Peace." *American Journal of Political Science* 32:590–615.

Lancaster, Kelvin. 1973. "The Dynamic Inefficiency of Capitalism." *Journal of Political Economy* 81:1092–109.

Lane, Ruth. 1986. "Artificial Intelligence and the Political Construction of Reality: The Case of James E. Carter." Paper presented at the American Political Science Association, Washington.

Leavitt, Michael. 1972. "Markov Processes in International Crises: An Analytical Addendum to an Events-Based Simulation of the Taiwan Straits Crisis." In *Experimentation and Simulation in Political Science*, J.A. Laponce and Paul Smoker, eds. Toronto: University of Toronto Press.

Leik, Robert K., and Barbara F. Meeker. 1975. *Mathematical Sociology*. New York: Prentice Hall.

Li, Richard Y.P., and William R. Thompson. 1975. "The 'Group Contagion' Hypothesis." *Journal of Conflict Resolution* 19:63–88.

Lien, Da-Hsiang Donald. 1987a. "Asymmetric Information in Competitive Bribery Games." *Economics Letters* 23:153–56.

Lien, Donald Da-Hsiang. 1987b. "A Note on Inducing Cooperation by Reciprocative Strategy." *Economics Letters* 25:131–35.

Luce, R. Duncan, and Howard Raiffa. 1957. *Games and Decisions: Introduction and Critical Survey*. New York: John Wiley.

Luenberger, David G. 1979. *Introduction to Dynamic Systems: Theory, Models and Applications*. New York: John Wiley.

Luterbacher, Urs, and Michael D. Ward, eds. 1985. *Dynamic Models in International Conflict*. Boulder: Rienner.

MacKuen, Michael B. 1981. *More Than News: Media Power and Public Affairs*. Beverly Hills: Sage.

Majeski, Stephen J. 1985. "Expectations and Arms Races." *American Journal of Political Science* 29, 2:217–45.

———. 1987. "A Recommendation Model of War Initiation: The Plausibility and Generalizability of General Cultural Rules." In *Artificial Intelligence and National Security*, Stephen Cimbala, ed. Lexington, Mass.: Lexington Books.

———. 1989. "A Rule Based Model of the United States Military Expenditures Decision-Making Process." *International Interactions* 15, 2:129–54.

Majeski, Stephen J., and David L. Jones. 1981. "Arms Race Modeling." *Journal of Conflict Resolution* 25:259–88.

Majeski, Stephen J., and David J. Sylvan. 1983. "A Formalization of Decision and Measurement Heuristics for War Initiation: The 1961 Vietnam Commitments." Paper presented at the American Political Science Association, Chicago.

———. 1984. "Simple Choices and Complex Calculations: A Critique of 'The War Trap.'" *Journal of Conflict Resolution* 28, 2:316–40.

———. 1985. "Decision and Recommendation Heuristics for War Involvement: The 1961 Vietnam Commitments, A Progress Report." Paper presented at the International Studies Association, Washington.

Mallery, John C., and Roger Hurwitz. 1987. "Analogy and Precedent in Strategic Decision-Making: A Computational Approach." Paper presented at the American Political Science Association, Chicago.

March, James G., and Johan P. Olsen. 1983. "The New Institutionalism: Organizational Factors in Political Life." Paper presented at the American Political Science Association meetings, September.

Marra, Robin F. 1985. "The New Institutionalism: Organizational Factors in Political Life." *International Studies Quarterly* 29, 4:357–84.

May, Robert M. 1974. *Stability and Complexity in Model Ecosystems*. Princeton: Princeton University Press.

———. 1976. "Simple mathematical models with very complicated dynamics." *Nature* 261:459–67.

Mayer, Thomas F. 1986. "Arms Race and War Initiation: Some Alternatives to the Intriligator-Brito Model." *Journal of Conflict Resolution* 30,1:1–28.

McCloskey, Donald M. 1983. "The Rhetoric of Economics." *Journal of Economic Literature* 21:481–517.

McGuire, Martin 1965. *Secrecy and the Arms Race*. Cambridge: Harvard University Press.

McKelvey, Richard D. 1976. "Intransitivities in Multidimensional Voting Models and Some Implications for Agenda Control." *Journal of Economic Theory* 12:472–82.

———. 1986. "Covering, Dominance, and Institution-free Properties of Social Choice." *American Journal of Political Science* 30:283–314.

McKelvey, Richard D., and Richard Niemi. 1978. "A Multistage Game Representation of Sophisticated Voting for Binary Procedures." *American Journal of Political Science* 18:1–22.

McKelvey, Richard D., and Norman Schofield. 1986. "Structural Instability of the Core." *Journal of Mathematical Economics* 15:179–98.

———. 1987. "Generalized Symmetry Conditions at a Core Point." *Econometrica* 55:923–33.

McPhee, William, and W. Glaser, eds. 1962. *Public Opinion and Congressional Elections*. Glencoe, Ill.: Free Press.

McPhee, William. 1963. *Formal Theories of Mass Behavior*. Glencoe, Ill.: Free Press.

Meadows, Donella H., Dennis L. Meadows, Jörgen Randers, and William W. Behrens. 1972. *Limits to Growth*. New York: Universe Books.

Mefford, Dwain. 1984. "Formulating Foreign Policy on the Basis of Historical Analogies: An Application of Developments in Artificial Intelligence." Paper presented at the International Studies Association, Atlanta.

———. 1985a. "Changes in Foreign Policy across Time: The Logical Analysis of a Succession of Decision Problems Using Logical Analogies: An Application of Developments in Artificial Intelligence." In *Dynamic Models of International Conflict*, Michael Don Ward and Urs Luterbacher, eds. Boulder: Reinner.

———. 1985b. "Inducing Decision Diagrams from Historical Cases: The Implementation of a Scenario-Based Reasoning System." Paper presented at the Merriam Seminar, University of Illinois.

———. 1986a. "What Morton Kaplan Wanted To Do, and Should Have Done: Balance of Power as a Rule-Based System." Paper presented at the International Studies Association, Anaheim.

———. 1986b. "Using Political Narratives to Structure Decisions and Games: The Design for an Expert System Shell." Paper presented at the International Studies Association, Anaheim.

———. 1987a. "The Cognitive Elements of a Theory of Foreign Policy: Part I." Paper presented at the American Political Science Association, Chicago.

———. 1987b. "Analogical Reasoning and the Definition of the Situation: Back to Snyder for Concepts and Forward to Artificial Intelligence for Method." In *New Directions in the Study of Foreign Policy*, Charles F. Hermann, Charles W. Kegley, Jr., and James N. Rosenau, eds. Boston: Allen and Unwin.

———. 1989. "Case-Based Reasoning, Legal Reasoning and the Study of Politics." Mimeo, Dept. of Political Science, Ohio State University.

Mertins, Jean-François, and Shmuel Zamir. 1985. "Formulation of Bayesian Analysis for Games with Incomplete Information." *International Journal of Game Theory* 14:1–29.

McGinnis, Michael. 1986. "Issue Linkage and the Evolution of International Cooperation." *Journal of Conflict Resolution* 30,1:141–70.

Midlarsky, Manus I. 1984. "Preventing Systemic War." *International Studies Quarterly* 28, 4:563–84.

———. 1986. "A Hierarchical Equilibrium Theory of Systemic War." *International Studies Quarterly* 30, 1:77–106.

———. 1970. "Mathematical Models of Instability and a Theory of Diffusion." *International Studies Quarterly* 14:60–84.

———. 1978. "Analyzing Diffusion and Contagion Effects: The Urban Disorders of the 1960's." *American Political Science Review* 72:996–1008.

———. 1981. "Equilibrium in the Nineteenth-Century Balance of Power System." *American Journal of Political Science* 25:270–96.

———. 1983. "Absence of Memory in the Nineteenth-Century Alliance System." *American Journal of Political Science* 27:762–84.

———. 1986. *The Disintegration of Political Systems: War and Revolution in Comparative Perspective*. Columbia: University of South Carolina Press.

Midlarsky, Manus I., Martha Crenshaw, and Fumihiko Yoshida. 1980. "Why Violence Spreads: The Contagion of International Terrorism." *International Studies Quarterly* 24:262–98.

Miller, Gary, and Terry Moe. 1983. "Bureaucrats, Legislators, and the Size of Government." *American Political Science Review* 77:297–322.

Miller, Gary. 1989. "Managerial Dilemmas: Political Leadership in Hierarchies." John M. Olin School of Business, Washington University, St. Louis.

Miller, Nicholas R. 1977. "Graph Theoretical Approaches to the Theory of Voting." *American Journal of Political Science* 21, 4:769–803.

———. 1980. "A new solution set for tournaments and majority voting." *American Journal of Political Science* 24:68–96.

Mintz, Alex. 1986. "Arms Imports as an Action-Reaction Process: An Empirical Test of Six Pairs of Developing Nations." *International Interactions* 12,3:229–44.

Mintz, Alex, and Philip A. Schrodt. 1987a. "A Conditional Probability Analysis of Regional Interactions in the Middle East." *American Journal of Political Science* 32,1:217–30.

———. 1987b. "Distributional Patterns of Regional Interactions in the Middle East and Europe." In *Interaction and Communication in the Global Arena*, Claudio Cioffi-Revilla, Richard L. Merritt, and Dina Zinnes, eds. Beverly Hills: Sage.

Mitchel, C.R., and Michael Nicholson. 1983. "Rational Models and the Ending of Wars." *Journal of Conflict Resolution* 27, 3:495–520.

Moe, Terry M. 1984. "The New Economics of Organization." *American Journal of Political Science* 28:739–77.

Morrow, James D. 1985. "A Continuous Outcome Expected Utility Theory of War." *Journal of Conflict Resolution* 29, 3:473–502.

———. 1986. "A Spatial Model of International Conflict." *American Political Science Review* 80, 4:1131–50.

———. 1987. "On the Theoretical Basis on a Measure of National Risk Attitudes." *International Studies Quarterly* 31, 4:423–38.

Most, Benjamin, and Harvey Starr. 1980. "Diffusion, Reinforcement, Geopolitics and the Spread of War." *American Political Science Review* 74:932–46.

Myerson, Roger B. 1978. "Refinements of the Nash Equilibrium Concept." *International Journal of Game Theory* 8:73–80.

———. 1985. "Bayesian Equilibrium and Incentive Compatability: An Introduction." In *Social Goals and Social Organization: Essays in Memory of Elisha Panzer*, Leon Hurwicz et al., eds. Cambridge: Cambridge University Press.

Nash, John F. 1950. "Equilibrium Points in n-Person Games." *Proceedings of the National Academy of Science* 36:48–49.

Nelson, Charles R., and Heejoon Kang. 1984. "Pitfalls in the Use of Time as an Explanatory Variable in Regression." *Journal of Business and Economic Statistics* 2:73–82.

Newell, Allen, and Herbert Simon. 1972. *Human Problem Solving*. Englewood Cliffs, N.J.: Prentice-Hall.

Nilsson, Nils J. 1980. *Principles of Artificial Intelligence*. Palo Alto: Tioga Publishing.

Niou, Emerson M.S., and Peter C. Ordeshook. 1986. "Balance of Power in International Systems." *Journal of Conflict Resolution* 30, 4:685–715.

———. 1987. "Preventive War and the Balance of Power." *Journal of Conflict Resolution* 31:387–419.

———. 1989. "The Geographical Imperatives of the Balance of Power in 3-Country Systems." *Mathematical and Computer Modelling* 12:519–31.

Niskanen, William. 1971. *Bureaucracy and Representative Government*. Chicago: Aldine.

Oliva, T.A., M.H. Peters, and H.S.K. Murthy. 1981. "A preliminary empirical test of a cusp catastrophe in the social sciences." *Behavioral Science* 26: 153–62.

Olinick, Michael. 1979. *An Introduction to Mathematical Models in the Social and Life Sciences*. Reading, Mass.: Addison-Wesley.

O'Neill, Barry. 1986. "Arms Races and War Initiation." *Journal of Conflict Resolution* 30, 1:33–50.

Ordeshook, Peter C. 1986. *Game Theory and Political Theory*. Cambridge: Cambridge University Press.

Ordeshook, Peter C., and Thomas Schwartz. 1987. "Agendas and the control of political outcomes." *American Political Science Review* 81:179–99.

Ordeshook, Peter C., and Thomas R. Palfrey. 1988. "Agendas, strategic voting, and signaling with incomplete information." *American Journal of Political Science* 32:441–66.

Owen, Guillermo. 1982. *Game Theory*. Second ed. New York: Academic Press.

Palfrey, Thomas R. 1984. "Spatial Equilibrium with Entry." *Review of Economic Studies* 51:139–56.

Palfrey, Thomas R., and Howard Rosenthal. 1985. "Voter Participation and Strategic Uncertainty." *American Political Science Review* 79:62–78.

Parkinson, F. 1977. *The Philosophy of International Relations*. Beverly Hills: Sage.

Perutz, M.F. 1978. "Hemoglobin Structure and Respiratory Transport." *Scientific American* 239:97–105.

Phillips, Warren R. 1987. "Alternative Futures in the Middle East: The Results from Three Simulations." In *Artificial Intelligence and National Security*, Stephen Cimbala, ed. Lexington, Mass.: Lexington Books.

Plott, Charles. 1967. "A Notion of Equilibrium and its Possibility Under Majority Rule." *American Economic Review* 57:787–806.

Polya, Georg. 1962. *Mathematical Discovery*. New York: John Wiley.

Powell, Robert. 1987. "Crisis Bargaining, Escalation, and MAD." *American Political Science Review* 81:717–36.

———. 1988. "Nuclear Brinksmanship with Two-Sided Incomplete Information." *American Political Science Review* 82:155–78.

Prieditis, Armand. 1987. *Analogica: Proceedings of the First Workshop on Analogical Reasoning*. Los Altos: Kaufmann.

Przeworski, Adam, and Michael Wallerstein. 1982. "The Structure of Class Conflict in Democratic Capitalist Societies." *American Political Science Review* 76, 2:215–38.

Przeworski, Adam, and John Sprague. 1986. *Paper Stones: A History of Electoral Socialism*. Chicago: University of Chicago Press.

Rapoport, Anatol. 1957. "Lewis F. Richardson's Mathematical Theory of War." *Journal of Conflict Resolution* 1:249–99.

Richardson, Lewis F. 1919. *Mathematical Psychology of War*. Oxford: William Hunt.

———. 1960a. *Arms and Insecurity: A Mathematical Study of the Causes and Origins of War*. Pittsburgh: Boxwood Press.

———. 1960b. *Statistics of Deadly Quarrels*. Pittsburgh: Boxwood Press.

Riker, William, and Peter C. Ordeshook. 1968. "The Calculus of Voting." *American Political Science Review* 62:25–42.

Riker, William. 1980. "Implications from the Disequilibrium of Majority Rule for the Study of Institutions." *American Political Science Review* 74: 432–46.

———. 1982. *Liberalism against Populism: A Confrontation between the Theory of Democracy and the Theory of Social Choice.* San Francisco: W.H. Freeman.

Rivers, Douglas. 1988. "Heterogeneity in Models of Electoral Choice." *American Journal of Political Science* 32:737–57.

Roemer, John E. 1981. *Analytical Foundations of Marxian Economic Theory.* Cambridge: Cambridge University Press.

———. 1982. *A General Theory of Exploitation and Class.* Cambridge: Harvard University Press.

———, ed. 1986. *Analytical Marxism.* Cambridge: Cambridge University Press.

Romer, Thomas, and Howard Rosenthal. 1978. "Political Resource Allocation, Controlled Agendas, and the Status Quo." *Public Choice* 33:27–43.

Saaty, Thomas. 1968. *Mathematical Models of Arms Control and Disarmament.* New York: John Wiley.

Sanjian, Gregory S. 1988a. "Arms Export Decision-Making: A Fuzzy Control Model." *International Interactions* 14, 3:243–66.

———. 1988b. "Fuzzy Set Theory and U.S. Arms Transfers: Modeling the Decision-Making Process." *American Journal of Political Science* 32, 4:1018–46.

Sankoff, David, and Joseph B. Kruskal, eds. 1983. *Time Warps, String Edits and Macromolecules: The Theory and Practice of Sequence Comparison.* New York: Addison-Wesley.

Saperstein, Alvin M., and Gottfried Mayer-Kress. 1988. "A Nonlinear Model of the Impact of SDI on the Arms Race." *Journal of Conflict Resolution* 32, 4: 636–70.

Schank, Roger C. 1987. "What is AI, Anyway?" *AI Magazine* 8:59–65.

Schelling, Thomas C. 1960. *The Strategy of Conflict.* Oxford: Oxford University Press.

———. 1971. "Dynamic Models of Segregation." *Journal of Mathematical Sociology* 1:143–86.

———. 1978. *Micromotives and Macrobehavior.* New York: W.W. Norton.

Schofield, Norman. 1978. "Instability of Simple Dynamic Games." *Review of Economic Studies* 45:575–94.

———. 1989. "Smooth social choice." *Mathematical and Computer Modelling,* 12:417–34.

Schofield, Norman, Bernard Grofman, and Scott L. Feld. 1988. "The Core and the Stability of Group Choice in Spatial Voting Games." *American Political Science Review* 82:198–211.

Schrodt, Philip A. 1981. "Conflict as a Determinant of Territory." *Behavioral Science* 26,1:37–50.

———. 1984. "Artificial Intelligence and International Crisis: An Application of Pattern Recognition." Paper presented at the American Political Science Association, Washington, D.C., August.

———. 1985a. "Precedent-Based Logic and Rational Choice: A Comparison." In *Dynamic Models of International Conflict*, Michael Don Ward and Urs Luterbacher, eds. Boulder: Reinner.

———. 1985b. "The Role of Stochastic Models in International Relations Research." In *Theories, Models and Simulations in International Relations*, Michael Don Ward, ed. Boulder: Westview.

———. 1987a. "Pattern Matching, Set Prediction and Foreign Policy Analysis." In *Artificial Intelligence and National Security*, Stephen Cimbala, ed. Lexington, Mass.: Lexington Books.

———. 1987b. "Classification of Interstate Conflict Outcomes using a Bootstrapped CLS Algorithm." Paper presented at the International Studies Association, Washington.

———. 1989. "Short Term Prediction of International Events Using a Holland Classifier." *Mathematical and Computer Modelling* 12:589–600.

———. 1990. "Pattern Recognition of International Event Sequences: A Machine Learning Approach." In *Artificial Intelligence and International Relations*, Valerie Hudson, ed. Boulder: Westview.

Schrodt, Philip A., Dina A. Zinnes, and John V. Gillespie. 1977. "Parameter Estimation by Numerical Minimization Methods." *International Interactions* 4:279–301.

Schrodt, Philip A., and Michael Don Ward. 1981. "Statistical Inference in Incremental and Difference Equation Formulations." *American Journal of Political Science* 25:815–32.

Selten, Reinhard. 1975. "Reexamination of the Perfectness Concept for Equilibrium Points in Extensive Games." *International Journal of Game Theory* 4:25–55.

Shepsle, Kenneth A. 1979. "Institutional Arrangements and Equilibrium in Multidimensional Voting Models." *American Journal of Political Science* 23:27–60.

Shepsle, Kenneth A., and Barry R. Weingast. 1984. "Uncovered Sets and Sophisticated Voting Outcomes with Implications for Agenda Control." *American Journal of Political Science* 28:49–74.

———. 1987. "The Institutional Foundations of Committee Power." *American Political Science Review* 81:85–104.

Shupe, M.C., W.M. Wright, K.W. Hipel, and N.M. Fraser. 1980. "The Nationalization of the Suez Canal—A Hypergame Analysis." *Journal of Conflict Resolution* 24,4:477–93.

Simaan, M., and J.B. Cruz. 1975. "Formulation of Richardson's model of the arms race from a differential game viewpoint." *Review of Economic Studies* 42:67–77.

Simon, Herbert. 1954. "Mathematical Modelling." In *Mathematical Thinking in the Social Sciences*, Paul Lazarfeld, ed. New York: Free Press.

Singer, J. David, and Melvin Small. 1972. *Wages of War*. New York: John Wiley.

Snyder, Glenn H., and Paul Diesing. 1977. *Conflict Among Nations*. Princeton: Princeton University Press.

Spear, Stephen E., and Sanjay Srivastava. 1987. "On Repeated Moral Hazard with Discounting." *Review of Economic Studies* 54:599–671.

Stokes, Donald E. 1963. "Spatial Models of Party Competition." *American Political Science Review* 57:368–77.

Stokes, Donald E., and Gudmund R. Iverson. 1966. "On the Existence of Forces Restoring Party Competition." In *Elections and the Political Order*, Angus Campbell et al., eds. New York: John Wiley.

Stoll, Richard J. 1987. "System and State in International Politics: A Computer Simulation of Balancing in an Anarchic World." *International Studies Quarterly* 31, 4:387–402.

———. 1982. "Let the Researcher Beware: The Use of the Richardson Equations to Estimate the Parameters of a Dyadic Arms Acquisition Process." *American Journal of Political Science* 26, 1:77–89.

Sylvan, Donald A., and Steve Chan, eds. 1984. *Foreign Policy Decision Making: Perception, Cognition and Artificial Intelligence*. New York: Praeger.

Sylvan, Donald A., Ashok Goel, and B. Chandresekaran. 1988. "An Information Processing Model of Japanese Foreign and Energy Policy Decision Making: JESSE." Paper presented at the International Studies Association, St. Louis.

Tanaka, Akihiko. 1984. "China, China Watching and CHINA-WATCHER." In *Foreign Policy Decision Making: Perception, Cognition and Artificial Intelligence*, Donald A. Sylvan and Steve Chan, eds. New York: Praeger.

Taylor, Michael. 1976. *Anarchy and Cooperation*. London: John Wiley.

———. 1987. *The Possibility of Cooperation*. Cambridge: Cambridge University Press.

Thorson, Stuart, and Donald A. Sylvan. 1982. "Counterfactuals and the Cuban Missile Crisis." *International Studies Quarterly* 26:537–71.

Tullock, Gordon. 1981. "Why So Much Stability?" *Public Choice* 37:189–205.

Ulmer, S.S. 1982. "Supreme Court Appointments as a Poisson Distribution." *American Journal of Political Science* 26, 1:113–16.

Vasquez, John A. 1976. "Statistical Findings in International Politics." *International Studies Quarterly* 20:171–218.

Von Neumann, John, and Oskar Morgenstern. 1944, 1947. *Theory of Games and Economic Behavior*, first and second edition. Princeton: Princeton University Press.

Wallis, W.A. 1936. "The Poisson Distribution and the Supreme Court." *Journal of the American Statistical Association* 31:376–80.

Ward, Michael D. 1984. "Differential Paths to Parity: A Study of the Contemporary Arms Race." *American Political Science Review* 78:297–317.

———, ed. 1985. *Theories, Models and Simulations in International Relations.* Boulder: Westview Press.

Ward, Michael Don, and Urs Luterbacher, eds. 1985. *Dynamic Models of International Conflict.* Boulder: Reinner.

Wilkenfeld, Jonathon. 1972. "Models of the Analysis of Foreign Conflict Behavior of States." In *Peace, War and Numbers*, Bruce Russett, ed. Beverly Hills: Sage.

Williams, J.D. 1954. *The Compleat Strategyst.* New York: Dover.

Winston, Patrick Henry. 1984. *Artificial Intelligence.* Second edition. Reading, Mass.: Addison-Wesley.

Wittman, Donald. 1983. "Candidate Motivation: A Synthesis of Alternate Theories." *American Political Science Review* 77:142–57.

Zadeh, Lotfi A., King-Sun Fu, Kokichi Tanaka, and Masamichi Shimura. 1975. *Fuzzy Sets and Their Application to Cognitive and Decision Processes.* New York: Academic Press.

Zinnes, Dina A. 1976. *Contemporary Research in International Relations.* New York: Free Press.

———. 1984. "An Event Model of Conflict Interaction." In *Conflict Processes and the Breakdown of International Systems*, Dina A. Zinnes, ed. Denver: University of Denver Monograph Series in World Affairs.

Zinnes, Dina A., J.L. Zinnes, and R.D. McClure. 1972. "Markovian Analysis of Hostile Communications in the 1914 Crisis." In *Crisis in Foreign Policy Decision Making*, Charles F. Hermann, ed. New York: Free Press.

Zinnes, Dina A., and John V. Gillespie, eds. 1976. *Mathematical Models in International Relations.* New York: Praeger.

Zinnes, Dina A., John V. Gillespie, Philip A. Schrodt, G.S. Tahim, and R. Michael Rubison. 1978. "Arms and Aid: A Differential Game Analysis." In *Exploring Competitive Arms Processes*, W.L. Hollist, ed. New York: Marcel Decker.

Zinnes, Dina A., and Robert G. Muncaster. 1984. "Hostile Activity and the Prediction of War." *Journal of Conflict Resolution* 28(2):187–203.

6

Gender Politics, Gendered Politics: The State of the Field

Virginia Sapiro

We reached a turning point in the study of gender in political science about twenty years ago. Earlier, gender was raised occasionally as a secondary and peripheral theme in political research. It was only rarely a primary focus of political research (Breckinridge 1933; Merriam and Gosnell 1924; Duverger 1955).

The rise of the new women's movement in the late 1960s affected many women (especially) in political science as it affected many women in other academic fields—as, indeed, it affected women throughout society. It brought gender into focus, and made people ask questions where previously there had been only assumptions. Within a few years a literature on women and politics began to develop, including a cottage industry of critiques of the gendered assumptions that underlay much of political research (Bourque and Grossholtz 1974; Elshtain 1979; Evans 1980; Goot and Reid 1975; Jaquette 1974; Keohane 1981; Morgan 1974; Sapiro 1979, 1987). Although the specific arguments of these pieces vary in theory and method, they share a common charge: where political scientists have claimed (or implied) gender neutrality in their work, they were wrong.

Many observers of the growth of women's studies within different disciplines have remarked on the path of development it seems to take (Andersen 1987; Schuster and Van Dyne 1984; Tetrault 1985). In the first phase in which women become at all visible, they are merely added

I would like to thank Barbara Bardes, Barbara Nelson, Joan Tronto, and Graham Wilson for their comments.

165

to old problems and questions—a phase often known within women's studies as "add women and stir."[1] In this phase a common research strategy is to take old research problems and strategies, and check to see whether the answer is different when we compare women and men, or look at women where we have been looking at men. This phase can also be viewed as "compensatory scholarship," in which we fill in the obvious gaps resulting from ignoring women. Most of us have done some of this work. The most obvious example of this approach in political science is simply to add controls for sex or look for gender differences in phenomena (such as turnout rates or partisanship) that have been studied before or to review political philosophers of the canon (Aristotle, Locke, Mill, Marx) to see what they said about women.

During the first phase of the development of feminist studies, gender may become a variable, and women a topic of research, but the models, methods, language, and theories remain by and large intact. They are still derived from scholarly practices informed almost exclusively by the experience of a gender-segregated and male-centered world.[2]

In the second phase we learn more directly from women and their experiences, less mediated by androcentrism. There is more attention to the gender-specific context of women's lives, to their subjectivity, to the things they have done and thought and felt that most men may have been unaware of. In political science this means, for example, investigating women's political activity not just in the arenas, organizations, and channels in which men most commonly participate, but in those where we find relatively few men. It means taking seriously the possibility— the probability—that in a social world in which there are deep gender divisions of labor and considerable gender segregation, if we have understood women and politics almost exclusively through androcentric frames, we are likely to get a lot wrong.

A third phase takes a shifted frame and looks beyond women. At this stage we criticize not just particular theories or assumptions as they have been applied to women, but as they are constructed and apply in any case.[3] As many people have argued, and I shall below, our very understanding of the meaning of *the political* may change as a result of what we learn through a shifted, gendered focus. Whereas in the earlier phases of the development of gender studies, many people believe we can become *gender-neutral*, either by eliminating gender as a structuring principle or by balancing the androcentric view with a newer gynocentric view, many scholars have come to believe the point is to take *gender-informed* stances, becoming reflexive in understanding the role that gender (including that of the observer) plays.[4]

The task of examining the state of the field in gender politics is therefore an ambiguous mission. It must include an assessment of issues and problems in the scholarly community of people who study women and politics. At the same time, there is no subfield of political science, conventionally understood, in which we do not find gender studies, and few areas in which there is nothing to say about gender. There has undoubtedly been more attention to gender in political behavior and political theory than in international relations and methodology, but to assess the whole field of gender or women and politics is to assess the whole discipline of political science. We need to look at the state of the field defined by those of us who focus on gender and politics. But we also need to look at the study of politics more generally, to evaluate both the incorporation of gender into political research, and its exclusion.

The remainder of this paper, therefore, identifies six important themes or problems in gender politics. Because, for reasons just discussed, I cannot cover the whole field,[5] I have used four criteria in selecting my themes. First, each of these strikes me as a central question both for political scientists interested in gender politics and for those who are not. They are problems worth tackling in order to learn about gender and politics, but for those who are not specialists in gender politics they serve as handles to larger questions. Second, each is broadly conceived, and can be investigated in a variety of ways on different specific objects of study. Third, these problems are still in early stages of research development within political science. Some, in fact, are better developed in related disciplines. Fourth (in order once again to deny comprehensiveness), they are questions in which I happen to be interested; not the only questions, I hasten to add, but some of them.

PROBLEM 1: IDENTITY POLITICS

Feminist scholars have returned repeatedly to Simone de Beauvoir's questions, "Are there women, really?" and "What is a woman?" (de Beauvoir 1952: xv). The definition of woman (multiple meanings of *definition* intended) has long been a central and framing preoccupation of feminist scholars and theorists. During an earlier phase of feminist writing, for example, the transcendentalist Margaret Fuller entitled her now most famous essay "The Great Lawsuit: Man *versus* Men; Woman *versus* Women," and not *Woman in the Nineteenth Century*, as her publisher apparently demanded (Fuller 1971).[6] Her original title implied a distinction between a cultural construction, myth, or ideal (man and woman) and actual, live, existent people (men and women). Most feminist theorists, psychologists, historians, and others today would generally see Fuller's contrast as only a first glimmering of the problem, and de Beauvoir's focus on situation, myth, and justification as much further down the road.

One of the tasks feminist scholars share across the disciplines—from literary theory to experimental psychology—is probing the definitions and constructions of sex, gender, and sexuality at all levels, from the cultural-linguistic to the social and institutional to the microprocesses of individual psychology. Political scientists should play important roles in these debates and investigations. The processes by which these categorizations are developed, maintained, and applied involve power, conflict, and other values any political scientists would accept as within our domain. Governmental institutions play crucial roles in the process (Gordon 1988a; Rifkin 1980; Sapiro 1986).

Although there are many routes one could take with this theme in political science, here I wish to emphasize the political psychology of identity as one particular take on the question of gender definition and politics. We can begin with a classic question of political socialization: How do individuals become formed into social and, ultimately, political beings? How, during the course of individuals' lives, do they incorporate into their own identity a sense—and any given *particular* sense—of relationship to other individuals, other people as part of social formations, and abstractions such as particular social groups, religions, and nations?

Notice that here I leave aside political socialization research that merely examines gender differences in political outlook and behavior over time to determine whether and at what pace females and males become similar or different political beings. Rather, I am focusing on the development of gender identity itself, and how initial self-identification as female or male becomes connected with other social and political significance. The question here is not simply whether and how women and men, on average, think or act differently (although that is an interesting question), but whether and how understanding of one's own and others' gender incorporates political content. Is politics at the individual level mediated through gender as it is through other types of identity, at least in some circumstances, such as nationality, partisanship, race, class, and religion?

Research on gender consciousness has begun to enrich our understanding of gender identity and politics (Conover 1988; Gurin 1985; Kalmuss, Gurin, and Townsend 1981; Klein 1984; Miller, Gurin, Gurin, and Malanchuk 1981). Research on the individual *development* of gender consciousness has not moved as far (Chapman 1987; Sapiro 1990). Part of this effort must involve probing the development of schemas that incorporate both gender and politics. Gender schemas are important in structuring people's perception and behavior (Frable 1989; Frable and Bem 1985). How and under what circumstances does politics become a part of or related to that identity? Focusing on this problem not only offers more sophisticated and conceptually powerful

access to questions of gender, political behavior, and political orientations, but also turns our attention to basic building blocks of selfhood
including, presumably, political selfhood.

Ultimately, the importance of understanding this political psychology of gender is the degree to which it helps to reveal the process of
mobilization of social identity and consciousness for political action.
Political science has long been marked by an interest in group-based
politics, but the psycho-dynamics of political mobilization are still not
well enough understood. What is the process by which and the conditions under which individuals' social identity becomes politicized?

Nancy Cott, in her splendid history of the women's movement in the
1910s and 1920s, identified a problem in the political mobilization of
women on the basis of gender politics that remains important today
(Cott 1987). Feminism rested on a claim that the fact that women share
gender gives them shared political interests. Women face certain
problems that need to be addressed through politics and, for the solving
of those problems, their shared gender takes primacy over other types of
identities and characteristics that may divide them. As she pointed out,
giving gender primacy in the organization of one's political outlook is
more likely for women whose other social characteristics and identifications are not equally or more apt to be identified as the source of oppression. In other words, gender-based politics is more likely to be central for
women whose other links to social groups would put them in privileged
positions, were it not for their sex. As Cott goes on to say, however:

> Nonetheless, that perception of "womanhood" as defining one's iden-
> tity has, at times in history, galvanized women of diverse sorts, and it
> has been the essential element of coalitions based on sex solidarity.
> [Cott 1987: 9]

Our question is why? Under what circumstances? How can one form of
identity not just "galvanize" people across diversity, but across forms of
diversity that are themselves bases of inequality and domination? What
form of gender consciousness can coalesce people who are also divided
by race, class, religion, age, or other grounds?[7]

Diversity among women, and its relationship to identity, consciousness, and political mobilization is one of the most prominent themes in
contemporary women's studies. Diversity is usually treated as an issue
among people as individuals, groups, or institutions. The question is,
How can diverse individuals be brought together in political relations?
Work on this question is far from complete. But political psychology
should also lead us to look at diversity, consciousness, and mobilization
as an issue *within* individuals. The question here is, How do socially complex individuals develop and use any kind of group consciousness?

Gender is widely regarded as less politically relevant than, for example, class or race. Indeed, many class- and race-based interest groups (as well as others) have taken pains to point out that gender politics is a "divisive" issue and in any case irrelevant to their (class- or race-based) group. This raises the question of politically relevant identity conflicts within individuals. Everyone "has" gender, race, class, age, national heritage, as well as a host of other identifications that may potentially become a part of political consciousness and serve as a point of political mobilization. What are the conditions of political consciousness-raising and mobilization given not just plural societies, but complex individuals (King 1988)?

PROBLEM 2: PERSONAL AND POLITICAL, PUBLIC AND PRIVATE

One of the ubiquitous themes of the study of women and politics is the distinction and relationship between the personal and political, the private and public. A number of feminist works discuss the historical development of the public-private split and the relegation of women and things "feminine" to the private and domestic world as distinct from the public, political world (Elshtain 1981; Landes 1988). Others also tackle the gendered relationship between public and private, political and personal, but focus on the crucial role that government has played in regulating sexuality and gender (Gordon 1988b; Petchesky 1984). Many have investigated the relationship between women's private roles and their political orientations and behavior (Sapiro 1983; Carroll 1984). Many writers (especially historians) have argued that because women have been defined as private and nonpolitical, we have missed seeing their political activity and influence even where it existed.

Although this theme has received considerable attention among students of women and politics, there is much left to do. In addition, while this theme holds perhaps the greatest potential contribution to the wider study of politics, as of yet it has had little serious impact on the discipline as a whole, in part because it requires substantial rethinking of the basic terms of politics.

As many scholars have pointed out, our definitions of public and private are historically created (Davidoff and Hall 1987; Elias 1978; Landes 1988). We have been able to define women as less political than men in part by defining politics around men's experiences, and not looking elsewhere. This has given the compensatory mode of scholarship plenty of room to grow; even where women were taking part and even leading in politics as it is conventionally defined, they have been ignored, forgotten, or trivialized until very recently.

Feminist scholars have also argued that just as there have been forms or locations of political activity that have been heavily male-segregated (including all the most powerful and public forms), so there are forms or locations of political activity that have been heavily female-segregated (such as, most obviously, feminist movements). The argument is not just that this political activity has been ignored because it involves women, but that it has sometimes been defined as something other than political activity, as in the case of some of women's community activism. If we exclude from our lens political activity that has been female-dominated, we may well be excluding not just *quantities*, but also *qualities* of political action. If, as we know, men and women act differently depending on whether they are in gender-segregated or -integrated situations, if we never focus on women in female-dominated situations, we may be missing something distinctive and very important.

Participants in the study of women and politics seem almost inevitably drawn to the question, What do we define as political and why? The "defining we" I am referring to is a double one. First is the "we" referring to scholarly and cultural observers and critics. With some exceptions, political scientists have defined the internal power dynamics of nongovernmental institutions and social relationships as out of our territory, even when those dynamics are shaped or regulated in part by government, and in turn may have important effects on political relationships more conventionally understood and even public policy.

When political scientists look at the family, they tend to see a corporate unit that produces new citizens, or a corporate unit that is the object of public policy. In fact the family is a unitary entity with pure common interest only in traditional common-law theory (i.e., in legal fiction). A more accurate picture shows divisions of labor and interest that have important political implications (Hartmann 1981). It is not just that there is not enough political analysis of private institutions and relationships. Because the family is the most obviously important institution involved in the creation and maintenance of gender, a reluctance to analyze the family as a political institution inhibits our ability to investigate the relationships between sex/gender systems and political systems.[8] This in turn weakens our ability to see the relationship between politics and the political system and people's day-to-day personal lives.

I am not arguing—and few feminist theorists within political science would argue—that a reexamination of the definition of the political means we should accept in any simple way the rhetorical device "the personal is political" as an utterly unbounded term. The point is that "the political," like other political concepts, is a historically, situationally, and *politically* shaped entity deserving of scholarly attention and analysis as such (Ball, Farr, and Hanson 1988). Because gender is so closely related to public-private distinctions, we have reason to suspect that gender politics plays a role in this definitional process.

Reopening the definition of the political returns us to some of the questions suggested in the context of Problem 1. It has long been said that women's political orientations and behavior are shaped by their private—that is, everyday—familial and work roles. For some years considerable research, based primarily on survey research, looked for relationships between parental or employment status and political behavior and attitudes. More recently some discussion, largely theoretical, has focused more on structuring principles of political morality and decision-making first suggested by Carol Gilligan's (1982) discussion of the rights/justice and obligation/care principles of morality, corresponding, she argued, to male and female voices. Although the evidence for these claims has been mixed, there is still good reason to investigate associations between people's most absorbing social relationships and activities, and their political orientations (e.g., Andersen and Cook 1985; Sapiro 1983).

A crucial framing question remains unanswered: Under what circumstances do people understand their personal situations in political terms? When do they see problems in their daily lives as stemming from public, communal, political decisions? Under what circumstances do people begin to define solutions for their problems in public, communal, political terms? It is true that scholars have approached parts of this question from very different points of view. The social movement literature is relevant, as is research on economic interests and voting behavior (Feldman 1982; Lau and Sears 1981; Weatherford 1983). Research on gender and sexuality offers particularly important cases for investigation because it focuses on aspects of life that have been so thoroughly regarded as private even while they are state-regulated in many respects (Hanmer and Saunders 1984; de Monteflores and Schultz 1978).

The history of women's political action includes fascinating examples of people who were probably very thoroughly socialized to believe that politics was something for other people but not themselves, who became politically mobilized on the basis of problems that were very clearly personal: feeding their families (Frank 1985). It also contains examples of people who engaged in political activity without necessarily defining that activity as political, and people whose apparently private and personal behavior was very evidently political (Jones 1985). This observation leads to another question that should be important not just for the study of gender politics but for the study of politics more generally: What difference does it make if people do or don't define their actions as political? What, in the end, is the meaning of politics to people, and what are the political implications of political subjectivity?

PROBLEM 3: THE POWERS OF THE UNPOWERFUL

It is no news to political scientists that power and its varietal forms is an important and complicated subject. Although all of us would agree that it is one of the most central concepts—if not the key concept—in the discipline, we still disagree among us about its meaning.

Observers of women and politics are particularly aware of and interested in relations of domination and political inequality, for obvious reasons, but they also have long had an appreciation for the *complexity* of and special issues raised by the nature of power within these types of relationships. At an early stage in the development of women's studies, scholars tended to emphasize the power disparity between women and men to the exclusion of all complicating issues. The result was a subfield that often seemed to have as its main theme the victimization of women. A number of scholars wrote critiques of this emphasis (Johansson 1976; Lerner 1976). As Lerner pointed out, using victimization or oppression as our central themes leaves us in the mold of androcentrism, valuing only those things that men and not women do or are. Even where there is victimization and domination, there may be something other than pure brute passivity.

Women have not held anything close to an equitable share of positions of political power, and especially authority. Women have been treated more as subjects than as citizens in many respects. But at the same time, women have found ways to have influence, even if it has not been recognized or remembered, and they have found ways of surviving and even asserting themselves even while their options and resources have been severely limited by conditions of patriarchal domination.[9] Many times women have worked within women's space, or networks that are female-segregated either by women's choice or not ("Communities of Women" 1985; Cook 1977; Freedman 1979; Ryan 1979; Ware 1981). Although one of the major objects of feminist political activity is influencing male-dominated institutions, including governmental institutions, a large proportion of feminist political activity—probably the majority—takes place within female space because it is aimed at influencing women and mobilizing them.

Some feminist observers of women's situation have also noted another problem of power within domination relationships: the powers exerted by the dominated against the dominant. As long ago as 1792, Mary Wollstonecraft, in her *Vindication of the Rights of Woman*, discussed the types of "unjust" powers used by women (Wollstonecraft 1975). Her argument, in brief, was that relationships based on inequality and domination are corrupting, and lead both parties to use power in an abusive fashion. In women's case, she observed, because women are left no resources but beauty and the fact that they are regarded as sexual objects, they use beauty and sexuality as their resources:

> Exalted by their inferiority (this sounds like a contradiction), they constantly demand homage as women, though experience should teach them that the men who pride themselves upon paying this arbitrary insolent respect to the sex, with the most scrupulous exactness, are most inclined to tyrannize over, and despise the very weakness they cherish. [Wollstonecraft 1975:145]

The powers of the weak are probably used most often for saving lives and dignity, for that is what is threatened when one is part of a dominated group. Power cannot be based on the same resources, or be used in the same fashion, for the weak and the strong (Janeway 1980). The powers of the weak is an important topic for further investigation, and not just by students of gender politics.

Women's studies scholars have also remarked many times on what might be considered the inverse of the powers of the weak: the dependencies of the strong. Those in power develop special kinds of dependencies; they depend, for example, on subordinates to carry out the tasks the powerful do not want to do themselves. They depend on others staying "in their place." Moreover, in certain kinds of power relations the powerful depend upon the subordinate for self-esteem. Men are still expected to marry someone younger than they are and someone whose job achievement will not "threaten" (that is, equal or better) their own. Given the dominant cultural expectations, it is something of an achievement for a man to retain his self-esteem if his wife has a higher-status job or better pay than he has. One can argue that it is in part this *dependence* of men on women's dependence and subordination that has motivated social policy that subordinates women; the power they have wielded is only the *mechanism* (Sapiro 1986).

PROBLEM 4: AMBIVALENT STATES

Is it best for the state to be loved or feared? Feminist theory and political action serves as a major and provocative case study of one of the most important dilemmas of political community and government. Because of the nature of the problems that feminism addresses, feminists have not had the luxury of being able to rest on one side or another of debates over the benefits or ills of an active state. The combination of issues that feminists address simultaneously lead them to have to grapple with both at once.

It is no wonder that feminist activists have long been in the forefront of demands for an affirmative state. Because of the various effects of their roles as mothers, their segregation into helping professions, the special forms of violence inflicted against them, and their disproportionate share of the nation's poverty, among other things, feminists have been strong advocates of expansion of the state's efforts to provide for and protect the health and welfare of the citizens, and especially those least powerful to provide for and protect themselves. Women played key roles in designing the directions of social welfare policy in the 1920s and New Deal era, and many did so at least in part with explicit grounding in gender consciousness (Hoff-Wilson and Lightman 1984; Lemons 1973; Nelson 1990; Ware 1981). The contemporary women's movement, and its various associated political organizations, have certainly taken consistent positions on the side of active government roles in health care and other social welfare provision, as well as urging active intervention in the labor market through antidiscrimination policy. It has also supported government intervention in social relations through policies against gender-based violence.

At the same time, feminists have had plenty of reason to refrain from regarding government intervention as an unmitigated good. Probably the vast majority of feminist political writing over the last two centuries has been devoted to showing the ills of governmental action. Indeed, much of the emphasis of feminist political writing has been to show how governmental interference in women's relationships, behavior, and opportunities has served to maintain women in subordinate position. Public policy has been based on enforcing a preference for segregation of women in domestic and auxiliary roles. Even when government has appeared to come to the aid of women through social policy, many feminists argue, the structure of the policy is still based on gender segregation and ultimately, female dependence (Gordon 1988a; Nelson 1984; Sapiro 1986). Certainly the history of women's battle for control over reproduction and access to their bodies exhibits awareness of confrontation between feminist definitions of women's interests and government regulation of individual behavior (Gordon 1974; Petchesky 1984).

Just as feminism has long been identified with the pursuit of governmental solutions such as rights and equality legislation, so is there a long and profound tradition of rejection of strategies aimed at change through governmental and conventional political institutions. One reason is that historical experience has shown women that government is not a neutral tool that can be used equally to anyone's advantage. Government is not independent of the values of the political community even if some decisions may occasionally offend public opinion, and in an androcentric society government cannot be an entirely trustworthy friend of women. From protective legislation to the most recent interpretations of the *Roe* and *Doe* abortion cases, decisions originally hailed as steps forward for women often end up being used to limit them in new ways. Protective legislation protected women out of jobs. The 1973 abortion cases have been used to justify making fetuses wards of courts, putting government, in the apparent interest of the fetus, in an adversarial legal position against the pregnant woman. The painful debates within the feminist movement over pornography are based in part on ambivalence over what can be left to government protection with what degree of safety.

Feminist theory as well as historical research on gender questions and political institutions and policy provide fruitful ground for returning to perennial questions about the relationship of the ends and processes of government. In careful study of feminist movements we can find case studies of decision-making through basic dilemmas of the weak seeking solutions through the strength of governmental authority, of people seeking individual freedom through communal action. Studying government through a feminist lens does not allow easy answers to questions over whether turning to government is "good" or "bad." Even in the process of constructing active social policy and community-based support systems, feminist political experience should lead us immediately to considering the possibility—rarely attained—of nonpatriarchal and nonpaternalistic forms.

PROBLEM 5: GENDERED STATES

Once upon a time most feminist observers seemed to assume that government was basically a gender-neutral tool that could be used, and generally was used, in gender-based ways. Feminist political theory based in liberalism tended to argue that the problem with government as it was constructed was that rights and democratic procedures were simply not extended far enough. The changes required to incorporate women as full citizens would be difficult to achieve, but were, theoretically speaking, not radical changes. Gender is not, in any direct sense, a part of the basic structure of a political system. Likewise, although feminist political theory based in Marxism called for radical changes in political structure, it has tended to define gender systems as derivative of production and ownership systems. Class is a direct part of the structure of the political system, but gender is not. Divergent theories, including feminist ones, regarded politics as such as gender-neutral in an important sense.

The influence of radical feminism, language-based theories of politics, and some psychological theory has led some feminist theorists to move gender and gender structures to center stage, not to replace other principles of social structure, but not as mere derivative either.

We need not see explicit mention of "male" or "female" in a term to understand the gender basis or associations of the term. When one is asked, for example, to list "women's policy issues," the list almost invariably includes family issues, including almost anything having to do with children. "Family problems" or "child care" are not women's issues because there is any explicit referent to women in the terms; rather, they are women's issues even though men too are in families and have children, because historically we have come to associate women, families, and children together. Many concepts that are apparently gender-neutral on the face do, in fact, have gender-based meaning to most people within a given culture.[10]

Politics is certainly one of those terms that has gendered meaning. Politics is masculine and the associated words most people probably think of most quickly—power, conflict, war, decision-making, corruption, competition—are masculine words. The problem of women and politics is not simply that women have been excluded from specific activities or arenas, but that politics itself has gender. But immediately upon saying this, it is important to add another twist: certain aspects of politics are regarded as feminine, even if it is still men who hold the most authoritative positions. Social welfare and education are feminine.

Some of the most interesting recent work on gender and politics investigates the historical path of the gendering of politics and specific forms of politics such as republicanism (Bloch 1987; Elshtain 1981; Kerber 1980; Landes 1988; Pitkin 1984). Studies of the gendered meaning of the ultimate "masculine" political institutions and process, defense agencies, and war are intriguing (Elshtain 1987; Cohn 1987). These are not just studies of women's involvement in defense policy and activities, although those are important as well. Rather, this type of work criticizes any simple notion, shared by many feminists and non-feminists alike, that war is a property of men, or at least that maleness is a property of war. The importance of these questions involves not just understanding women's relationship to politics, but asking what these aspects of politics mean to us as gendered people in a gendered society. Likewise, many feminist scholars have become involved in asking how we come to regard some aspects of politics as feminine, and what that means to a political community as a whole (Tronto 1987).

Cultural definitions of the health and normality of specific personality characteristics and patterns of behavior in people are gender-based. What is defined as health for women and men is different (for a review, see Sapiro 1990a). The body politic and its component parts are also gendered, so much so that metaphors of gender can replace serious political reflection with scripts constructed by androcentric gender ideology. The literature developing in this field suggests that assessments of the health and appropriateness of characteristics of the political system depend on the gender of the part we are discussing. Just as aggression, competition, and toughness are regarded as characteristics of healthy men but not women, so they are regarded as normal and healthy characteristics of politics. Candidates, for example, who act otherwise are "wimps": not masculine enough. Stereotypic views of women's peace orientation are not just viewed as alternative viewpoints that should be represented at the highest levels in a pluralistic democratic system, but as inappropriate, unhealthy, irrational (overidealistic) stances toward something as masculine as defense and foreign policy.

Feminist theorists and activists have devoted considerable effort to attempting to construct visions of political organization and action that are alternatives to what many have defined as masculine ways. They argue (in very different ways) that feminists, in reconceptualizing the stereotypic masculine virtues of competition, aggression, toughness, abstracted rational decision-making as not necessarily normal, have a lot to contribute to democratic theory and practice (Bunch 1987a; Dietz 1985, 1987; Elshtain 1982; Hooks 1989). A good example of this type of exercise is Mansbridge's *Beyond Adversary Democracy*, which, although not presented as feminist analysis, is very much an example of the tradition (Mansbridge 1980). The point is not that there is anything essentially masculine or feminine about different modes of political organization and process, but like notions of masculinity and femininity themselves, they are shaped and understood through historical processes and language.

PROBLEM 6: BRINGING HISTORY BACK

After a period of virtual exclusion of history from the study of political institutions, processes, and behavior, we are now witnessing a renewed interest in history. In many areas of political inquiry scholars are coming to the conclusion that snapshots, especially those without any time referents, are not the best pictures and most informative pictures of politics. The study of women and politics is certainly beginning to benefit in many ways from the work of historians and from historical studies by political and other social scientists.

Historical research and the grounding of political research in history serves a most important purpose in gender studies. One of the most insidious myths is that gender is as it always was (except, perhaps, for recent changes), as are the family and family roles, or constructions of sexuality. Gender, the family, the structure of private life and sexuality are all at least in part historically constructed (Davidoff and Hall 1987; Russett 1989; Weeks 1981). The result is an awareness that aspects of life that are usually culturally defined as natural, eternal, and essential are in fact the result of processes not just of evolutionary changes, but of conflict and negotiation, often explicitly political debate. We can certainly witness this process in current political arguments over family and sexual policy.

One very important area of inquiry is gender and policy history. Those of us who have taught women and politics become very aware that a common conception of gender and history is that once upon a time (in the olden days) women's roles were very restrictive, and law and policy did not allow women to do much of anything. Then, when Western democracies were invented, and especially in the United States, women "were given" or "were granted" more rights, beginning with the vote in 1920, and then continuing with everything else in the last twenty years. This development seems to be understood as natural and even inevitable because of the Enlightenment-based rule of history: things used to be very bad because people were parochial and not well informed, and things have gotten much better because we are more modern and enlightened.

Two crucial points (at least) are missing here. First, women were not just "granted" or "given" rights, any more than any social group was just given or granted important changes in their political status. These changes involved political conflict and strategic political action. Second, the path of policy history is not a straight line from restriction to enlightenment but rather, a much more interesting and complex process of change (for examples, see Petchesky 1984; Pleck 1989; Sapiro 1984).

A related point is that historical studies of law and policy, especially when developed in social and political context, are revealing the important role that gender plays in political life. A number of scholars are arguing, for example, that the particular development of the social welfare state in the United States depended not just on the politics of class formations, but also on gender as a basic part of the structure of society (Abramowitz 1988; Gordon 1988a; Nelson 1984; Sapiro 1986).

Another role that historical study is playing is to expand our understanding of women's political involvement. There is an especially interesting literature on women's movements and feminisms that does much more than simply fill in the gaps in women's political action. It restores a large, missing sector to our understanding of political action per se (Berg 1978; Becker 1981; Cott 1987; DuBois 1978; Evans 1979; Freeman 1975). In addition, however, historical studies offer a critical handle on expanding our understanding of political activity, and women's political activity in particular, outside the channels of political activity most commonly investigated.

The importance of bringing history back in does not mean just focusing more on the past. It does not mean attempting to "write history." Indeed, some feminist historians, while applauding the greater use of historical materials in other disciplines, remark on the problems raised as those of us not trained in historiography and historical methods press ahead nevertheless (Offen 1989). Rather, the point is that even those of us who spend most of our time investigating the present and perhaps especially those of us who focus to a large degree on the microprocesses of politics, need to maintain a more profound sense of the historical context and forces at work in our field of view. This is something that is particularly rare, for example, in the study of political behavior.

A final, but perhaps most important problem of history for the construction of future research on gender politics concerns the uses of traditions of political theory. The literature on feminist theory and women and political theory is now massive. Much of it, especially in political science, is devoted to critical analysis of the treatment of gender questions or women specifically in the work of particular historical traditions, periods, or figures.

Feminist theory is not simply a critique of the past. Many people have worked in a self-conscious way to develop feminist theory as an approach that can be used to understand politics. This effort seems inevitably to involve reviewing traditions of theory to find the sources of distinctively feminist frameworks. Many theorists attempt to build very directly from specific schools or traditions of thought, working to build a feminist socialism, a feminist psychoanalysis, a feminist poststructuralism/postmodernism, or other versions.

An interesting problem of history in all this is the degree of self-consciousness among theorists engaging in this feminist reconstruction of their relationship to the tradition that is feeding them and to the goal for which they are striving. The problem of traditions is linked to its root meaning, *to hand over*, presumably from one generation to the next.

There are two possible meanings of the handing over in feminist theory. One is that the feminist theorist takes what is given and tries to adapt it to feminist purposes. The other is that in the process of developing feminist theory the theorist is informed by the traditions, but is much more active in choosing what one shall accept from the package that is handed over. Too often feminist theorists seem to accept what has been handed over for the sake of inheriting the name, as in "liberal feminist" or "socialist feminist" or "postmodern feminist." Keeping someone else's name may not be worth it, depending on what baggage is handed over at the same time. Many years ago Charlotte Bunch observed the pressure to be true to categorizations and compartmentalizations of theory and called for a "nonaligned feminism" (Bunch 1987b). Her point remains important, and not just for political theorists. The problem for feminist scholars who break from or criticize tradition is that they may be regarded as committing intellectual treason. Indeed, *tradition* and *treason* are derived from the same root.

CONCLUSION

The state of the field of gender politics is that we began in earnest less than twenty years ago and now have a literature of hundreds of articles, scores of books, a journal, and an organized section of the American Political Science Association. Some areas of inquiry have been worked very thoroughly, such as women and voting behavior and political recruitment of women.[11] There is much more work on U.S. politics than on gender in other area studies. At the other end of the scale, there is relatively little research on women and politics that attempts real cross-cultural comparison (for exceptions, see Christy 1987; Haavio-Mannila et al. 1985; Jennings 1983; Lovenduski 1986; Meehan 1985; Randall 1987).

I have attempted to identify a few themes and problems that seem to "work" in a number of different specific areas of inquiry. These assessments are directed in two directions: the state of gender studies among those of us who specialize in the area and the significance of gender studies in political inquiry regardless of one's specific specialization. The list I have constructed is necessarily partial. There are many areas of inquiry I have not even touched. I have not even mentioned some of my favorite pieces of past research.

One overriding conclusion is that the study of women and politics has far exceeded many initial expectations. One early suspicion has not been fulfilled: this has not been a minor exercise in filling small gaps. Rather, we have found increasingly as time has gone on, that focusing on the relationship between gender and politics alters our understanding of both.

NOTES

1. In describing these phases I do not imply they follow a clear chronological sequence either across or, indeed, within individuals.

2. On gender and the practice of research, particularly in the sciences, see Eichler 1988; Harding 1986.

3. This is one of the reasons why many of us are not entirely sure what the best title for our field is. "Women's studies" implies that the object of study is women, which is not always the case. "Gender studies" may be used to indicate what it is about women but also men, social institutions, processes, and so forth, we are interested in. "Feminist studies" indicates both the historical generation of the field and also a body of theory.

4. For empirical evidence, see, for example, Eagly and Carli 1981; Lyons and Serbin 1986.

5. My own research and teaching leads me to spend the most time with

relevant work in political psychology, political theory, and policy, and these primarily with a U.S. focus. Even that would provide too much ground to be covered in anything resembling a comprehensive fashion.

6. They're like that, aren't they?

7. Many theorists have been tackling this problem in recent years including especially Bunch 1987a; Hooks 1984, 1989; Rich 1979.

8. "Sex/gender system" is a term parallel to "political system" or "economic system." The term was first developed in Rubin 1975.

9. I share with many feminist theorists a dislike of the term "patriarchal" when used to describe any and all androcentric sex/gender systems. Here, however, I am referring to historical patriarchal relations.

10. I discuss the gendered meanings of apparently neutral terms further in Sapiro 1990, ch.9.

11. I do not mean to say there is nothing left to do.

REFERENCES

Abramowitz, Mimi. 1988. *Regulating the Lives of Women*. Boston: South End.

Andersen, Kristi, and Elizabeth Cook. 1985. "Women, Work, and Political Attitudes." *American Journal of Political Science* 29:606–25.

Andersen, Margaret L. 1987. "Changing the Curriculum in Higher Education." *Signs* 12:222–54.

Ball, Terence, James Farr, and Russell Hanson, eds. 1988. *Political Innovation and Conceptual Change*. New York: Cambridge University Press.

de Beauvoir, Simone. 1952. *The Second Sex*. New York: Knopf.

Becker, Susan D. 1981. *The Origins of the Equal Rights Amendment: American Feminism between the Wars*. Westport, Conn.: Greenwood.

Berg, Barbara J. 1978. *The Remembered Gate: Origins of American Feminism*. New York: Oxford University Press.

Bloch, Ruth H. 1987. "The Gendered Meanings of Virtue in Revolutionary America." *Signs* 13:37–58.

Bourque, Susan C., and Jean Grossholtz. 1974. "Politics as an Unnatural Practice: Political Science Looks at Female Participation." *Politics and Society* 4: 255–66.

Breckinridge, Sophinisba. 1933. *Women in the Twentieth Century: A Study of their Political, Social, and Economic Activities*. New York: McGraw-Hill.

Bunch, Charlotte. 1987a. *Passionate Politics: Feminist Theory in Action*. New York: St. Martin's Press.

———. 1987b. "Beyond Either/Or: Nonaligned Feminism." In *Passionate Politics*. New York: St. Martin's Press: 46–60.

Carroll, Susan. 1984. *Women as Candidates in American Politics*. Bloomington: Indiana University Press.

Chapman, Jenny. 1987. "Adult Socialization and Out-Group Politicization: An Empirical Study of Consciousness-raising." *British Journal of Political Science* 17:315–40.

Christy, Carol A. 1987. *Sex Differences in Political Participation: Processes of Change in Fourteen Nations*. New York: Praeger.

Cohn, Carol. 1987. "Sex and Death in the Rational World of Defense Intellectuals." *Signs* 12:687–718.

"Communities of Women." 1985. A symposium in *Signs* 10:633–740.

Conover, Pamela J. 1988. "The Role of Social Groups in Political Thinking." *British Journal of Political Science* 18:51–76.

Cook, Blanche W. 1977. "Female Support Networks and Political Activism: Lillian Wald, Crystal Eastman, Emma Goldman." *Chrysalis* 3:43–61.

Cott, Nancy. 1987. *The Grounding of Modern Feminism*. New Haven: Yale University Press.

Davidoff, Leonore, and Catherine Hall. 1987. *Family Fortunes: Men and Women of the English Middle Class, 1750–1850*. Chicago: University of Chicago Press.

Dietz, Mary. 1985. "Citizenship with a Feminist Face: The Problem with Maternal Thinking." *Political Theory* 13:19–35.

———. 1987. "Context Is All: Feminism and Theories of Citizenship." *Daedalus* 116:1–24.

DuBois, Ellen. 1978. *Feminism and Suffrage*. Ithaca: Cornell University Press.

Duverger, Maurice. 1955. *The Political Roles of Women*. Paris: UNESCO.

Eagly, Alice H., and L.L. Carli. 1981. "Sex of Researchers and Sex-Typed Communications as Determinants of Sex Differences in Influenceability: A Meta-analysis of Social Influence Studies." *Psychological Bulletin* 90:1–20.

Eichler, Magrit. 1988. *Nonsexist Research Methods: A Practical Guide*. Winchester, Mass.: Allen and Unwin.

Elias, Norbert. 1978. *The History of Manners*. New York: Pantheon.

Elshtain, Jean Bethke. 1979. "Methodological Sophistication and Conceptual Confusion: A Critique of Mainstream Political Science." In Julia Sherman and Evelyn Beck, eds., *The Prism of Sex: Essays in the Sociology of Knowledge*. Madison: University of Wisconsin Press: 229–52.

———. 1981. *Public Man, Private Woman: Women in Social and Political Thought*. Princeton: Princeton University Press.

———. 1982. "Feminist Discourse and its Discontents: Language, Power, and Meaning." *Signs* 7:603–21.

———. 1987. *Women and War*. New York: Basic Books.

Evans, Judith. 1980. "Attitudes to Women in American Political Science." *Government and Opposition* 15.

Evans, Sara. 1979. *Personal Politics: The Roots of Women's Liberation in the Civil Rights Movement and the New Left*. New York: Vintage.

Feldman, Stanley. 1982. "Economic Self-Interest and Political Behavior." *American Journal of Political Science* 26:446–66.

Frable, Debra E.S. 1989. "Sex-Typing and Gender Ideology: Two Facets of the Individual's Gender Psychology That Go Together." *Journal of Personality and Social Psychology* 56:95–108.

Frable, Debra E.S., and Sandra L. Bem. 1985. "If You Are Gender Schematic, All Members of the Opposite Sex Look Alike." *Journal of Personality and Social Psychology* 49:459–68.

Frank, Dana. 1985. "Housewives, Socialists, and the Politics of Food: The 1917 New York Cost-of-living Protests." *Feminist Studies* 11:255–86.

Freedman, Estelle. 1979. "Separatism as Strategy: Female Institution Building and American Feminism." *Feminist Studies* 5:512–29.

Freeman, Jo. 1975. *The Politics of Women's Liberation*. New York: Longman.

Fuller, Margaret. 1971. *Woman in the Nineteenth Century*. New York: W.W. Norton

Gilligan, Carol. 1982. *In a Different Voice*. Cambridge: Harvard University Press.

Goot, Murray, and Elizabeth Reid. 1975. *Women and Voting Studies: Mindless Matrons or Sexist Scientism?* Beverly Hills: Sage.

Gordon, Linda. 1974. *Woman's Body, Woman's Right: A Social History of Birth Control in America*. Baltimore: Penguin.

———. 1988a. "What Does Welfare Regulate?" *Social Research* 55:609–30.

———. 1988b. *Heroes of Their Own Lives*. New York: Viking.

Gurin, Patricia. 1985. "Women's Gender Consciousness." *Public Opinion Quarterly* 49:143–63.

Haavio-Manilla, Elina, et al., eds. 1985. *Unfinished Democracy: Women in Nordic Politics*. New York: Pergamon.

Hanmer, Jalna, and Susan Saunders. 1984. *Well-Founded Fear: A Community Study of Violence to Women*. London: Hutchinson.

Harding, Sandra. 1986. *The Science Question in Feminism*. Ithaca: Cornell University Press.

Hartmann, Heidi. 1981. "The Family As the Locus of Gender, Class, and Political Struggle: The Example of Housework." *Signs* 6:366–94.

Hoff-Wilson, Joan, and Marjorie Lightman. 1984. *Without Precedent: The Life and Career of Eleanor Roosevelt*. Bloomington: Indiana University Press.

Hooks, Bell. 1984. *Feminist Theory: From Margin to Center*. Boston: South End.

———. 1989. *Talking Back: Thinking Feminist, Thinking Black*. Boston: South End.

Janeway, Elizabeth. 1980. *Powers of the Weak*. New York: Morrow.

Jaquette, Jane S. 1974. "Introduction: Women in American Politics." In J.S. Jaquette, ed., *Women in Politics*. New York: John Wiley.

Jennings, M. Kent. 1983. "Gender Roles and Political Inequalities in Political

Participation: Results From an Eight-Nation Study." *Western Political Quarterly* 36:364–85.

Johansson, Sheila R. 1976. " 'Herstory' as History: A New Field or Another Field?" In B. Carroll, ed., *Liberating Women's History*. Urbana: University of Illinois Press: 400–430.

Jones, Jacqueline. 1985. *Labor of Love, Labor of Sorrow: Black Women, Work, and the Family from Slavery to the Present*. New York: Basic Books.

Kalmuss, Deborrah, Patricia Gurin, and Aloen Townsend. 1981. "Feminist and Sympathetic Feminist Consciousness." *European Journal of Social Psychology* 11:131–47.

Keohane, Nannerl. 1981. "Speaking from Silence: Women and the Science of Politics." In Elizabeth Langland and Walter Gove, eds., *A Feminist Perspective in the Academy: The Difference It Makes*. Chicago: University of Chicago Press: 86–100.

Kerber, Linda K. 1980. *Women of the Republic: Intellect and Ideology in Revolutionary America*. Chapel Hill: University of North Carolina Press.

King, Deborah K. 1988. "Multiple Jeopardy, Multiple Consciousness: The Context of a Black Feminist Ideology." *Signs* 14:42–72.

Klein, Ethel. 1984. *Gender Politics*. Cambridge: Harvard University Press.

Landes, Joan B. 1988. *Women and the Public Sphere in the Age of the French Revolution*. Ithaca: Cornell University Press.

Lau, Richard, and David Sears. 1981. "Cognitive Links between Economic Grievances and Political Responses." *Political Behavior* 3:279–302.

Lemons, Stanley. 1973. *The Woman Citizen: Social Feminism in the 1920s*. Urbana: University of Illinois Press.

Lerner, Gerda. 1976. "Placing Women in History: A 1975 Perspective." In B. Carroll, ed., *Liberating Women's History*. Urbana: University of Illinois Press: 349–56.

Lovenduski, Joni. 1986. *Women and European Politics: Contemporary Feminism and Public Policy*. Boston: Northeastern University Press.

Lyons, Judith A., and Lisa A. Serbin. 1986. "Observer Bias in Scoring Boys' and Girls' Aggression." *Sex Roles* 14 (March): 301–13.

Mansbridge, Jane J. 1980. *Beyond Adversary Democracy*. New York: Basic Books.

Meehan, Elizabeth M. 1985. *Women's Rights at Work: Campaigns and Policy in Britain and the United States*. London: Macmillan.

Merriam, Charles, and Harold Gosnell. 1924. *Nonvoting*. Chicago: University of Chicago Press.

Miller, Arthur, Patricia Gurin, Gerald Gurin, and Oksana Malanchuk. 1981. "Group Consciousness and Political Participation." *American Journal of Political Science* 25:494–511.

de Monteflores, Carmen, and Steven J. Schultz. 1978. "Coming Out: Similarities and Differences for Lesbians and Gay Men." *Journal of Social Issue* 34: 59–72.

Morgan, Jan. 1974. "Women and Political Socialization: Fact and Fantasy in Easton and Dennis and in Lane." *Politics* 9:50–55.

Nelson, Barbara. 1984. "Women's Poverty and Women's Citizenship: Some Political Consequences of Economic Marginality." *Signs* 10:209–31.

———. 1990. "The Gender, Race, and Class Origins of Early Welfare Policy and the Welfare State: A Comparison of Workmen's Compensation and Mothers' Aid." In Louise Tilly and Patricia Gurin, eds., *Women, Change, and Politics*. New York: Basic Books.

Offen, Karen. 1989. "The Use and Abuse of History." *Women's Review of Books* 6:15–16.

Petchesky, Rosalind P. 1984. *Abortion and Women's Choice*. New York: Longman.

Pitkin, Hannah F. 1984. *Fortune Is a Woman*. Berkeley: University of California Press.

Piven, Francis F., and Richard Cloward. 1988. "Welfare Doesn't Shore Up Traditional Family Roles: A Reply to Gordon." *Social Research* 55:631–48.

Pleck, Elizabeth H. 1989. *Domestic Tyranny: The Making of American Social Policy against Family Violence from Colonial Times to the Present*. New York: Oxford.

Randall, Vicky. 1987. *Women and Politics*. Chicago: University of Chicago Press.

Rich, Adrienne. 1979. *On Lies, Secrets, and Silence: Selected Prose, 1966–1978*. New York: W.W. Norton.

Rifkin, Janet. "Toward a Theory of Law and Patriarchy." *Harvard Women's Law Journal* 3:83–96.

Rubin, Gayle. 1975. "The Traffic in Women: Notes on the 'Political Economy' of Sex." In Rayna Reiter, ed., *Toward an Anthropology of Women*. New York: Monthly Review Press: 157–210.

Russett, Cynthia E. 1989. *Sexual Science: The Victorian Construction of Womanhood*. Cambridge: Harvard University Press.

Ryan, Mary P. 1979. "The Power of Women's Networks: A Case Study of Female Moral Reform in Antebellum America." *Feminist Studies* 5:66–85.

Sapiro, Virginia. 1979. "Women's Studies and Political Conflict." In J. Sherman and E. Beck, eds., *The Prism of Sex: Essays in the Sociology of Knowledge*. Madison: University of Wisconsin Press: 253–66.

———. 1983. *The Political Integration of Women: Roles, Socialization, and Politics*. Urbana: University of Illinois Press.

———. 1984. "Women, Citizenship, and Nationality: Immigration and Naturalization Policies in the United States." *Politics and Society* 13:1–26.

———. 1986. "Gender and Social Policy." *Political Science Quarterly* 101: 221–38.

———. 1987. "What Research on the Political Socialization of Women Can Tell Us about the Political Socialization of People." In C. Farnham, ed.,

The Impact of Feminist Research in the Academy. Bloomington: Indiana University Press: 148–73.

――――. 1990a. *Women in American Society*. Mountain View: Mayfield.

――――. 1990b. "The Women's Movement and the Creation of Gender Consciousness: Social Movements as Socialization Agents." In O. Ichilov, ed., *Political Socialization, Citizenship Education, and Democracy*. New York: Teachers College Press.

Schuster, Margaret, and Susan Van Dyne. 1984. "Placing Women in the Liberal Arts: Stages of Curriculum Transformation." *Harvard Educational Review* 54 (November): 413–28.

Tetrault, Mary K.T. 1985. "Feminist Phase Theory." *Journal of Higher Education* 56 (July/August): 363–84.

Tronto, Joan. 1987. "Beyond Gender Difference to a Theory of Care." *Signs* 12: 644–64.

Ware, Susan. 1981. *Beyond Suffrage: Women and the New Deal*. Cambridge: Harvard University Press.

Weatherford, M. Stephen. 1983. "Economic Voting and the 'Symbolic Politics' Argument: A Reinterpretation and Synthesis." *American Political Science Review* 77:158–74.

Weeks, Jeffrey. 1981. *Sex, Politics, and Society: The Regulation of Sexuality since 1800*. New York: Longman.

Wollstonecraft, Mary. 1975. *Vindication of the Rights of Woman*. Baltimore: Penguin.

7

Paradigms and Paradoxes: Political Science and African-American Politics

Michael C. Dawson and Ernest J. Wilson, III

THE CURRENT STATUS OF THE FIELD

When writing an essay on the future of a controversial field in contemporary politics, it is helpful to gain perspective by taking a step or two back and pretending that one is a visitor from long ago and far away, like Alexis de Tocqueville. Such an acute observer, looking at the study of politics and race in contemporary America, might discover several disturbing paradoxes. First, while the place of race in the *practice* of American politics is, arguably, quite central (Carmines and Stimson 1989; Kinder et al. 1989; Huckfeldt and Kohfeld 1989), the place of race in the *study* of American politics is surprisingly peripheral. Second, if our returned French observer read widely in the social sciences, he would discover that while race is indeed central to politics (and hence should be central to the work of political scientists), there is more intellectual segregation by race in political science then in its sister disciplines of history and sociology (E. Wilson 1985). Third, after a close and careful reading of the relevant texts our visitor would also discover that black and white political scientists tend to produce different kinds

The authors wish to thank the following for their helpful comments on earlier drafts of this paper: Lucius Barker, Robert Brown, Cathy Cohen, Donald Culverson, Kimberly James, Mack Jones, Donald Kinder, Diane Pinderhughes, Steve Rosenstone, Jocelyn Sargent, Todd Shaw, and Ronald Walters. Any errors of fact or interpretation are our own.

of scholarship when studying black politics, even when they use the same theoretical model.

These three findings about the study of race—within political science; between political science and other disciplines; and between black and white political scientists—emerge quite clearly from our critical evaluation of the field of black politics. Curiously, we began the essay with another question in mind—that is, how different social science paradigms analyze black politics. Still, the findings are no less valid for being somewhat unanticipated.

In this essay we examine major themes and models in the field, and suggest new directions that the field might take over the coming decade. However, this is decidedly not a review of all major and minor works in the field. (Indeed, we devote less attention to individual authors and books than we would in a conventional essay.) Instead, we are concerned with explicating the underlying logic of theories of politics and identifying themes or issues that will be important in the years ahead. But, before we take up these theories or models of politics, let us return briefly to the paradoxes of centrality of race in politics and the marginalization of black politics within political science.

Some scholars have argued persuasively that the politics of racial conflict and antagonism has reshaped the American party system. From the local level (in cities such as Chicago and Philadelphia) to the national level, racial politics has helped to elect several conservative presidents, including the most conservative Democratic and Republican presidents since the Depression. Scholars of race and American politics are now beginning to examine the role of race in realigning party and class politics within the United States (Carmines and Stimson 1989; Huckfeldt and Kohfeld 1989). Students of the politics of race (such as Alexis de Tocqueville, Gunnar Myrdal, Robert Dahl, Dianne Pinderhughes, and Jennifer Hochschild) in many different generations have used racial politics as the prime lens to show the dark side of American democracy. Profound public policy questions such as slavery, civil rights, welfare reform, the professionalization of the military, health care, and the viability of urban economy and society are all intimately tied to the politics of racial attitudes and behavior.

Further, many scholars of African-American politics such as Adolph Reed (1986), Michael Preston (1987), Ronald Walters (1988), Paul Kleppner (1985), and Rufus Browning and his associates (1984) claim that there has been a profound change in black politics, which they have labeled "the new black politics." Jesse Jackson's campaign for president is an empirical example of the importance of the shift from protest to electoral politics for the American polity as a whole.

But the politics of race and black politics are hardly studied within American politics. The major journals usually do not feature articles on the subject. Black politics is marginalized too in graduate studies programs, in American politics textbooks, and in the research priorities of agencies like the National Science Foundation.

In addition to the paradox of the centrality of black politics and its marginalization in the discipline, there are rather paradoxical differences between the treatment of African-American materials in political science and in other disciplines. In his 1985 article in *PS*, Wilson presents quantitative and qualitative evidence demonstrating that in its treatment of black materials political science consistently ranks third behind sociology and history (E. Wilson 1985). His analysis of "all journal materials (articles, book reviews, research notes, etc.) published between 1977 and 1985 on or about African-Americans in three leading journals in each of the three disciplines that concern us," shows political science with the lowest absolute number of entries and lowest percentage of black to white subject entries. Furthermore, black subjects accounted for only 16 percent of all Ph.D. dissertation topics between 1979 and 1984, the lowest of the three fields. But far more important than merely counting dissertations or journal entries is the higher visibility and status African-American materials enjoyed in other disciplines. For better or worse, there simply is no equivalent in political science to the scholarly prominence and intellectual impact of books like *Time on the Cross* by Robert W. Fogel and Stanley L. Engerman (1974) in history or William Wilson's *The Declining Significance of Race* (1978) in sociology. We suggest reasons for this below.

The third major finding of our survey of writings in the field is that black and white scholars tend to approach the study of African-American politics in different ways, driven by different research questions and using different methods and evaluative criteria. We were able to extract a set of decision rules and criteria that demonstrate what we call two distinct communities of discourse that cross paradigmatic boundaries. We have two discourses, separate and perhaps unequal, certainly unalike. We return to these epistemological concerns in the conclusion.

The paradoxes we identify are especially critical because the study of African-American politics is at an important historical juncture. The last twenty-five years have witnessed a vast explosion in the scope of African-American politics. These changes are both quantitative and qualitative. Quantitatively, on the positive side, we see a dramatic expansion of the political arena. Twenty-five years ago the single most salient feature of black political life was its near total exclusion, through means official and unofficial, from the formal arenas of political action. Black politics now has gone well beyond the black church and the black voluntary associations like the NAACP and the Urban League. Now the meaning of black politics includes participation in a much wider array of political arenas, at the federal, state, and local levels, including executive, judicial, and legislative bodies.

In addition, while changes have occurred at all levels in the political hierarchy, from mass to elite politics, there have been especially notable changes at the higher levels of American politics. These changes have been both symbolic and substantive. Blacks like Representatives William Gray of Philadelphia and Charles Rangel of Harlem now occupy senior positions in the U.S. House of Representatives. The presidential bid of Jesse Jackson was important in and of itself as an expression of this new elite participation, and because it appeared to have had a galvanizing impact that drew other political aspirants into the fringes of senior levels of the presidential political arena. Ronald Brown's election to head the National Democratic Party reflects this newly emerging elite structure. However, these positive political changes within the elite have been accompanied by more negative changes at the mass level. The growing economic distress of the African-American inner cities has led to a growing political and social disorganization of the black community (Marable 1983; W. Wilson 1987). This is reflected in the serious epidemic of drug use and crime that afflicts African-American communities. Social disorganization is accompanied by a kind of political aimlessness, a drift in the direction of major black groups. We find a kind of deinstitutionalization of some leading organizations. Membership in the NAACP and the National Urban League has dropped precipitously, and other organizations like the Black Panther Party have disappeared altogether. Political weaknesses appear on the black left and center in nationalist organizations and in integrationist ones. Only the black right seems to be on the rise, and then only weakly.

To what extent have social science and social science models kept up with these new, often contradictory, societal and political changes? Here, too, the record of success and failure is quite mixed. On the positive side there has been a considerable increase in the number of works on various aspects of African-American politics. A recent review by Hanes Walton (1988) (shockingly, one of only a few such reviews that we found in the literature) enumerates a number of new works on the expanded scope of participation. Looking at studies published since 1977, he describes, in descending numerical order, new studies on black presidential politics, and on black protest and pressure politics; also on leadership, ideology, black urban politics, followed by electoral studies, judicial studies, and public policy. Conversely, reading the professional journals will reveal a small increase in the treatment of black politics. Still, this new work on various aspects of African-American politics certainly is welcome.

At the same time, one should temper one's enthusiasm by noting several caveats. First, as E. Wilson (1985) argues in his examination of the field, one is starting from a very low base. The sad fact remains that the study of African-American politics still is the stepchild of the discipline. The most recent and authoritative volume on the state of the discipline (Finifter 1983) devotes nineteen chapters to separate studies of topics in political science, including a chapter on gender politics. There is no chapter on race, only a handful of references to race, and only one or two African-American scholars cited for their work on black politics.

Before considering recommendations for future directions the field might take, we turn to its strengths and weaknesses. We identify three major failings. Taken singly, these limitations certainly are not unique to African-American politics, but taken together they do indicate a particular syndrome and unless corrected will limit the possibilities that the field will advance as it should.

First, there is insufficient attention to theoretical models and paradigms as a guide to research and scholarship. This fact comes through very clearly in our readings. There is very little sense in most of the writing that an author is tackling a subject because she or he is driven by challenging theoretical anomalies that need to be resolved. There is a disturbing lack of self-consciousness in the field as to which models or theories might best describe and explain African-American politics. Does a conflict or cooperation model best capture the dynamics of black-black and black-white political interactions? Such issues rarely are raised. (An interesting exception is the "race vs. class" debate of the mid-1970s.) Instead, most studies appear to be driven by a kind of contributionist imperative—that is, the black politics of city X or Y has not yet been described, so the author does so. The same holds for other levels of government and institutions. Certainly, in a relatively young or understudied area new information is valuable and helps push back the frontiers of ignorance. Still, while this is an important reason to study certain aspects of black politics, it is not sufficient to build a mature and dynamic field or to attract top-notch students.

This is not to deny the presence of some good critical work in the field. As we demonstrate below, some authors will level criticisms against particular components of one model, and point out that model's flaws. Not surprisingly, given pluralism's historically reigning position in American political science and the fact that unlike pluralism's current main challenger, social choice theory, pluralist writers have addressed race. Pinderhughes (1987), Hamilton (1973), and Hochschild (1983) have taken pluralism to task over its superficial treatment of racial politics. Standing firmly on the terrain of group interactions, they selectively expand, or redefine and reject, certain aspects of the paradigm in order to make it more applicable to African-American or racial politics. They do not, however, move far from the same theoretical terrain that pluralism calls its own. Instead, they continue to work within a modified form of pluralist analysis. (Contrast this with the probing essay of Manley [1983] who severely criticizes the pluralist model for overlooking such issues as inequality, and tries to reorient political thinking more toward Marxism.) Few who study the field of black politics seem inclined to compare and contrast whole paradigms as distinct theoretical alternatives. This is true even for otherwise contentious authors like Reed (1986) who are quite critical of current practice and theory of black politics, but do not provide explicit alternative theories except implicitly through example (see Willingham in Reed 1986). Part of the problem may be that radical critics like Willingham have not published very much in the major journals of the discipline, and hence their work is less accessible to most readers. Some of this work exists in a samizdat of conference papers that circulate through rather narrow circles. It is also certainly the case that American politics as a subfield suffers more than others (say, comparative politics) from the reluctance to justify paradigmatic or theoretical choices.

A second major weakness is the absence of consistency in the type of methodological approaches and tools necessary to confirm or invalidate theoretical propositions on African-American politics. We find insufficient emphasis on the kinds of appropriate rules of evidence in the work of many political scientists in this area. Formal and multivariate quantitative approaches are almost unknown in this field. It will be difficult to construct and implement sound research programs in black politics without a thorough understanding of the major theoretical and methodological questions that face us. We will continue to be plagued by methodological haphazardness without such research programs to guide our empirical work. This criticism holds for scholars using qualitative models as well as quantitative ones.

Where is the field of African-American politics likely to go in the coming years? What topics will grow in importance? No one can predict this with confidence. The best one can do is to suggest several substantive issues that scholars in the field may wish to tackle in the future. We generate this list of important topics from our understanding of African-American politics, mainstream American political science, and world politics.

1. What is the internal political experience of the African-American community? There is a shortage of sophisticated treatments of the internal political dynamics of African-American communities and populations. Sociologists are producing a fascinating and rapidly growing literature on the sociological dynamics within black communities, especially work on the black underclass. There is less available than we originally thought on political institutions, behaviors, and actors solely or mostly within black communities. This basic knowledge is a prerequisite to both good work on black politics and good comparative work between blacks and whites.

2. What are the political manifestations of social structural changes in African-American communities? What changes have actually oc-

curred in the political life of the black community as a result of new kinds and amounts of social stratification? This seems at first glance to be an empirical question; however, it has been systematically ignored by prevailing paradigms and their mainstream adherents. This suggests it is really an issue of theoretical focus. There has been very good analysis of the raw sociological dimensions of this issue. We have excellent descriptions of these changes (Farley and Allen 1987); we have analyses of particular strata (middle class blacks, Landry 1987; and the underclass, W. Wilson 1987); and we even have some good theorizing by sociologists like William J. Wilson (1978) about the origins of these changed patterns of social stratification. Yet there has been surprisingly little analysis that relates patterns of social transformation to new patterns of politics. For example, what new political behaviors do we find in the black middle class, or the black underclass?

3. What has been the nature of the racial transitions in urban government? What have been the consequences (or shared causes) for economic and political opportunities and constraints?

4. A fourth and related issue is the continued leftward slant and growing political isolation of African-Americans within the American policy. African-Americans not only continue to be the most "liberal" group in American politics, but with the rightward move in the American polity, blacks are more isolated than ever. Black-white attitude differences are on the increase along many dimensions. The evidence for this finding lies in the recent polling data on political attitudes, and in black preferences for national policies and leadership during the last presidential campaign that were far more liberal than those of the white population—a finding that replicates results from the 1960s, 1970s, and 1980s. Stated somewhat differently, how can we account for the attitudinal and behavioral differences between black and white Americans?

5. A fifth area for investigation is the intersection of gender, race, and class in the black community. On the one hand, black women are to some degree concentrated at the bottom of the social structure. On the other hand, their voting rates are higher than for black men. These differences have not been systematically explored or explained. "Typically" it has been argued that lower socio-economic status has been correlated with lower voting rates (see Preston 1987 for a critique of the SES model of political participation and African-Americans).

6. Another tremendously neglected area is the comparative dimension to the study of black politics. How does what we call "racial politics" manifest itself in other national contexts? One should study racial and ethnic conflicts in other postmodern societies, including Europe (east and west). Here one could address such current political concerns as the relationship between the rise of right-wing conservatism and the

political mobilization of ethnic and racial minorities. Ira Katznelson's (1981) brilliant but problematic work on race and politics and urban politics owes much to his comparative breadth.

7. There is a whole series of important public policy questions that are directly or indirectly informed by race that should be addressed and answered. Some work in these areas exists already, but more attention is paid to them by sociologists and economists than political scientists. These include the effects of the shift from manufacturing to a service economy on black politics; crime and drugs; African-Americans and United States foreign policies; and the politics of full employment.

8. Finally, those interested in African-American politics should also explore ways in which the study of African-American politics can enrich the discipline as a whole. Kilson's call for political scientists to look at black politics as an excellent example of differential rates of political mobilization and modernization is one of a few such instances (Kilson 1977).

These eight issues, some emerging, others whose history can be traced back to Bunche and Du Bois, are important in their own right, and they also lend themselves to the kind of reorientation that we suggest—letting theoretical questions drive research, and greater self-consciousness about the kinds of models and methods used by scholars of African-American politics.

THE STUDY OF SOCIAL STRATIFICATION AMONG AFRICAN-AMERICANS

Because we lack the space in this essay to demonstrate how one could go about addressing each of the preceding questions, we select one that touches on many of the issues raised—that of social stratification and its political manifestations. We can think of no more important question for understanding the major dynamics within African-American communities, and between those communities (or individuals or groups) and nonblack individuals, groups, classes, or communities. This is a theoretically important question that touches on many current debates in several disciplines. It is also a theoretically important issue that is central to contemporary public policy debates (i.e., the black underclass). In addition, the subject also illuminates the ways that major contending social science models handle the question of racial politics.

There are a number of commonsense queries that one might make under the heading of the political consequences of social stratification. For example, one might examine the ways in which the leadership of the black communities has changed as a result of social stratification. Under this rubric, one might consider the rise of Jesse Jackson in class terms—

to what extent did Jackson articulate the sentiments of, if he did not actually "represent," the interests of new or reorganized segments of the black community (Reed 1986)? We could also ask whether stratification has changed the content of African-American ideology. For example, if the last twenty to forty years has indeed seen the rise of a new black middle class, several theories would predict the rise of new ideologies or the adoption of more mainstream, formerly "white," ideologies. Did the neoconservatism of Glenn Loury, Thomas Sowell, or Alan Keyes articulate this new ideology, or were they yet another creation of white politicians? Or, as Adolph Reed (1986) suggests, is "affirmative action" the new ideology of the black middle class? Does the black working class still, to the degree it ever did, look to the black middle class for leadership and ideas? Finally, one might also ask whether the forms and forums of political participation have been changed as a result of forty years of fairly rapid stratification? Have working class participation patterns changed? Is there any political significance to the institutionalization of the Congressional Black Caucus' national networks created and sustained through their annual Washington workshops and social events, which each year draw thousands of middle-class blacks to Capitol Hill?

For the following section of the essay we want to emphasize in the strongest possible terms that we have two distinct but related purposes in organizing the material in the way that we have. Our purposes are pedagogical, and they are theoretical and conceptual. As teachers in a field with insufficient material available to the student that evaluates and compares one model after another in a critical way, we feel obligated to proceed in precisely this fashion. As scholars interested in theory building and theory testing, we also feel it important to evaluate alternative models and theories critically. Yet if we were only interested in the latter, and not interested in the pedagogy of the field, we might shorten the following section and move more directly to apply only selected models to the research problem we have identified. However, we do believe that analyzing each model one by one will prove helpful to students when, for example, they prepare for field and qualifying examinations.

SOCIAL SCIENCE PARADIGMS AND AFRICAN-AMERICAN POLITICS

How then do the leading social science paradigms treat racial politics? We use the Kuhnian (Kuhn 1970) sense of paradigm. Shared paradigms include common sets of assumptions, scientific practices and methodologies, foundation works, and a research program that includes both settled questions and agreement on what questions are open for investigation (Kuhn 1970). Racial politics will fit centrally in some paradigms; for others, race will at best fit uneasily as a residual category. In the following sections we examine the ways that leading social science paradigms treat race and racial politics. There are two parts to this exercise: one at the level of the logical structure of the general model; the second, the ways in which the model has been applied to racial politics in actual studies by selected social scientists. At the most general level, we demonstrate how the logical structure of a particular paradigm leads an analyst to structure the problem of racial or black politics in a particular way. The way in which a Marxist will organize an inquiry into black politics will differ from the way a pluralist will do so. In order to compare and contrast the paradigms in the limited space available to us, we simply sketch the outlines of the paradigm, and, using criteria that we selected to bring out critical aspects of African-American politics, we estimate the ways that black politics will be treated within it.

After evaluating the model according to these criteria, we turn to examine the predictions that the model would make about the political consequences of social stratification. Given the kind of social stratification that sociologists tell us has occurred since the Second World War, what kinds of political changes would each paradigm predict? This approach allows us to pinpoint with some confidence the strengths and weaknesses of each of the paradigms. We should be able to identify where more conceptual or empirical work needs to be done. We can thereby evaluate each model and use the best and attempt to combine them in ways that seem to capture more of African-American politics than any single paradigm could capture by itself.

Some paradigms are more likely than others to treat racial politics as an important and serious subject. In all cases, however, we did want to show how the subject matter was handled by the paradigm, even if racial politics was not necessarily central to a paradigm's theoretical concerns. We analyze the following paradigms: Marxism, social choice, Weberian analysis, modernization, and nationalist perspectives.

Pluralism and the Study of African-American Politics

Pluralist theory is the dominant theoretical paradigm in the study of American politics, although it has been challenged in recent years by social choice theory. Pluralist theory has been formally stated and empirically tested in the work of Robert Dahl in the 1950s and 60s. There have been, of course, numerous statements and tests of the theory since Dahl published his formal statement in *Preface to Democratic Theory* (1954), and the study and test of pluralism in the context of urban politics, *Who Governs* (1961). His early statements still serve as a useful expression of the key elements of the pluralist paradigm, particularly as it relates to race and politics.

The core elements include the following. Democracy is a method, according to pluralist theory, which insures that policy selections are as close as possible to the preferences of the majority. Preferences represent the full range of options available in the polity. Each citizen's political preferences are assigned equal weight. Therefore, social and economic inequalities are not cumulative. They do not transfer into the political sphere.

Agendas are open, and citizens can get their preferences on the table for debate and to be voted on. Crosscutting cleavages due to individuals' multiple interests and memberships ensure that no single group becomes organized into a faction that develops such strong interests as to threaten political stability. Elections are instruments of governance whereby individual preferences are aggregated (elections are the highest form of decision). It is assumed that orders of elected officials are executed. This is crucial as political elites are the representatives of the citizens' preferences.

One of the critical problems of democracy is the question of the intensity of conflicting policy preferences. Another major problem identified by Madison in *Federalist 10* is the problem of the tyranny of majority. Simply stated, and of critical importance to the study of racial politics, how does a pluralist democracy accommodate a minority with intense preferences?

What Dahl calls the American hybrid is not a pure pluralist system. He discusses various theorists' answers to the problem presented by the tyranny of the majority and highly polarized groups within a democratic polity. One solution he considered was the system of social checks and balances found in the Constitution. Another often-proposed counterargument is that of overlapping memberships and moral suasion (moral suasion is supposed to work on individuals who belong to groups that contain minorities in other circumstances). Dahl's analysis shows that none of these distributions can guarantee minority rights, and have not in the past, when there have been intensely held and different preferences found in two groups with a bimodal split of the distribution.

Despite his gloomy assessment of the efficacy of the pluralist system, Dahl's key statement concerning pluralist theory and racial politics is "all active and legitimate groups in the population can make themselves heard at some crucial stage in the process of decision" (1961:137). That is to say that groups can punish if politicians are not responsive. Decisions are made through endless bargaining by groups. Therefore black Americans, like all Americans, have access to the system and participate in the bargaining process. We will return to his explicit discussion of what he calls ethnic politics when we make predictions concerning pluralist theory and African-American social stratification.

Students of race and politics and African-American politics work on the same terrain as the classical pluralists but often come to radically different conclusions. Writers such as Dianne Pinderhughes, Linda Williams, Jennifer Hochschild, and Hanes Walton, Jr., examine the bargaining process, the incremental nature of pluralist policy-making, and the ability of African-Americans to translate political gains into economic advancement (as the pluralists have argued that other "ethnic" groups have been able to do). Groups with intensely held preferences not only lose in the bargaining process, they often are not even given access to the policy-making process. They concluded that the incremental nature of the policy process is inadequate to rectify the massive problems facing the black community. Economic and social inequalities are cumulative and further weaken African-Americans in all spheres—social, economic, and political. Hence, at least for black Americans, pluralist theory does not work.

Most writers in the widely used and cited text, the *New Black Politics* (Preston et al. 1987), are also pluralists, but are more optimistic and, despite reservations and criticisms of the political system, utilize many of the features of the pluralist paradigm. The Introduction by the editors, the article on the presidency by Henderson, and many of the articles on black mayors all emphasize the successful mobilization of black voters, and the entrance of African-Americans into the bargaining process as black elected officials come to the fore. A key element of these scholars' work is the emphasis on the transformation of African-American politics from a politics of protest to one of electoral politics. While many of these writers eventually would expect to see more political heterogeneity with increased social and economic heterogeneity, they would see this process as being retarded by continuing racial conflict.

The Challengers

In every scholarly or professional field there is inevitably a set of individuals whose work does not fit neatly into the conventional categories. In the study of African-American politics there is also such a collection of individuals. For the most part, these are scholars who accept the very broad strictures of the pluralism model. They accept the level and unit of analysis (groups, group-elite interaction, etc.); they accept many of the core concepts, and so forth. However, we consider them challengers because they deliberately raise sharp and serious questions about some of the major tenets of the pluralism paradigm. In African-American politics and the politics of race this group includes Hochschild, Pinderhughes, Hamilton, Williams, Walters, and several others. From an earlier period, we would include Ralph Bunche (1941), the first black Ph.D. in political science.

While each "challenging" scholar is different, a few common themes run through their work. First, they are each consistently broad in the topics the author covers, including public policy, elite-elite relations, elite-mass relations, and ideology. Secondly, they will often question the discipline's focus on the "political." Williams (1987), for example, argues that successful mass political mobilization did lead to successful, increased political participation and political rewards. However, unlike more conventional analysts, black or white, she then asks whether these political rewards have substantially translated into improved standards or quality of life for nonelite African-Americans. The "challengers" also express misgivings about the ability of conventional political science to capture other important components of African-American politics.

Predictions

The classic pluralist model would make the following predictions. Dahl (1961) describes how ethnic politics first develops and then falls apart within the American pluralist system. The main prediction is that social heterogeneity leads to political heterogeneity and the decline of ethnicity as a political factor. Dahl describes three stages of ethnic politics in *Who Governs*.

In the first stage, members of the ethnic group are primarily "proletarian." During this stage political entrepreneurs emerge and function as intermediaries between the old political system and the low-status, new ethnic group. Ethnic loyalty, ethnic politics, and political homogeneity are high during this stage, according to Dahl.

In the second stage, there is more socio-economic heterogeneity. Ethnic leaders are sometimes given larger roles in the local and other levels of the party. But, because of the increased arena, ethnic politicians have to become cautious, and most embrace issues that are not divisive along ethnic classes. The political system, in many versions, is used to help "bootstrap" the community economically.

In the third stage one finds a high degree of socio-economic heterogeneity. The middle class seeks to assimilate and is "embarrassed" by lower-class cousins. The middle class finds ethnic politics useless. Crosscutting cleavages within the ethnic group lead to low levels of political homogeneity. According to Dahl, the Germans, Irish, eastern Europeans, and Italians went through the first stage in about fifty years or less, the second stage in twenty to forty years, and now have entered the third stage. African-Americans have gone through the first stage, but it took 170 years by his count, and have been in stage two since 1961. To recapitulate, the pluralists make an unambiguous prediction of increases in African-American socio-economic stratification and political heterogeneity. There should be increasing heterogeneity among blacks and convergence along class lines with whites.

WEBER

The structure, logic, and key concepts of Weberian analysis should in principle lend themselves to the study of African-American politics. Weber stressed elements of the political economy and society that correspond to African-American historical realities. First, Weber built his sociology upon the concept of control and *domination*. For Weber, power is exercised along two axes, through a "constellation of interests," as in competition through markets; and second, through "established authority," or domination (Bendix 1946). Domination of the ruled by the ruler(s) takes three forms, which vary across communities or nations, and through time: charismatic authority, traditional authority, and legal/rational authority. The Weberian emphasis on several forms of domination should match the black historical experience.

Second, Weber placed at the center of his model of society the universal tension between societal position determined by economic relations and social position determined by noneconomic status relations, which includes traditional notions of hierarchy and deference. He thought it important to study the intersection of class and status. In distinction to Marx, Weber does not dismiss but emphasizes the ways that culture and traditional values intersect with class relations. Race, culture, and values fit easily under the Weberian framework, and indeed are central to it.

Weber emphasized several other dimensions of society directly relevant to African-American politics including the importance of history, the character of linkages between elites and masses, and the role of the state. He argued that as societies move from more traditional to more modern behaviors and attitudes, political and social relations are rendered more formalized and predictable by legitimate laws and regulations, and other rules.

We have selected two scholars who work directly on this subject and have recently produced widely reviewed and praised books on social stratification in the African-American population: William J. Wilson *(The Declining Significance of Race)* and Bart Landry *(The New Black Middle Class)*. Although both are sociologists, their writing is directly related to the topic of this essay. Both authors analyze the system of ethnic and social stratification in society, which they see as partly determined by economic imperatives, and partly by social belief systems somewhat independent of class. Wilson's study aims to explain the historical evolution of racial domination in the United States, which he traces through several phases, beginning with a paternalist racism by the landed classes, through a more competitive market-based stratification system propped up by the competition between white and black workers. This competition reinforces the racism of the former and the subordinate status of the latter. Like Weber, Wilson sees domination expressed through uneven market competition; for blacks, the consequence is a legacy of racially determined low status now maintained by their class position. Landry focuses more directly on the internal dynamics of one part of the social structure—the old and new middle classes. Both authors present evidence suggesting major quantitative and qualitative changes in the social structure over the past two or three decades—a larger middle class, a larger unskilled working class and "underclass," a smaller skilled working class. For the political scientist, however, the insightful sociological analyses of both authors leave underdeveloped (and almost unexamined) the power and political relations associated with these structural changes. They examine potential lines of cleavage and conflict neither within the black community, nor between those communities and whites. They do not seriously examine, for example, whether there are changing political relations between members of the black middle class and the black working or underclass. Landry offers some data on the organizational involvement of the new middle class, which he describes as moving more toward professional and personal development activities, away from the social clubs, fraternities, and sororities of earlier middle-class blacks. He attributes this to "the civil rights movement," but he does not specify the exact mechanisms through which this shift is brought about.

Predictions

Despite their neglect of the political, we can nonetheless extrapolate what the Weberian model would predict about black politics. First, middle-class black involvement in the political arena would begin more and more to resemble the behavior of white counterparts in voting, lobbying, and other direct forms of political activities. In the area of the "informal" political dynamics of institutions like the church, the Weberian model would permit some "autonomy" and continuity of the cultural and religious. Race and racism can persist even though the economy changes. Indeed, cultural values should influence the market-based behavior of individuals from that culture. There might be convergence of values between middle-class blacks and whites, but less than under the Marxist, modernization, or pluralist models.

Political relations within the black community should also change according to a Weberian logic (William Wilson). Wilson expresses this most strongly in his work (including his latest, *The Truly Disadvantaged*, 1987). The social distance between middle-class and underclass blacks has grown dramatically as the former escape the ghettos and the latter remain. This reduces the opportunities for shared folkways, and shared self-interest in local schools, services, and so forth, to be maintained across class lines. Changed material conditions should result in changed attitudes and interests. Though operating within the same paradigm, Landry is much more cautious about the extent and permanency of these changes, and the degree of interclass separation. His data suggest that middle-class blacks are still much more likely to live in neighborhoods with nonmiddle-class families than are whites.

A Weberian would probably predict that working-class or underclass African-Americans should show some changes, but would retain some of the previous patterns. Anomie is as likely an outcome as revolt for the urban and rural black poor. The poor and nonpoor continue their past associations with church and other social organizations.

The net result would be some convergence toward white values and participation among middle-class blacks, and some divergence from interaction and interests with nonmiddle-class blacks, but not so much interclass divergence as under other models. Traditional values and persistent social status awareness would mute economic stratification. The Weberian model would predict, therefore, medium levels of divergence and convergence.

MARXISM AND THE STUDY OF AFRICAN-AMERICAN POLITICS

We identify several core elements of a Marxist paradigm. In sum, the analysis situates the particular issue to be studied within a structural and historical context of class struggle that results from the attempt by capitalists to extract surplus value from working people. The motor that drives the system is surplus extraction, and all political action is, in the final instance, related to the struggle of classes over the extraction and disposition of that surplus. Politics is therefore somewhat residual in Marxist analyses, and enjoys little autonomy of its own apart from the class struggle. Like politics, culture, race, and gender are superstructural expressions of society's economic foundations.

The more modern Marxist and neo-Marxist formulations devote more attention to political activity and to the state. In studies of Third World and First World social formations, there is more effort to bring political behavior, political institutions, and political leadership back into the analysis. The current "statist" literature is especially noteworthy in this regard.

With a few exceptions like O'Connor (1973), movement toward a more political approach has reduced the attention given to issues of surplus extraction and capital accumulation. At the margins, the work of Miliband (1969) and other instrumentalists melds into expansive and radicalized versions of pluralist analyses, "expansive" since they examine far more levels of analysis and a wider range of phenomena than do pluralists and radicals because they focus on the causes and the consequences of social inequality. But since many neo-Marxists focus on interest groups and elites, albeit within the broader structure of a dominant class, there is a methodological proximity to pluralism that shapes the neo-Marxist work. The internal sociology of the ruling class, not the relationship between the rulers and the ruled, becomes the center of attention. The social inequality of state policies and the creation of class hegemony become legitimate objects of inquiry. It is against this background that we examine Marxist studies of African-American politics.

Marxists do not typically have race as a central aspect of their analyses. A particularly telling example of the limited treatment of African-American materials by Marxists is found in the survey of major themes in Marxist studies edited by Bertell Ollman and Edward Vernoff (1982). Their discipline-by-discipline analysis examines major concerns of Marxist scholars, and criticizes mainstream approaches. Only in the chapter on psychology is there a separate heading on race, while history and economics give race and gender a few paragraphs. Kesselman's (Ollman and Vernoff 1982) chapter on political studies gives race only a passing and perfunctory nod.

Those Marxist scholars who have considered race and black politics traditionally have tended toward two surprisingly undialectical views of African-Americans' place in society and in political conflict. One such view characterizes African-Americans as being economically marginal, politically backward, and noncentral to the major questions of class conflict and accommodation facing the American working class. A very sophisticated, analytical version of this tendency can be found in the writings of Adam Przeworski (1985). A more classic version of this view, which sees African-Americans as being similar to other oppressed backward peasant groups, can be found in the work of Stanley Aronowitz (1973).

Aronowitz argues that black workers preferred the planters to the socialists in the late nineteenth and early twentieth century (coercion does not enter the picture for him) and that young white workers who challenged work rules at the Youngstown auto plant were more revolutionary than the revolutionary black workers movement that swept from the DRUMS of the Detroit auto plants to Mawah, New Jersey. DRUM (Detroit Revolutionary Union Movement) chapters were radical black worker caucuses that enjoyed broad support in Detroit during the 1960s and early 70s. Those factory organizations had their base in the auto plants but eventually spread to other industries. As did other black radical groups of the period, they disintegrated due to a combination of external pressure and internal ideological disunity. He argues that jazz is a bourgeois art form that contributes to the fragmentation of the working class, while rock music is progressive and working-class based. Racism, for Aronowitz, is the same as ideologies that stigmatized peasant groups from Czarist Russia to Italy. Black working-class history is marked by the use of blacks as strikebreakers.

Przeworski's profoundly more reasoned arguments end with similar conclusions. Working-class anger toward those such as blacks is based to a degree on proletarian moral anger directed toward parasites from below (welfare recipients, etc.). Blacks occupy increasingly marginal locations within the working class, and are falling out of the working class altogether. To the degree that struggles such as those of blacks become prominent, they detract from the overall struggle of the working class.

The second traditional trend among Marxist scholars is the Black Vanguard tendency. Prevalent among both activists and scholars involved in the groups that emerged from the New Left Movement, this strand views blacks as a revolutionary vanguard of the working class. While these scholars (most clearly Mike Davis, but also elements of this view can be found in Katznelson's *City Trenches* [1981], and Castells's article "Wild City," and book, *The City and the Grassroots* [1983]), celebrate the revolutionary potential of African-Americans because they view the oppression and struggle of African-Americans as challenging the entire hegemonic system of economic, political, and cultural roots of American capitalism, they are as suspicious of nationalist tendencies among African-Americans as their less enthusiastic colleagues (Castells 1983; Davis 1986; Katznelson 1981). They view African-American political conflict as central to the degree that it challenges the class relations of American society. To the degree that African-Americans do not take up the struggle of the class as a whole they are doomed to remain oppressed and exploited (Castells 1983; Katznelson 1981). For these scholars, racism and nationalism are the unequal sides of the same coin; both divide the working class and prevent the revolutionary potential of African-Americans from being fulfilled (Davis 1986; Katznelson 1981). African-American political progress serves to demobilize the revolutionary potential of African-Americans and co-opt the African-American petty bourgeoisie (Davis 1986; Katznelson 1981).

Both tendencies view the civil rights movement as being profoundly incomplete due to the lack of black working-class leadership within the movement. Both schools define the only road to the end of black exploitation as unity with the other progressive and potentially revolutionary sectors of the working class. Both approaches are marked by an unsophisticated and often erroneous analysis of the internal contradictions and dynamics of the various classes and strata that form the African-American community and upon which African-American political movements, both traditional and radical, are based.

A different approach can be found in the work of African-American Marxists such as Manning Marable (1983). Like his white counterparts, Marable argues that increasing class contradictions among African-Americans will eventually lead to a "rupture" of the black working classes with the black petty bourgeoisie. Unlike his counterparts, however, he believes that organizations based on opposition to racial and sexual oppression not only have a progressive role to play in the period before successful transformation of society and seizure of state power but would have a progressive role to play in the postrevolutionary period. Black liberation and similar nonclass movements based on racial or gender oppression are not only progressive but central to a potential socialist revolution in the United States (Marable 1983). This perspective is markedly different from that of the great majority of white Marxist approaches to analyses of American society and politics. Some of the differences between Marable and other Marxists are found in Table 7.1.

Predictions

The predictions of Marxists are similar to those of pluralists, although the normative evaluation is different. From Marable to Aronowitz, non-Gramscian Marxists would predict that increases in socio-economic heterogeneity or, put within the appropriate vernacular, increased class contradictions, will lead directly to increased political contradictions between African-American classes. Gramscians, such as Przeworski, who view cultural hegemony as being firmly grounded in the return of part of the product of extracted surplus value to various segments of the working class, would predict that growing political heterogeneity would depend on whether enough of the returned surplus value was distributed among African-American petty bourgeoisie and upper working classes to buy loyalty to the state. Some European variants of Gramsci would predict continued political homogeneity among African-Americans to the degree that antihegemonic forces within the African-American community were able to organize successfully and promote an alternative worldview. But most Marxists would predict growing class conflict within black communities.

MODERNIZATION

Modernization theory has been employed mainly to explain social and political change in non-U.S. settings. The model has also been employed on occasion by writers like Kilson and others to account for po-

Table 7.1
Marxism, Black and White

	Przeworski	Marable
Theoretical views on race:		
central	X	central and potentially revolutionary
peripheral	X	tend toward reactionary core of working class
Status of racial struggle:		
black elite	tends toward negative/diverting	
black masses	not treated	
	not treated fully; part of lower section of out-of-labor force sector	
black underclass victims	reactionary (justifies white racism to a degree; *my interpretation*)	
status of race	just another group	precapitalist formation with nearly status of class
View of "politics":	part of Gramscian struggle	bourgeois politics bankrupt except in tactics situations
	distribution profits, not deterministic, some workers (white) benefit in short to medium run	
conflict/coop		
zero-sum or positive sum	varying, in democracy usually positive sum diverting/reactionary	tends toward zero sum/progressive
Links of politics with model:		
high		
medium		
low		

Table 7.1
continuing

Empirical levels of analysis:		
individual		
group	X	X
institution	X	X
class	X	X
Predictions of model		
Social structure:		
convergence		
no change		
divergence		
Value structure:		
convergence	not discussed	
no change		
divergence		X
Dependent variable:	socialist success	black movement, socialist movement revolutionary bloc, state
Empirical validation:	class/race analysis invalidated by Marxist Erik Olin Wright empirical class analysis and a historical treatment race and gender mathematical models	historical and some demographical

litical changes in this country as well. We feel the model has a particular utility for understanding social change among blacks, and has on occasion been so employed.

Briefly, what are the core arguments and concepts of this paradigm? First, changing attitudes, norms, and values held by individuals and groups lie at the center of the model. It draws a sharp distinction between traditional attitudes and practices, on the one hand, and modern ones on the other. Traditional values stress social solidarity, ascriptive criteria, religious orientations, and, like Weber, charismatic authority. Modern values are secular, achievement-oriented, and more individualistic. Social differentiation and social mobilization of underlying populations occur for a variety of reasons, but when they do, new values and ideologies may arise within groups. While differentiation does produce tension within and between individuals and groups, the model assumes a core central cohesion in societies may be achieved if leaders and formal organizations help to integrate the new entrants into their new roles and activities, and ultimately into the social whole. Thus, while class and ethnic differences arise, they are often mitigated by new ideologies articulated by new leaders.

Modernization assigns an important place to political linkages between modernizing elites and more traditional masses as a critical nexus in the movement from one kind of society to another. These linkages take a variety of forms, and tend to occur more between segments of the population that are more mobilized than those that are not mobilized. Indeed, part of the "function" of political elites and subelites is to help guide this transformation into channels that will normalize participation and enhance leverage of the new groups to gain goods and services from government. This typically occurs through formal organizations such as political machines led by the modernizing elite.

The relevance of this paradigm for African-American politics is considerable. One can analyze the movement of black Americans from their rural agricultural roots into a more urban and variegated political culture through the lens of the modernization paradigm. Drawing partly from his use of the modernization paradigm in his work on the politics of African nationalism and decolonization, Martin Kilson applies the model to black America (Kilson 1977). In a similar way that a rising class of "modernized" African elites in the liberal professions of law, medicine, and journalism challenged simultaneously the dominance of the European colonial oligarchy and the privileged status of the traditional, tribal elites, so the appearance of a parallel black professional class challenged white American racism and the modest privileges of more established black "brokers" or buffers. In the 1960s the civil rights oligarchy was itself challenged as Uncle Tom conservatives by the rising tide of radical black nationalists who sought to mobilize the black popular classes through their own organizations, using the new ideology of black power. The status of this stratum was in turn challenged by the growing influence of black elected officials, who, as Reed argues (1986), had the greater capacity to deliver modern material goods and services. Ideologies of black nationalism, separatism, and integration are taken seriously in this model.

Predictions

What implications for politics and stratification can we derive from this paradigm? First, the model does focus directly on social stratification and its political consequences. The ideological, behavioral, and institutional consequences are seen as important objects of study. It recognizes that social change will lead to new interests and new groups mobilized, often in conflict with one another. To that extent it shares some perspectives with Marxism. On the other hand, like pluralism, it posits the possibility, indeed the likelihood, that value integration will overcome the centrifugal forces of class differentiation. Whereas pluralism sees this as almost inevitable, and Marxism as almost impossible, modernization theories remain somewhat more agnostic. While the long-term outlook for racial integration is seen as positive, political development depends heavily upon the political and organizational skills of the political class at the time. One would predict some conflict of interests, with newly mobilized elements of the black population competing with established black elites for control over resources and the definition of the public agenda. Within the black community, values should diverge, organizations and traditional community links should die away, reform, and restructure. Between the black and white populations, there should be some convergence, but nationalism and potential class conflicts should remain. However, the outcome is indeterminate.

THE DOG THAT DIDN'T BARK IN THE NIGHT: SOCIAL CHOICE THEORY AND THE STUDY OF AFRICAN-AMERICAN POLITICS

Several observers of political science, especially of the study of American politics, have commented on the ascendancy of social choice theory and formal modeling within the field (Przeworski 1985; Sims 1989). It is apparent within the major journals and other scholarly work. However, and at least partly due to the strong emphasis on the individual as the appropriate unit of analysis, there is an absence of work on racial politics and African-American politics within this paradigm. Even though social choice analysis does not currently address all the materials, the rapid rise of the model in the field warrants at least a passing consideration. We will outline the core elements of social choice theory and then construct, based on one of our own works, a utility maximizing model drawing on the theories of Simon (1985) that seeks to explain and predict African-American group behavior and group consciousness.

Elster (1986) describes three core elements of social choice theory. The individual is assumed to consider the full set of social choices available to him or her. Second, the individual possesses a causal model of how her or his actions could plausibly lead to one alternative or another. Finally, possible choices or actions are ranked on the basis of the desirability of the outcomes to which each choice is presumed to lead. Individuals are assumed to be rational, and rationality is defined as the maximization of their own (or perhaps their families') utility. Extensions of the basic theory include modifications based on when individuals make choices under varying degrees of uncertainty, when information costs are taken into account, and so forth. Most importantly, groups are not an appropriate level of analysis, because they are assumed to be difficult to form due to free rider problems, because individual circumstances are supposed to overwhelm any group circumstances in calculating utility, and because the individual level of analysis provides a more parsimonious and powerful theory of social choice than group-based analyses. Elster concludes that social choice theory denies even the possibility of collective desires or collective beliefs—making it even more difficult for the theory to explain or predict African-American political behavior (Elster 1986).

This theory has been challenged on several grounds. Several leading psychologists including scholars such as Simon argue that humans are not intuitive scientists or statisticians. Simon has proposed the theory of "satisficing" behavior as an alternative to the utility optimizers of social choice theory and neoclassical economists (Simon 1985).

It can be argued within the American context, and particularly in the case of African-Americans, that political behavior and beliefs can best be explained through both group membership and group consciousness. The argument can be constructed within this framework as follows. The historical and institutional context, and of African-American social history, has forged a common experience in which, up to at least the past decade, one's life chances were overdetermined by group membership. Therefore individuals' decision-making, choice processes, and utility maximization would be greatly economized by using the status of the group as a proxy for individual status in making social decisions. However, we do not claim that all individuals "possess" the same degree of group consciousness. The seeming homogeneity of African-American social behavior and beliefs are due to three major factors:

1. The continued utility of substituting group measures of well-being as proxies for individual well-being as a satisfying, efficient, procedurally rational (Simon 1985) method of individual utility.

2. The constraint of the American political ideological space by comparative standards masks much variation among African-Americans as to the strategies to pursue common goals. Some of the variation can be explained by class differences manifested as policy and tactical differences.

3. Individual differences among African-Americans can be explained by different conditions of socialization (e.g., differences of socialization between age cohorts, or between those socialized in urban or rural environments), severity and saliency of individual experiences with discrimination, and so forth.

Predictions

The strong version of social choice theory would make the straightforward prediction that as social heterogeneity increases and African-Americans enter the primary labor market, one would see as much and similar political heterogeneity as with white Americans. The "soft satisfying" version of the theory would temper its predictions by stating that as long as perceptions remained that race was the salient feature in determining black life chances (which the great majority of black Americans still believed as of 1988) we would expect to see the continuation of strong group consciousness and political homogeneity. Further, the heuristic of substituting group utility for individual utility would persist as long as the real differences persist and perhaps longer as the social institutions and political entrepreneurs of the black community sought to reinforce possibly anachronistic modes of behavior.

RACE AS CENTRAL: THE PARADIGM

If some paradigms like social choice virtually ignore race, others put race as central to political life. The black nationalist paradigm is a term we apply to cover political analysts like Ron Karenga, James Turner, and others whose writings exhibit the features that define a particular paradigm—shared assumptions, shared basic texts, common methods, and agreement as to what constitutes important problems and research questions. It is the latter element that is especially important—the main problematique is to produce scholarship that is engaged and relevant to improving the current conditions of black communities. It is highly normative, deliberately designed to change the world, and not simply to describe it. To this degree it shares some features with the "public policy" paradigm within political science.

Understanding this perspective is important for two kinds of work. First is writing centrally located within the paradigm; second is writing significantly informed by the paradigm but which operates using other recognizable paradigms. There are some works, for example, that fit methodologically into a pluralist or Marxist framework, in which we can identify important elements of a nationalist evaluative or normative underpinning. We analyze the latter group in our conclusion. In this section we focus mainly on core nationalist writers like Karenga (1982) or (early) Amiri Baraka or the sociologist Alphonso Pinkney (1984).

What are the modal features of a nationalist perspective? First and foremost, the empirical focus is Afro-centric. Nationalist writers are especially likely to analyze the internal dynamics of the black community. (It is certainly not the case, however, that all writers who focus on black politics are nationalists!)

Along our conflict dimension, the greatest conflict is assumed to exist between blacks and whites (this parallels the Marxist assumption of class contradiction and inevitable class conflict); greater cooperation is assumed to exist among blacks. There is typically an assumption of domination and exploitation as the modal relationship between the races, with resistance and struggle occupying a large part of the picture. The idea of black resistance to white domination is glorified, and victories celebrated. The preferred focus of nationalist writers is on resistance, while collaboration or other forms of black-white accommodation are often downplayed or considered the work of race traitors. The domination-resistance relationship is seen as multifaceted, affecting all areas of public and private life, from the family to the firm, by no means restricted to the "political" alone. The domination-resistance relationship is almost always viewed through the lens of history. One almost always finds contemporary accounts set within a historical setting or references made to historical antecedents. Some writers also introduce references to Africa in their discussion of black American politics (see Walton's inclusion of an entry or two on South Africa in his recent review of works on black American politics). An interesting, and slightly more class-conscious variant of this approach, is the "internal colony model," which likens the situation of U.S. ghettos to Third World colonies, with self-interested black elites serving as a comprador class facilitating the white exploitation of the black masses. When nationalist writers take up the challenge of evaluating other models, they assert that the uniqueness of the African-American experience requires a unique and particular method of analysis, which they claim their approach satisfies.

Predictions

The nationalist predictions are rather straightforward. First, the model would deny or strongly resist the ideas that much social stratification has occurred, or will occur within the black community. Second, to the degree that some stratification may occur, it insists that the forces of white racism are still so pervasive and so powerful as to obviate or counteract the divisive tendencies of social stratification. In short, race will overcome class. The more populist strain of nationalist writing may criticize any attempts by individuals or groups to move away from a grassroots, race-based communal orientation. The black elite may attempt to escape from its blackness, but American racism will force that elite to live in black areas or attend black schools, and the pressures of racism will sustain traditional forms and degrees of social interaction between groups—that is, between upper-class, middle-class, and working-class blacks. In short, this paradigm predicts continuing value consensus on black politics among all elements of the community. Class differences should not lead to value dissensus. The paradigm predicts that differences between black and white attitudes would remain or even grow. Politics will (and should) remain racially-based.

It is worth extending our discussion of this approach a bit further, in part because we have found that the nationalist approach is not only interesting in and of itself, but also because authors sometimes conjoin it with other explanatory models. In our discussion of the use of particular models by African-American scholars whether Marxist, pluralist, or otherwise, we found a number of intriguing features that seemed to hold across all the models. Thus, a black scholar may employ the conceptual apparatus of the pluralist model—including its primary focus on group structure, power, and competition to secure political resources in various policy arenas. However, in those areas where evaluative factors can come most heavily into play—such as the initial choice of subject (i.e., "black politics"); the selection and articulation of the "problematique" (what is the exciting puzzle to be explained, i.e., the "independent variable"); the evaluation of the goodness and the badness of political outcomes and political processes—there we found interesting differences between the way that black and white scholars employed the model.

DETERMINING THE POLITICAL CONSEQUENCES OF SOCIAL STRATIFICATION

In this section we suggest how one might go about testing the predictions delineated in the previous section. This discussion is not meant to be and is not a definitive empirical validation or refutation of any of the paradigms that have been discussed. Instead we offer a heuristic that can help to guide subsequent research and writing in the subfield. While we present some very preliminary quantitative evidence, other more qualitative modes of investigation serve as equally fruitful alternatives and complements to the multivariate causal modeling in which our research projects are engaged. These alternative modes of investigation, which have produced some of the best work in black politics, include careful historical analysis, in-depth interviewing, hermeneutic interpretation of texts, and other qualitative analytical methods of empirical research.

If the very preliminary evidence that we have analyzed holds up, the theories we have examined leave something to be explained. Tables 7.2 and 7.3 show that on occupational dimensions and with regard to income there has been continuing social stratification over the entire century and an apparent acceleration in economic polarization over the last two decades.

Table 7.2 in the last graphic shows the occupational middle stratum shrinking, while bottom and top of the occupational structure gets larger. The distribution of income by the late 1980s is the most unequal since 1947. The top 5 percent has the most it has had and the bottom fifth has less than ever. This increasing income inequality among blacks occurred during times of overall declining black incomes.

We can make firmer judgments when we further probe the association between economic stratification and African-American public opinion and political behavior. Table 7.3 shows simple bivariate relationships between poverty status in 1988 and various items of black public opinion, partisanship, and political choice. The black urban poor are compared to the black urban nonpoor. The economic distress described by Wilson, Marable, and others, has not only grim social effects on inner-city communities but also has led to grave levels of political disorganization and demobilization (Marable 1983). In many ways, we expect to find the most severe status-associated political divisions between different strata of African-Americans to be between the urban poor and other African-Americans. Table 7.3 displays the relationship between poverty status and public opinion for black urban residents. Table 7.3 indicates differences in public opinion between those above and below the poverty line in 1988.

Conventional conceptions of political differences, partisanship, and choice show little or no distinction between the urban black poor and black nonpoor. Specifically, we did not find any substantive or statistically significant class-type differences using traditional measures such as approval ratings of the president, party identification, or indicators of how hard the two major parties work on "black issues." For example, no differences are found between the urban poor and nonpoor in 1988 in levels of approval for former President Reagan, nor any differences between the poor and nonpoor.

If analysis stopped with the conventional measures, we would have to conclude that the preliminary evidence provides scant support for theses relating social stratification to black public opinion. Hence, the predictions of the nationalists would be supported, and pluralists, social choice practitioners, and Marxists would be undercut.

However, we believe that the conventional conceptions and their measures are inadequate, at least within the realm of African-American politics. Conventional conceptions of American politics inadequately capture issues such as strategic and tactical differences that periodically appear within black communities, especially when seen in long historical perspective. These would include the firey debates between Frederick Douglass and Henry Highland Garnett; W. E. B. Du Bois and Booker T. Washington; Marcus Garvey and the radical black intellectuals of the early twentieth century; and more recently the Nation of Islam versus the NAACP. Our different conception of the important issues and historical development of black politics leads us to believe that we need different indicators of political division within the black community.

However, traditional surveys of American politics do not include measures adequate for studying these debates—for example, among integrationists and black nationalists. New survey instrumentation is required. The data we use are from the National Black Election Study whose originators were concerned with these types of issues. When one examines these new measures of nationalism and redistribution of wealth displayed in Table 7.3, one does find significant status differences associated with political divisions between the black urban poor and nonpoor. The poor are more black nationalist in orientation. They display greater support for an independent black political party. They more firmly believe that African-Americans should always vote for a black candidate and that blacks should work in black-only organizations. This political nationalism is accompanied by an even more radical posture toward redistribution of wealth than their more affluent African-American cousins. They more strongly support both a government guarantee of job or income and special consideration of minorities in hiring due to past discrimination. Multivariate log-linear analysis supports the relationships between poverty and the indicators of black political nationalism (Dawson 1989). Work to extend the multivariate analysis to the other relationships suggested in Table 7.3 continues. This preliminary analysis suggests that the urban poor are both more nationalist and more classically in support of redistribution.

If these preliminary results are confirmed by subsequent multivariate quantitative analysis and various qualitative forms of research, the applicability of many of the major paradigms discussed above for black politics would have to be rethought. Perhaps the mainstream of black politics is sufficiently different from the mainstream of white politics to require us to frame more carefully both our theoretical and empirical propositions on black politics. Certainly, researchers in the field have no a priori reason to assume that empirical measures and analytical models

Table 7.2
Changing Black and White Occupational Structure 1910–1981

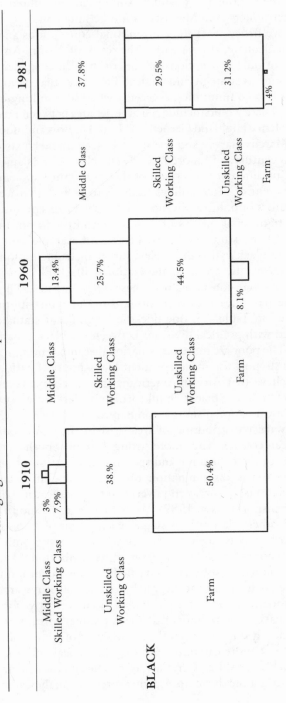

BLACK

1910

Middle Class 3%
Skilled Working Class 7.9%

Unskilled
Working Class 38.%

Farm 50.4%

1960

Middle Class 13.4%

Skilled
Working Class 25.7%

Unskilled
Working Class 44.5%

Farm 8.1%

1981

Middle Class 37.8%

Skilled
Working Class 29.5%

Unskilled
Working Class 31.2%

Farm 1.4%

Table 7.2
continuing

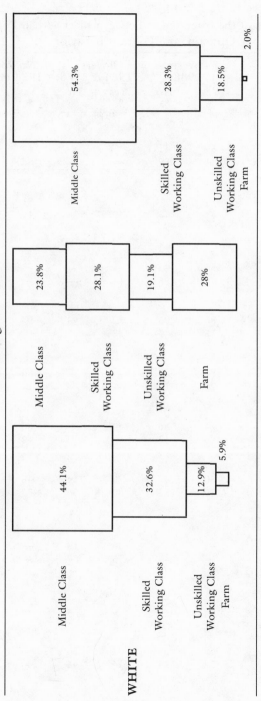

Source: Bart Landry (1987), *The New Black Middle Class*, pp. 21, 68, and 219. Sums do not equal 100% because of those for whom no occupation was reported.

Table 7.3

Selected Examples of the Interactions between Black Urban Poverty, Public Opinion, and Political Behavior

Issue Area	Poverty 1988 Yes %	Poverty 1988 No %	Poverty 1984 & 1988 Yes %	Poverty 1984 & 1988 No %	No Poverty 1984 or 1988 Yes %	No Poverty 1984 or 1988 No %
Personal Efficacy						
Officials don't care?						
agree	59[a]	41	[b]	—	42	57
disagree	41	59	—	—	58	43
Government run by few big interests?						
agree	—	—	51	76	81	62
disagree	—	—	49	24	19	38
Group Political Efficacy						
White officials get own way?						
agree	56	45	—	—	—	—
disagree	44	55	—	—	—	—
Black vote makes difference in local elections?						
agree	85	95	72	93	97	82
disagree	15	5	28	7	3	18
Political Engagement						
Care which party wins?						
yes	74	85	—	—	86	75
no	26	15	—	—	14	25
Interest in political campaign?						
yes	74	86	—	—	88	74
no	26	14	—	—	12	26
Read black newspapers or magazines?						
yes	30	47	20	44	48	32
no	70	53	80	56	52	68
Partisanship						
How hard do Democrats work on black issues?						
very hard	—	—	36[c]	13	—	—
not hard	—	—	5	7	—	—
How hard do Republicans work on black issues?						
very hard	—	—	—	—	1[c]	12
not hard	—	—	—	—	39	32
Blacks better off when work within system?						
agree	68	56	84	56	—	—
disagree	32	44	16	44	—	—

continued

Table 7.3
continuing

Black Nationalism						
Support independent black political party?						
yes	32	20	—	—	—	—
no	68	80	—	—	—	—
Always vote for black candidate?						
agree	34	15	47	18	15	32
disagree	66	85	53	82	85	68
Blacks should work in black only organizations?						
agree	64	57	68	31	30	46
disagree	36	43	32	69	70	54
Redistributive Policies						
Government guarantee job or income?						
agree	83	73	88	74	73	80
disagree	17	27	12	26	27	20
Special consideration for minorities in hiring because of past discrimination?						
agree	73	68	75	68	—	—
disagree	27	32	25	32	—	—
Political Participation						
Go to meeting, dinner, or speech?						
yes	17	28	—	—	28	18
no	83	72	—	—	72	82
Contact public official?						
yes	30	55	20	52	59	33
no	70	45	80	48	41	67
Sign petition?						
yes	48	77	35	72	77	53
no	52	23	65	28	23	47
Boycott, sit-in, picketted?						
yes	3	15	—	—	16	3
no	97	85	—	—	84	97
Political Choice						
Reagan job approval?						
approve	22[d]	24	—	—	—	—
disapprove	78	76	—	—	—	—

Source: 1984–1988 National Black Election Panel Study, Program for Research on Black America, The Institute for Social Research, the University of Michigan, Ann Arbor.

[a]All reported statistical differences (for example, between those poor in 1988 and those not poor in 1988) are significant at least at the .05 level and have correlations between the political item and difference in poverty status of at least 0.20.

[b]Dashes represent findings that do not meet the test in note [a] above.

[c]Totals do not sum to 100% because of omission of intermediate categories.

[d]Not statistically significant differences between poor and nonpoor.

constructed to understand mainstream mainly white American politics would have more than limited utility in explaining black politics. African-American political experience is a result of a different historical experience and continued separate social reality. Therefore, new models, constructs, and indicators must be developed to capture fully the dynamics of black politics. The question remains, however, whether there are sufficient divisions between blacks to require separate analysis of strata within the black community. Our theoretical work must confront these questions.

First, careful theoretical propositions that are testable will have to be derived from the theories being evaluated. Second, both historical analysis of the dynamics of the black community and well-specified multivariate causal models of the dynamics of black communities need to be constructed and estimated. In both cases careful specification of the hypotheses under study, variables of importance, and evidence of either theoretical confirmation or falsification will be necessary. Wherever possible, when strong evidence for theoretical falsification is found, analysts need to suggest alternative theoretical approaches or adjustments to the existing model. This kind of investigation has a nearly century-old history with roots in the work of Du Bois and others. Not all research works need to cover all the steps that we call for within the same scholarly article or research report. However, we do believe that all research work should be conducted within the framework of an explicit and comprehensive research program. The cumulative process of constructing theory, empirically testing theory, and refining theory is critical for all social scientists whether one is interested primarily in scientific investigation, reforming the system, or maintaining the system.

CONCLUSION

In this essay we selectively reviewed the field of African-American politics in order to identify its strong and weak points, and we suggested a set of major research issues the field should address in the coming years. In addition, and as importantly, we suggested a way of organizing the field, paradigm by paradigm, that will advance its theoretical rigor, its appeal to a broad range of political and social scientists, and will advance our ways of teaching for students in the field.

We were especially concerned with the capacity of six leading social science paradigms to capture important aspects of black politics. One key aspect in this essay was the paradigms' treatment of the relationship between social stratification and political changes.

Through our evaluation of the literature we reached two kinds of findings. The primary finding is that the theoretical structure of some paradigms did indeed make them more sensitive to racial politics than others. Writers using some paradigms devoted considerably more attention to the politics of race than other authors. Paradigms most frequently used by scholars interested in black politics included pluralist, nationalist, and Weberian/modernization approaches.

On one substantive issue very important for black politics, social stratification, we found strong indications (but could not conclude conclusively) that some models will predict (or retrodict) actual political outcomes better than others. These findings about the likely empirical foci, the theoretical orientation, and the relative explanatory power of alternative paradigms are, we hope, a modest contribution to the field. (In this we follow on the work of previous writers like Milton Morris [1985], Hanes Walton, Jr. [1989], and several others.)

Less conventional and perhaps more controversial are our secondary findings. Through our research we discovered that not only do scholars differ in the selection of the paradigms in which they choose to work, but they also may differ along other dimensions that are, in some sense, "extraparadigmatic" or metaparadigmatic. These are features that we uncovered as we read and reread the work of many scholars writing across a variety of different paradigms. We found that despite the paradigm or model in which black scholars worked, there were among many such scholars commonalities that transcended paradigmatic differences and united their inquiries into black politics. What are these shared features?

1. The Strategic Imperative. Black authors demonstrated a very clear concern with political tactics and strategies aimed at empowering blacks or reducing the constraints on their political choices. This focus holds for both the descriptive aspect of their work, and the normative orientation as to what should occur. In this respect the subfield is similar to the subfield of public policy, which also is concerned with strategic and normative issues.

2. Internal Dynamics. Authors focus on the internal dynamics of African-American communities. The concern is to explain shifts in political power within the population—for example, changes in the relative power of black elected officials and of community leaders. Research problems are less driven by the degree to which the "black problem" impinges on the majority society (often found among white writers), and more by internal dynamics within African-American communities. The extensive work by black scholars on the 1972 Gary convention is one outstanding example. We know of no work on this important topic by white political scientists. Among black authors there appears to be less concern with drawing contrasts between black and white samples, or tracing linkages between white and black political actors.

3. Historical References. An author makes reference to, or draws extensively upon, historical antecedents or developments to elucidate or account for contemporary phenomena. Resistance to historical oppression, the continuity of struggle, and a sense of historical mission are common themes.

4. The Normative Imperative. Here the author introduces normative concerns throughout the piece (not just at the opening or the conclusion), often underscoring the failure of the American political system to meet its formal obligations of equal access and equality. Authors stress the gap between promise and performance of the American political system. Because the system has not been fully realized for blacks, the author may deny the democratic tenets of the system as a whole.

5. The "Blame the Victor" Imperative. This is the reverse of the "blame the victim" approach where the fault for economic inequality and political powerlessness is assigned to the poor and the powerless. As we identify this feature, black authors are more likely than white ones to blame white racism for unequal societal outcomes.

It may not be inaccurate to sum up these parts of the meta-paradigmatic differences in terms of the *purposes* of scholarship. One respected black colleague wrote to us that while black scholars are and should be concerned with the further refinement and development of the discipline and the field of black politics, the primary challenge for black political scientists is black political empowerment and advancement. This is a sentiment one encounters frequently at gatherings such as the National Conference of Black Political Scientists. This sentiment is less evident in meetings of the American Political Science Association or in the pages of the *American Political Science Review*.

We do not wish to argue that all black political scientists exhibit these features in their work, nor that no white political scientists share these features. That is not at all what we conclude. We do find, however, that these features seem to appear disproportionately in the work of black scholars.

Randall Kennedy (1989) is also a discontented critic of his discipline who is concerned with racial splits between black and white legal scholars. In a scathing article in the *Harvard Law Review* entitled "Racial Critiques of Legal Academia," Kennedy identifies key issues where he feels black scholars have failed to substantiate their claims of racism in the profession. We are sympathetic with his criticisms, but we try to go beyond the limits of criticism to begin to account for and explain the differences between black and white scholars. Unlike Kennedy, we also question whether there are possible and valid trade-offs among the institutional criteria used to evaluate academic performance. We assert that learning and emulation can be a two-way street between minority and majority discourses, and that the dominant discourse of our discipline could usefully learn from the historical, engaged, and contextual approach of minority scholars.

If we identify differences between the two bodies of literature, we cannot in this already overlong essay speculate about all their causes or their likely consequences. We will simply list some competing hypotheses about the origin of the differences.

First, differences in scholarship may significantly reflect the values of the scholar's community of origin. We have already demonstrated, using survey research data, that there is a real discontinuity in the political attitudes of the black and the white populations in America. The former is shifted much further to the left (on standard dimensions) than the latter. Given that, we might expect to see some divergence between scholars who come from these two populations. This might result from early socialization, or from experiences later in life. The very different structural positions and material conditions of their community or their community of origin may push black scholars to pursue different subjects in different ways. Different experiences with racism and discrimination may account for differences in scholarship.

Second, the existence of two communities of discourse may express different sets of institutional incentives for black and white scholars. Many black scholars work at smaller colleges, especially historically black colleges and universities (HBCU). The incentives, resources, and professional orientations at smaller schools are different from those of larger research universities, where many white scholars who shape the discipline are located. Black colleges stress teaching and student motivation. Different institutional norms and incentives may account for the two communities of discourse.

Third, there is certainly anecdotal evidence to suggest that the average black scholar is more pressed by various societal and political demands into a wider range of pro bono activities than the average white scholar. This may push certain values to the fore, such as a greater concern with normative and strategic issues.

Fourth, minority scholars who reject the mainstream paradigms or evaluative criteria may feel sufficiently alienated from the discipline that they choose not to get involved with mainstream professional activities such as publishing in the principal journals. Minority professional organizations such as the National Conference of Black Political Scientists (NCOBPS) may provide sufficient recognition, and intellectual challenge, that attendance at the APSA meetings is less desirable. This may reinforce and institutionalize the existence of two discourses.

Rather than pursue this line of investigation, we choose simply to accept our findings of difference as fact, and to suggest that however we term this pattern ("ideology," "evaluative framework," "ways of knowing") it seems to reinforce and to express the existence of two very different "communities of discourse." By community of discourse we mean networks of individuals who share certain ideas and values that are communicated through various media—journal articles, conferences, teaching, books, circulating samizdat articles, public and private disputes, telephone calls, and at times collective action. Such communities are bounded by implicit frontiers recognized as such by the community. It is to this community of discourse that authors, in the isolation of their studies, typically address their writings. The community of discourse is the writer's intended audience. In the case at hand, black writers seem to aim their work to one community of discourse, white writers another. Clearly there are overlaps; but the circles of discourse, of audience, often are distinct and not coterminous.

It is widely recognized that different populations with different demographic profiles and social histories may have different intellectual styles, research agendas, and methods. Social science as practiced in Continental Europe and in Great Britain, for example, has long had different approaches to explanation and theory. In general, the intellectual traditions of Europe, especially France, tend toward broad structuralist interpretations in a highly systematized and formal framework. By contrast, the British are better known for analytic works that stay closer to the empirical data. In political science, the contrasts between the militantly structuralist treatises of Nicos Poulantzas (1968) and the more empirically rooted and positivist studies of Ralph Miliband are cases in point. Along the same lines, David McKay, of the European Consortium for Political Research, clearly identifies two distinct communities of discourse on each side of the Atlantic, as seen through American and European journals, professional training, conferences, and "distinct theoretical and empirical approaches" (McKay 1988).

Our attention to the epistemological questions that inform positivist political science research has direct parallels in other disciplines. In sociology, Walter Allen has carefully analyzed the theoretical, methodological, and ideological (or evaluative) components of work on the black family. He identifies an "objective" orientation (choice of model), and a "subjective" one that interprets black family structure and behavior as either deviant, identical to or different from the white "norm." He too looks at the race of the investigator, but finds little correlation between race and the content of the scholarship (Allen 1979). McLloyd (1984) pursues similar questions in her work on psychology. In her study of the "Segregated Scholar," Francille Rusan Wilson identifies a number of dimensions along which black and white scholars of the first half of the century differed (including historians, sociologists, and economists) (F. R. Wilson 1988). Gates has several thoughtful pieces on questions of race, voice, audience, and praxis (Gates, Jr. 1986).

The arguments we make here about the particularities of a racial perspective have their parallels in the work of others who focus on gender, nationality, or class as partial determinants of scholarly orientation. Feminist scholars contend that there is a unique perspective that women bring to the discipline. This rests in part on their exclusion from conventional forms of political participation. Remedying the exclusion of women, as of blacks, may have profound impacts on the field. Githens (1983) argues that the "political" has come to be defined as the political behavior of "affluent white males"—the wielders of power, the owners of resources. "The notion that there is one mode of political participation must be rejected; . . . A new construct based on more than just the political activity of affluent white males is now needed." We need "a new research agenda focusing on what women define as political and what they see as appropriate political behavior within this context. To achieve this, methodological tools, frameworks, and concepts to pursue such investigation must be developed" (Githens 1983).

Finally, we would be remiss if we did not address an important question of the institutionalization of these communities of discourse. For many black scholars, good work on African-American materials is the highest of callings. Yet for the discipline as a whole, it seems the lowest of callings. Why this discrepancy? Why do not more white scholars choose to enter the field? There is anecdotal evidence that black and white graduate students are steered away from the study of black politics by their faculty advisors. There seems a bias against the field that suggests that if you work on African-American materials, then by definition you are not as good as those who work on other materials. If some of the best students are steered away from the field, then we create a self-fulfilling prophecy. The presumption of inferiority may be somewhat reduced if the student also develops expertise in a "nonblack" field. Despite positive inducements to enter the field, it is likely that latent negative stereotyping of the field will continue to keep students out, especially white students.

Second, the intrepid white scholar who seriously studies black politics runs the risk of facing politically motivated nationalist pressures within the classroom and beyond. Black students, faculty, administrators, or others may readily find fault with one's interpretations in this arena where racial sensitivities are so close to the surface. Some scholars simply decide it is not worth the hassle. (For example, there were several episodes of this pressure at the University of Michigan in 1988–89.)

Third, black scholars show their own ambivalences about greater white involvement in black political studies. On the one hand, thoughtful black scholars complain about the marginalization of the field as a further expression of white racism. On the other hand, mainstreaming would increase the number of people from the other community of discourse with its distinct intellectual, methodological, and extraparadigmatic traditions. For example, there is some resistance—as Reed states explicitly—to introducing quantification into a field long marked by more historical and qualitative methods of the minority discourse (Reed 1986). We find this resistance problematic. More whites in the field, it is implied, would lower the quality of the field. Some of these same concerns are expressed by scholars at historically black colleges and universities about the work and professional orientation of black scholars at white universities.

Furthermore, independently of the particular issues at hand, continuing nationalist sentiments among black intellectuals lead them to bridle at full integration. These nationalist concerns are probably intellectual (the discourse problem) and personal, political, and professional—there are some benefits of scholarly control and legitimacy that accrue to black scholars by keeping black politics the nearly exclusive preserve of black scholars. Of course, one sees similar "turf" conflicts in other disciplines like history where white scholars are more active and prominent in using African-American materials in their work. Since there do appear to be genuine differences of scholarly interpretation and method, the racial split takes on greater significance than if the disputes were purely personal power grabs.

In other words, we find in political science a microcosm of the same ambivalences among and between whites and blacks that have long been manifest in American intellectual life. What we still have not explained, however, is why political science appears to be more segregated into two discourses than other disciplines. Is it mainly the discipline's focus on the wielders of power, the political life of the victors rather than the victims, or are there other paradigmatic and institutional reasons for the divided discourses?

Still, we feel that just as war is too important to be left to generals, and other fields too important to be the preserve of whites, black politics is too important and too interesting to be left to any single group of scholars. There are more than enough important substantive and theoretical questions that can occupy all our attentions for the foreseeable future. The first step is for those in the dominant discourse to recognize that a serious challenge—and great opportunities—exist, and to take steps to take the challenging discourse seriously.

NOTES

1. See "The Political Economy of International Energy Markets" for a similar substantive review of a field (Wilson 1986).

2. McLoyd and Randolph carefully analyze this same issue in psychology (McLoyd and Randolph 1984).

3. We use paradigm in a sense similar to Kuhn (1970). Shared paradigms represent theoretical approaches to scientific problems that set the organization of the field, the field's research agenda, major models, shared methods, instruction in the field, etc. Of particular interest for our problem is that the "normal science" conducted under a field defines interesting problems capable of being solved by the paradigm. Black political development and dynamics may provide ambiguous cases, we argue, for most of the mainstream theories of politics. Whether these challenging cases will lead to further "articulation" of extant theories, or to a "scientific revolution" in the study of black politics, which brings to the fore new theories and associated paradigms, rests on the work we believe needs to be done in the future.

4. We borrow this term from Frey's survey of the field of political economy in which he identifies half a dozen challengers to the neoclassical paradigm.

5. This table is an example of the type of analysis that could be done for all of the major discussed paradigms.

6. For the purposes of this exercise, we use the simple income-to-needs ratio defined by the official U.S. government definition of poverty. In future extensions of this work we will use more sophisticated measures of black poverty.

7. It should be pointed out that interracial differences still overwhelm intraracial differences on these questions. See Kinder et al. 1989.

8. See "The Elusive Paradigm: Gender, Politics and Political Behavior" in Ada W. Finifter, ed., *Political Science: The State of the Discipline*, pp. 471–502. In this review of the field, black political scientists, the study of black politics, and the study of race and politics are almost totally absent.

REFERENCES

Aberbach, Joel, and Jack Walker. 1973. *Race in the City*. Boston: Little, Brown.

Allen, Walter R. 1978. "The Search for Applicable Theories of Black Family Life." *Journal of Marriage and the Family* 117–29.

Barker, Lucius J., and McCorry, Jr. 1980. *Black Americans and the Political System*. Second edition. Cambridge: Winthrop Publishers.

Barongo, Yolamu. 1983. *Political Science in Africa: A Critical Review*. London: Zed Books.

Bendix, Reinhard. 1946. *Max Weber: An Intellectual Portrait*. Garden City, N.Y.: Anchor Books, Doubleday.

Black Studies: A Catalogue of Selected Doctoral Dissertation Research. 1985. Ann Arbor: University Microfilms International.

Blacks and the 1988 Democratic National Convention. 1988. Washington, D.C.: Joint Center for Political Studies.

Blackwell, James E., and Morris Janovitz. 1974. *Black Sociologists. Historical and Contemporary Perspectives*. Chicago: University of Chicago Press.

Browning, Rufus, Dale Rogers Marshall, and David H. Tabb. 1984. *Protest is*

Not Enough: The Struggle of Blacks and Hispanics for Equality in Urban Politics. Berkeley: University of California Press.

Bunche, Ralph. 1941. "The Negro in the Political Life of the United States." *Journal of Negro Education*, X.

Carmines, Edward G., and James A. Stimson. 1989. *Issue Evolution: Race and the Transformation of American Politics*. Princeton: Princeton University Press.

Castells, Manuel. 1979. "The Wild City." In Joe Feagin, ed., *The Urban Scene: Myth and Reality*. New York: Random House.

———. 1983. *The City and the Grassroots: A Cross-Cultural Theory of Urban Social Movements*. Berkely: University of California Press.

Cavanagh, Thomas E. 1987. *Strategies for Mobilizing Black Voters: Four Case Studies*. Washington, D.C.: Joint Center for Political Studies.

Cox, Oliver Cromwell. 1948. *Caste, Race and Class*. Garden City, N.Y.: Doubleday.

Dahl, Robert. 1954. *Preface to Democratic Theory*. Chicago: University of Chicago Press.

———. 1961. *Who Governs*. New Haven: Yale University Press.

Davis, Mike. 1986. *Prisoners of the American Dream*. London: Verso Press.

Dawson, Michael C. 1989. "Continuity and Change: Interactions between African American Urban Poverty and Individual Political Beliefs and Political Behavior." Paper prepared for delivery at the annual meeting of the American Political Science Association, Atlanta, August 30–September 3.

Drake, St. Claire. 1945. *Black Metropolis*. New York: Harcourt, Brace and World.

DuBois, W.E.B. 1899. *Philadelphia Negro*. Philadelphia: University of Pennsylvania Press.

Elster, Jon. 1983. *Sour Grapes: Studies in the Subversion at Rationality*. New York: Cambridge University Press.

———, ed. 1986. *Rational Choice*. New York: New York University Press.

Farley, Reynolds, and Walter R. Allen. 1987. *The Color Line and the Quality of Life in America*. New York: Russell Sage Foundation.

Finifter, Ada A., ed. 1983. *Political Science: The State of the Discipline*. Washington, D.C.: American Political Science Association.

Fish, Stanley Eugene. 1980. *Is There a Text in This Class?* Cambridge: Harvard University Press.

Fogel, Robert W., and Stanley L. Engerman. 1974. *Time on the Cross: The Economics of American Negro Slavery*. Boston: Little, Brown.

Frazier, E. Franklin. 1957. *Black Bourgeoisie: The Rise of a New Middle Class*. New York: Free Press.

Frey, Bruno. 1978. *Modern Political Economy*. New York: John Wiley.

Gates, Henry Louis, Jr. 1986. *Race, Writing, and Difference*. Chicago: University of Chicago Press.

———. 1989. "Whose Canon is it Anyway?" *The New York Times Book Review*, February 26.

Genovese, Eugene D. 1974. *Roll, Jordan, Roll: The World the Slaves Made*. New York: Random House.

Githens, Marianne. "The Elusive Paradigm: Gender, Politics and Political Behavior." In *Political Science: The State of the Discipline*. Ada A. Finifter ed., 1983. Washington, D.C.: American Political Science Association: 471–503.

Gosnell, Harold F. 1935. *Negro Politicians: The Rise of Negro Politics in Chicago*. Chicago: University of Chicago Press.

Hamilton, Charles. 1973. *The Bench and the Ballot: Southern Federal Judges and Black Voters*. New York: Oxford University Press.

Hochschild, Jennifer L. 1984. *The New American Dilemma: Liberal Democracy and School Desegregation*. New Haven: Yale University Press.

Holden, Matthew. 1973. *The Politics of the Black Nation*. New York: Chandler.

———. 1983. "Moral Engagement and Combat Scholarship: Contemporary Notes on a Black Scholarly Tradition." McLean, Va.: Court Square Institute.

Howard, Lawrence C., Lenneal J. Henderson, Jr., and Deryl Hunt. 1977. *Public Administration and Public Policy: A Minority Perspective*. Pittsburgh: Public Policy Press.

Huckfeldt, Robert. 1986. *Politics in Context: Assimilation and Conflict in Urban Neighborhoods*. New York: Agathon Press.

———, and Carol Weitzel Kohfeld. 1989. *Race and the Decline of Class in American Politics*. Urbana: University of Illinois Press.

Irish, Marian D. 1968. *Political Science: Advance of the Discipline*. Englewood Cliffs, N.J.: Prentice-Hall.

Jackson, James, Shirley Hatchet, and Ronald Brown. 1985. "Racial Consciousness and Electoral Choice among Black Voters." Presented at the annual meeting of the National Conference of Black Political Scientists, Columbus.

Karenga, Maulana. 1982. *Introduction to Black Studies*. Inglewood, Calif.: Kawaida Publications.

Katznelson, Ira. 1981. *City Trenches: Urban Politics and the Patterning of Class in the United States*. New York: Pantheon.

Kennedy, Randall. 1989. "Racial Critiques of Legal Academia." *Harvard Law Review* vol. 102 (June): 1745–819.

Key, V.O. 1949. *Southern Politics*. New York: Random House.

Kilson, Marion D. de B. "Afro-American Social Structure, 1790–1970." In *The African Diaspora*: 414–55.

Kilson, Martin. 1977. "Political Science and Afro-Americans: Normative Problems of American Politics." In *Teaching Political Science: The Professor and the Polity*, Vernon Van Dyke, ed. Atlantic Highlands, N.J.: Humanities Press.

———. 1987. "Politics of Race and Urban Crisis: The American Case." In Benyon and Solomos, eds., *The Roots of Urban Unrest*. New York: Pergamon Press.

Kinder, Donald, Tali Mendelberg, Michael C. Dawson, Lynn M. Sanders, Steven J. Rosenstone, Jocelyn Sargent, and Cathy Cohen. 1989. "Race and the 1988 Presidential Election." Paper prepared for delivery at the annual meeting of the American Political Science Association, Atlanta, August 30–September 3.

Kleppner, Paul. 1985. *Chicago Divided: The Making of a Black Mayor*. De Kalb: Northern Illinois University Press.

Kuhn, Thomas S. 1970. *The Structure of Scientific Revolutions*. Chicago: University of Chicago Press.

Landry, Bart. 1987. *The New Black Middle Class*. Berkeley: University of California Press.

Lindblom, Charles. 1982. "Another State of Mind." *American Political Science Review* 76:9–21.

Manley, John F. 1983. "Neo-Pluralism: A Class Analysis of Pluralism I and Pluralism II." *The American Political Science Review* 77:368–83.

Marable, Manning. 1983. *How Capitalism Underdeveloped Black America: Problems in Race, Political Economy, and Society*. Boston: South End.

———. 1985. *Black American Politics: From the Washington Marches to Jesse Jackson*. London: Verso.

McKay, David. 1988. "Why is There a European Political Science?" *PS* Fall: 1051–56.

McLoyd, Vonnie C. and Suzanne Randolph. 1984. "The Conduct and Publication of Research on Afro-American Children: A Content Analysis." In *Human Development*, vol. 27:65–75.

Miliband, Ralph. 1969. *The State in Capitalist Society*. London: Winfield and Nicholson.

Morris, Aldon. 1984. *The Origins of the Civil Rights Movement*. New York: Free Press.

Morris, Milton. 1975. *The Politics of Black America*. New York: Harper and Row.

National Research Council. 1983. *Summary Report 1983: Doctorate Recipients from United States Universities*. Washington, D.C.: National Academy Press.

O'Connor, James. 1973. *The Fiscal Crisis of the State*. New York: St. Martin's Press.

Ollman, Bertell, and Edward Vernoff. 1982. *The Left Academy: Marxist Scholarship on American Campuses*. New York: McGraw-Hill.

Painter, Nell Irvin. 1977. *Exodusters: Black Migration to Kansas after Reconstruction*. New York: Knopf.

Pettigrew, Thomas F., and Denise A. Alston. 1988. *Tom Bradley's Campaign for Governor*. Washington, D.C.: Joint Center for Political Studies.

Pinderhughes, Dianne. 1987. *Race and Ethnicity in Chicago Politics*. Urbana: University of Illinois Press.

Pinkney, Alphonso. 1984. *The Myth of Black Progress*. Cambridge: Cambridge University Press.

Poulantzas, Nicos. 1968. *Political Power and Social Classes*. London: New Left Books.

Preston, Michael B., and Maurice Woodard. 1984. "The Rise and Decline of Black Political Scientists in the Profession." *PS* 17:787–92.

Preston, Michael B., Lenneal J. Henderson, Jr., and Paul L. Puryear. 1987. *The New Black Politics: The Search for Political Power*. New York: Longman.

Przeworski, Adam. 1985a. *Capitalism and Social Democracy*. Cambridge: Cambridge University Press.

———. 1985b. "Marxism and Rational Choice." *Politics and Society* 14(4): 379–409.

Reed, Adolph, Jr. 1986. *Race, Politics, and Culture: Critical Essays on the Radicalism of the 1960s*. New York: Greenwood Press.

———. 1986. *The Jesse Jackson Phenomenon*. New Haven: Yale University Press.

Simms, Margaret C., and David H. Swinton. 1988. "A Report on the Supply of Black Economists." *The Review of Black Political Economy* 17, 1:67–88.

Simon, Herbert A. 1985. "Human Nature in Politics: The Dialogue of Psychology with Political Science." *American Political Science Review* 79:293–304.

Sims, Valerie T. 1989. "What's not Going on Here: Theories and Textbooks." *The Political Science Teacher* 2:20–21.

Skocpol, Theda, and John Ikenberry. 1983. "The Political Formation of the American Welfare State in Historical and Comparative Prospective." *Comparative Research* 6:92–119.

Skowronek, Stephen. 1982. *Building a New American State: The Expansion of National Administrative Capacities, 1877–1920*. New York: Cambridge University Press.

Somit, Albert, and Joseph Tanenhaus. 1964. *American Political Science: A Profile of a Discipline*. New York: Atherton Press.

———. 1967. *The Development of American Political Science: From Burgess to Behavioralism*. Boston: Allyn and Bacon.

Thorpe, Earl E. 1971. *Black Historians: A Critique*. New York: Morrow.

Turner, James. 1976. "Implications of Class Conflict and Racial Cleavage for the U.S. Black Community." *Review of Black Political Economy* 6(2): 133–44.

Van Dyke, Vernon. 1977. *Teaching Political Science: The Professor and the Polity.* Atlantic Highlands, N.J.: Humanities Press.

Walters, Ronald W. 1988. *Black Presidential Politics in America: A Strategic Approach.* Albany: SUNY Press.

Walton, Hanes, Jr. 1972. *Black Politics: A Theoretical and Structural Analysis.* Philadelphia: Lippincott.

———. 1988. *When the Marching Stopped: The Politics of Civil Rights Regulatory Agencies.* Albany: SUNY Press.

———. 1989. "The Current Literature on Black Politics." *National Review of Political Science* 1:152–68.

Williams, L. F. 1987. "Detroit Politics and Urban Theory: The More Things Change, The More They Stay the Same." Paper presented at the National Conference of Black Political Scientists' annual meeting, April 22–28.

Wilson, Ernest J., III. 1985. "Why Political Scientists Don't Study Black Politics, But Historians and Sociologists Do." *PS* Summer: 600–607.

———. 1987. "World Politics and International Energy Markets." *International Organization* 41,1:1250–149.

Wilson, James Q. 1960. *Negro Politics: The Search for Leadership.* Glencoe, Ill.: Free Press.

Wilson, William J. 1978. *The Declining Significance of Race: Blacks and Changing American Institutions.* Chicago: University of Chicago Press.

———. 1987. *The Truly Disadvantaged.* Chicago: University of Chicago Press.

Woodard, Maurice, and Michael B. Preston. 1985. "Black Political Scientists: Where Are the New Ph.D.s?" *PS* 18:80–88.

Notes on Contributors

Terence Ball received his doctorate in political science from the University of California at Berkeley in 1973. His areas of special interest include political theory, the history of political thought, the comparative study of political ideologies, and the history and philosophy of the social sciences. He has been a visiting professor at Oxford University (1978–79) and has lectured widely in North America and Europe. The author of some fifty professional articles, he has also written or edited several books, among them *After Marx* (1984), *Idioms of Inquiry* (1987), *Conceptual Change and the Constitution* (1988), *Transforming Political Discourse* (1988), and *Political Innovation and Conceptual Change* (1989). He is currently writing a book about our obligations to future generations.

William Crotty is professor of political science at Northwestern University. He received his Ph.D. from the University of North Carolina at Chapel Hill in 1964. His areas of interest include political parties and election processes, policy-making, and American and comparative governing institutions. He has served as president of the Political Organizations and Parties Section of the American Political Science Organization, the Midwest Political Science Association, and the Policy Studies Organization. He is the author of a number of articles and books, including *Decision for the Democrats* (1978), *Party Reform* (1983), *The Party Game* (1985), *American Parties in Decline* (co-author, 1980, 1984), *Presidential Primaries and Nominations* (co-author, 1985), and *Political Parties in Local Areas* (co-author, 1987). Professor Crotty has been the recipient of an American Political Science Association Fellowship to study the national political parties and he has served as a member of a number of commissions invited to observe elections and democratic processes in Latin America.

Michael C. Dawson is assistant professor of political science and Afro-American and African studies, University of Michigan, Ann Arbor. He received his Ph.D. degree from Harvard University in 1986. Dr. Dawson is currently co-principal investigator of the 1988 National Black Election Study. His research interests include the development of quantitative models of African-American political behavior and public opinion. This work includes delineating the differences in African-American political behavior from that of white Americans. Dr. Dawson is the author of articles on African-American political behavior and race and American politics, which have appeared in the *American Political Science Review*, the *National Review of Political Science*, and other publications.

Donald M. Freeman is John L. Igleheart Professor of Political Science at the University of Evansville. He completed his Ph.D. at the University of North Carolina, Chapel Hill, in 1963. In 1985/86 he was Fulbright Senior Lecturer in Political Science at the National University of Singapore. Among his writings are *Political Parties and Political Behavior* (co-editor, 1966, 1971); *Foundation of Political Science: Research, Methods, and Scope* (editor and contributor, 1977); *Governing a Changing America* (co-author, 1984); and *Parties and Politics in the Post-Reagan Era* (author, 1988).

Paul Edward Johnson, assistant professor of political science at the University of Kansas, is currently visiting at the Yale School of Organization and Management. He received his Ph.D. from Washington University in St. Louis in 1988. He has published scholarly articles in the *Journal of Politics, American Journal of Political Science, Public Choice,* and other journals. He is editor of *Formal Theories of Politics: Mathematical Modelling in Political Science*, a Pergamon Press volume, and co-author of *American Government: People, Institutions, and Policies*, published recently by Houghton Mifflin Company.

Kristen Renwick Monroe was graduated with honors from Smith College (1968) and received her M.A. (1970) and Ph.D. (1974) from the University of Chicago. She was a LaVerne Noyes Fellow at the University of Chicago (1975–76), a Killam Fellow in political economy and econometrics at the University of British Columbia (1975–76), and a Fellow at the Center of International Affairs at Princeton (1983–84). Currently an associate professor in politics and society at the University of California at Irvine, she has also taught at N.Y.U., Princeton, and the State University of New York at Stony Brook. She was founder and chair of the International Political Science Association's research group on political support and alienation for ten years and is also active in the APSA. Monroe is the author of *Presidential Popularity and the Economy* (1984) and the editor of *The Political Process and Economic Change* (1983) and *The Economic Approach to Politics* (1991).

J. Donald Moon received his Ph.D. from the University of Minnesota and now teaches political science at Wesleyan University. He is the author of the chapter "Logic of Political Inquiry" in the *Handbook of Political Science*, and has published a number of articles on the philosophy of social inquiry. He is the co-editor of *Dissent and Affirmation*, has edited *Responsibility, Rights, and Welfare* (1988), and has written a number of articles on the political theory of the welfare state.

Virginia Sapiro is professor of political science and women's studies at the University of Wisconsin-Madison. She received her Ph.D. from the University of Michigan in 1976. Her books include *The Political Integration of Women: Roles, Socialization, and Politics* (1983), *Women in American Society: An Introduction to Women's Studies* (1986, 1990), and *The Political Theory of Mary Wollstonecraft* (forthcoming), and she edited *Women, Biology, and Public Policy* (1985). She has also published scholarly articles in most of the major political science journals. She received awards for her work on women and politics from the Midwest, Western, and Southern Political Science Associations. In 1986 she received the Erik Erikson Award for Early Career Contributions to Political Psychology from the International Society for Political Psychology.

Philip Schrodt received an M.A. in mathematics and a doctorate in political science from Indiana University. His areas of interest include mathematical and computational models of political behavior, international relations, and foreign policy decision-making. Prior to joining the faculty at the University of Kansas, he taught at Northwestern University, where he helped develop, and later directed, the Mathematical Methods in the Social Sciences honors program. Schrodt is the author of some forty articles on international relations, mathematical modeling, and social science statistics. His books include *Microcomputer Methods for Social Scientists* and *Preserving Arms Distributions in a Multi-Polar World*. For the past five years he has been developing artificial intelligence models of international behavior, and is presently completing a book on that topic.

Ernest J. Wilson III received his B.A. from Harvard University and his Ph.D. from Berkeley. He is the author of "Why Political Scientists Don't Study Black Politics, But Historians and Sociologists Do," *PS* 1985, the new Introduction to Harold Cruse's second edition of *The Crisis of the Negro Intellectual* (1984), and articles on blacks and U.S. industrial policy and energy policy. His works on comparative political economy have appeared in *International Organization, Comparative Politics, Daedalus*, and other publications. He is the co-author of *The Decade of Energy Policy* (1984) and author of *Politics and Culture in Nigeria* (1988). Dr. Wilson is associate professor of political science and public policy, and director of the Center for Research on Economic Development, the University of Michigan.